陆小明　编著

英汉对照
附赠音频

晨读夜诵 · 每天读一点

经典希腊神话故事

Moment with English · Greek and Roman Mythology

華東理工大學出版社
EAST CHINA UNIVERSITY OF SCIENCE AND TECHNOLOGY PRESS
·上海·

图书在版编目(CIP)数据

晨读夜诵. 每天读一点经典希腊神话故事 ：附赠音频 / 陆小明编著. —上海 ：华东理工大学出版社，2019.9

ISBN 978-7-5628-5947-5

Ⅰ. ①晨… Ⅱ. ①陆… Ⅲ. ①英语-阅读教学-自学参考资料 Ⅳ. ①H3

中国版本图书馆 CIP 数据核字(2019)第 188881 号

项目统筹 / 刘　璇
责任编辑 / 刘　璇　芮建芬
装帧设计 / 徐　蓉
出版发行 / 华东理工大学出版社有限公司
地址：上海市梅陇路 130 号，200237
电话：021-64250306
网址：www.ecustpress.cn
邮箱：zongbianban@ecustpress.cn
印　　刷 / 杭州日报报业集团盛元印务有限公司
开　　本 / 890mm×1240mm　1/32
印　　张 / 10.625
字　　数 / 428 千字
版　　次 / 2019 年 9 月第 1 版
印　　次 / 2019 年 9 月第 1 次
定　　价 / 39.80 元

List of Gods and Goddesses in Greek and Roman Mythology

希腊罗马神话诸神对照表

One of the difficulties in reading Greek and Roman mythology lies in the numerous exotic names of the gods and goddesses, and the frequent confusion between the Greek names and their Roman counterparts. Therefore, the following table is meant to provide you with ready and immediate assistance once you embark on a journey into the mythological world. Have fun.

希腊罗马神话之所以难懂,原因之一在于不仅神的数量众多、名字拗口,而且这些神的希腊名和罗马名时常被混用,因此,在大家踏上神话阅读之旅前,请收藏下表以备不时之需。祝阅读愉快!

Greek Name 希腊名	Sex 性别	Chinese Name 中文名	Roman Name 罗马名	Chinese Name 中文名	Notes 备注
Zeus	M	宙斯	Jupiter	朱庇特	couple 夫妻
Hera	F	赫拉	Juno	朱诺	
Hades	M	哈迪斯	Pluto	普路托	couple 夫妻
Persephone	F	珀耳塞福涅	Proserpina	普罗塞耳皮娜	
Poseidon	M	波塞冬	Neptune	尼普顿	couple 夫妻
Amphitrite	F	安菲特律特	Salacia	塞蕾希耳	
Athena	F	雅典娜	Minerva	密涅瓦	智慧女神
Apollo	M	阿波罗	Apollo	阿波罗	twins 双胞胎
Artemis	F	阿尔忒弥斯	Diana	狄安娜	
Ares	M	阿瑞斯	Mars	马耳斯	战神

（续表）

Greek Name 希腊名	Sex 性别	Chinese Name 中文名	Roman Name 罗马名	Chinese Name 中文名	Notes 备注
Aphrodite	F	阿芙洛蒂忒	Venus	维纳斯	couple 夫妻
Hephaestus	M	赫菲斯托斯	Vulcan	伍尔坎	
Eros	M	厄洛斯	Cupid	丘比特	小爱神
Demeter	F	得墨忒耳	Ceres	刻瑞斯	女农神
Hermes	M	赫耳墨斯	Mercury	墨丘利	使者
Hestia	F	赫斯提	Vesta	维斯太	女灶神
Dionysus	M	狄俄尼索斯	Bacchus	巴克斯	酒神
Heracles	M	海格立斯	Hercules	赫丘利	大力神

目录
Contents

Part Ⅰ Myths of Creation
第一部分 创世神话

Part Ⅱ The Divinities
第二部分 神的谱系

Part Ⅲ Nature Myths
第三部分 大自然的神话

Part Ⅳ Myths of Love
第四部分 爱的神话

Part Ⅴ Myths of Human Nature
第五部分 人性的神话

Part Ⅵ Myth and Customs
第六部分 神话与习俗

Part Ⅶ　Myth and Fantasy
第七部分　神话与奇幻

Part Ⅷ　Myth and Legend
第八部分　神话与传奇

Part Ⅰ Myths of Creations

第一部分
创世神话

扫一扫,听本部分音频

Chapter 1 The Chaos
第一章 混沌太始

Word Knowledge 词汇知识

Chaos(混沌)

How did the universe come into being? Legends on it vary from country to country, but they all have one thing in common: the chaos, a confused and shapeless mass.

The English word "chaos" comes from a Greek root meaning "vast chasm" or "void", while the Chinese word "*hundun*" refers to the primeval state of the universe before the earth was first separated from the heavens.

In modern English, the word "chaos" is often used to mean a state of complete confusion or lack of order, and its adjective form is also frequently seen in news reports such as "Heathrow airport is absolutely chaotic."

宇宙是如何产生的？关于这个问题，不同的国家有不同的传说故事，但它们却有一个共同点：那就是"混沌"，一种混乱、无形的状态。

英语"chaos"这个词源自希腊语的一个词根，意思是"大裂口"或"空白"，而汉语中的"混沌"则是指天地分离之前宇宙所处的原始状态。

在当代英语中，chaos一词常用来表示一片混乱或杂乱无序的状态，而其形容词也经常出现在新闻报道中，比如"希斯罗机场简直混乱不堪"。

Centimani(百臂巨人)

We are now in the 21st century. How long is a century? One hundred years. What does centimeter mean? One-hundredth of a meter. The word "centigrade" actually denotes a thermometric scale on which the interval between the freezing point of water and the boiling point of water is divided into 100 degrees. Hence the prefix "*centi-*" represents the number of 100 in Latin. Centimani were the first three children of Uranus (Heaven) and Gaea (Earth). They were huge, powerful monsters with fifty heads and one hundred hands. They were so ugly and troublesome that even their father did not like them. Eventually Uranus imprisoned them in a place called Tartarus, which was below the underworld.

我们如今生活在21世纪,那么一个世纪有多长呢?一百年。厘米是什么意思?百分之一米。"摄氏度"这个词是指温度计的刻度,从冰点到沸点划分为100度。因此,centi-这个词缀在拉丁语中代表了数字100。Centimani是天父乌拉诺斯和地母盖亚最早生下的三个孩子,他们体型庞大、威力无比,是有着五十个脑袋和一百只胳膊的怪物,因为相貌丑陋,且成天惹事,就连亲生父亲都嫌弃他们,最终把他们囚禁到了地狱之下一个叫作塔尔塔罗斯的地方。

Cyclops(独眼巨人)

Although the word "Cyclops" may be new to you, I am sure you know the word "bicycle". What about *tricycle*, *monocycle*, *motorcycle* and *cyclist*? Once you are acquainted with these words, you are likely to get the hint of this Cyclops. In Greek and Roman mythology, it is one of the one-eyed giants, children of Uranus (Heaven) and Gaea (Earth). As the huge giant had only one big eye in the middle of its forehead, it looked very much like a wheel.

Do you know what an encyclopedia is? If your answer is no or you find it difficult to remember, try to divide the word into three parts: *en-* + *cyclop* + *-pedia*, which, based on the etymological explanation, might be interpreted respectively as "to make" "a Giant" of "knowledge/education". In fact, encyclopedia could also be spelt cyclopedia, a book or books dealing with every branch of knowledge. Now does the word make sense to you?

虽然你可能不知道 Cyclops 这个词,但是我猜你一定知道"自行车"这个词吧。那么 tricycle(三轮车)、monocycle(独轮车)、motorcycle(摩托车)、cyclist(骑手)这些词呢?一旦你熟悉了这些词,你就很可能猜到 Cyclops 的意思。在希腊罗马神话中,它是独眼巨人之一,是天父乌拉诺斯和地母盖亚的孩子。因为独眼巨人的脑门上只有一只大眼睛,所以看上去很像一个轮子。

你知道 encyclopedia 是什么吗?假如你的回答是否定的,或者你觉得这个单词太难记了,不妨将它这样拆开来看:en- + cyclop + -pedia,根据词源学的解释,这三部分对应的意思分别是"使成为""知识/教育"的"巨人"。事实上,encyclopedia 也可以拼作 cyclopedia,意思是"百科全书"。现在你是不是觉得这个词容易理解了呢?

The Myths 神话故事

Although there were different versions about the origin of the world, the generally accepted notion was that before earth and sea and heaven were created, all things were gathered in a confused mass of shapeless elements called Chaos, in which slept the seeds of all things. Chaos then grew gradually into two widely different substances: one is light, and the other, heavy. Thus out of the heavy and solid mass came into being the first great deity Gaea, or Mother Earth, who gave birth to Uranus, Father Sky, who became her husband and protector.

In fact, Gaea and Uranus were not the only offspring of Chaos. There were two mighty powers co-existing with them. They were Erebus (Darkness) and Nyx (Night), who formed a striking contrast to the cheerful light of heaven and the bright smiles of earth. Erebus and Nyx gave birth to many children, such as Aether (Brightness), Hemera (Day), Hypnos (Sleep) and Thanatos (Death). Tartarus was described as the homes of Nyx and her children Hypnos and Thanatos. Nyx and her daughter Hemera took turns to leave Tartarus, representing the alternating of night and day.

In Greek and Roman mythology, Uranus and Gaea produced three distinctly different races of beings: Centimani, Cyclopes and Titans. The Centimani were three hundred-handed giants. Each possessed a hundred hands and fifty heads. They could shake the universe and produce earthquakes. They were hideous to look at and extremely destructive. Feared that the great power of these turbulent offspring might be hurtful to himself, Uranus hurled the Centimani into Tartarus, the deep abyss served as a dungeon.

After the Centimani, three Cyclopes were born. They were giant monsters, each of which had only one eye in the center of his forehead. One Cyclops represented thunder, another lightning, and the last the lightning bolt. They served as builders, blacksmiths, and craftsmen, but they were strong and stubborn. Again Uranus worried about their mighty power, and threw them into Tartarus as well.

The third race of beings created by Gaea and Uranus were the Titans. Huge and powerful as they were, they were not as ugly as their elder brothers. They were twelve in number: six male and six female. Their names were: Oceanus, Ceos, Crios, Hyperion, Iapetus, Cronus, Theis, Rhea, Themis, Mnemosyne, Phoebe, and Tethys. The Titans inherited from their parents both great physical power and intellectual qualifications. They set about creating things like the seas, the moon, mountains, forests, and plains. They married each other and gave birth to a great number of other beings.

Gaea felt hurt about the imprisonment and oppression of her children, the Centimani and the Cyclopes, so she fashioned a stone scythe and persuaded the Titans to rebel against their father Uranus. Only Cronus, the youngest and the bravest of the Titans, was willing to do the deed. One day, when Uranus spread himself over the earth, Cronus leapt up and cut off his "vital organ" with the scythe. The organ fell into the ocean and produced a white foam, from which emerged the goddess of love, Aphrodite.

Cronus succeeded in dethroning his father, who, enraged at his defeat, cursed his rebellious son, foretelling that one of Cronus' children would rise up against him, just as what Cronus had done to his father. Uranus withdrew from Earth, and from that time on, the sky and the earth never touched again. Cronus made himself the supreme ruler of the universe. He married his own sister Rhea and made his brother Hyperion the sun god and his sister Phoebe the moon goddess.

关于世界的起源有着不同的说法，普遍认可的版本是在大地、海洋和天空出现之前，一切都处在一种混沌无形的状态，而这种混沌又孕育了一切。混沌逐渐演化成两种截然不同的物质：一轻，一重。从重而实的物质中诞生了第一位伟大的神：盖亚——大地之母。她生下了乌拉诺斯——天空之父，后者成了她的丈夫和保护者。

事实上，盖亚和乌拉诺斯并不是混沌的唯一后代，与他们同时存在的还有另外两个神：埃里伯斯（黑暗）和尼克斯（夜晚），他们与天空的快乐光芒和大地的明媚笑容形成了鲜明的对照。埃里伯斯和尼克斯有许多孩子，譬如以太（光明）、赫墨拉（白昼）、修普诺斯（睡眠）和塔纳托斯（死亡）。据说塔尔塔罗斯就是尼克斯和她孩子们的家，尼克斯和女儿赫墨拉轮流离开塔尔塔罗斯，便有了日夜的更替。

在希腊和罗马神话中，乌拉诺斯和盖亚生下了三个截然不同的物种：百臂巨人、独眼巨人和提坦巨人。百臂巨人是三兄弟，他们每人都有五十个脑袋和一百只胳膊，他们可以撼动宇宙、引发地震，并且奇丑无比、极具破坏力。因为害怕三兄弟有可能对自己造成伤害，乌拉诺斯便把他们锁进了塔尔塔罗斯，那个被用作地牢的万丈深渊。

百臂巨人之后，三个独眼巨人出生了。他们是巨大的怪物，每个人的脑袋中间都只有一只眼睛。三兄弟分别代表雷鸣、闪电和霹雳。作为建造者、工匠和手艺人的他们都异常强壮和倔强，这让乌拉诺斯再次感到担忧，于是，这三个独眼巨人也被关进了塔尔塔罗斯。

盖亚和乌拉诺斯诞下的第三类后代是提坦巨人。尽管他们也是力大无比的巨人，但是却没有哥哥们那般丑陋。他们一共有十二个：六男六女。他们的名字分别是：俄刻阿诺斯、西耳斯、克瑞耳斯、许珀里翁、伊阿珀托斯、克罗诺斯、忒弥斯、瑞亚、西弥斯、摩涅莫辛涅、福柏和蒂锡斯。提坦巨人不仅继承了他们父母的强壮身体，还遗传了他们的聪明智慧，他们开始着手创造海洋、月亮、山脉、森林和平原，他们彼此结合，繁衍出更多的后代。

自己的孩子百臂巨人和独眼巨人遭到囚禁和迫害，令盖亚非常难过，于是她制作了一把巨大的石镰，并劝说提坦巨人反抗他们的父亲乌拉诺斯。然而，只有最小最勇敢的克罗诺斯愿意付诸行动。这天，当天父乌拉诺斯拥抱地母之际，克罗诺斯一跃而起，挥舞石镰割掉了他的"命根子"，器官坠落大海之后，掀起无数白色的泡沫，爱神阿芙洛蒂忒从这些泡沫中诞生了。

克罗诺斯成功地推翻了父亲的王位，恼羞成怒的乌拉诺斯诅咒他的不孝子，预言克罗诺斯也将遭受和自己一样的命运：他的一个孩子将和他作对并推翻他的王位。从此以后，乌拉诺斯退出了历史舞台，大地和天空永久分离。克罗诺斯成为宇宙中至高无上的主宰，他娶了自己的妹妹瑞亚，封哥哥许珀里翁为太阳神，姐姐福柏为月亮女神。

Extra 拓展测试

1. Which of the following is likely to be a Cyclops?
下面哪一个有可能是独眼巨人?

A

B

2. Uranus is one of the planets in our solar system. Do you know which it is?
乌拉诺斯是太阳系八大行星之一,你知道是哪一颗吗?

(1. 答案:A)
(2. 答案:天王星)

CHAPTER 2 The Clash of Gods
第二章　诸神之战

Word Knowledge 词汇知识

Oceanus(俄刻阿诺斯)

There are various theories about Oceanus, which, in Greek mythology, means the vast expanse of ever-flowing water around the earth. One theory depicts him as the first-born child of Uranus and Gaea, for the formation of the ocean involves the rains from the sky and the streams flowing on the earth, a combined influence of Uranus and Gaea. Another theory sorts him with the Titans, the third race of beings created by Gaea and Uranus. Whichever theory it is, Oceanus married his sister Tethys, who gave birth to the three great rivers known to the Greeks, including the Nile in Egypt. They had more than three thousand other children. Their sons were called Oceanids, and their daughters were Nymphs or Oceanides. Each became the minor god or goddess of a river, stream, spring, lake, or pond.

In modern English, there are many words which could be traced back to the Greek word Oceanus: *ocean*, *Oceania*, *occanarium*, *oceanography*, to name a few.

在希腊神话中,"俄刻阿诺斯"的意思是环绕地球流淌的大片水域,关于他的起源有不同的版本,其中之一认为他是乌拉诺斯和盖亚的第一个孩子,因为海洋的形成需要来自天空的雨滴和来自大地的流水,即乌拉诺斯和盖亚的共同影响。另一个版本则将他归入提坦巨人,即乌拉诺斯和盖亚所生的第三类物种。但不管是哪个版本,一个普遍的说法是俄刻阿诺斯娶了他的妹妹蒂锡斯，诞下了对于希腊人来说非常重要的三条河流，其中就包括埃及的尼罗河。此外，他们还有超过三千子嗣，其中的男孩被称作俄刻阿尼得，女孩则叫宁芙或俄刻阿尼得斯。他们作为小神仙、小仙女，各自掌管着世界上众多的河流、溪水、清泉、湖泊和池塘。

在现代英语词汇中，有许多单词可以追溯到俄刻阿诺斯这个希腊名字，例如：ocean（海洋）、Oceania（大洋洲）、oceanarium（大型海洋水族馆）、oceanography（海洋学）等。

Atlas(阿特拉斯)

Do you know that the Atlantic Ocean in English actually means "sea of Atlas"? Atlantis, the legendary and mysterious island believed to represent lost civilization, could be interpreted as "island of Atlas". In modern English, atlas refers to a book of maps or charts. In Greek mythology, Atlas was one of the Titans who revolted against the Olympians in the war Titanomachy. When the Titans were defeated, most of them were confined to Tartarus, but Zeus condemned Atlas to stand at the western edge of Gaea and hold up the sky on his shoulders, preventing the two from resuming their primordial embrace.

你知道吗？在英语中"大西洋（Atlantic）"的意思是"阿特拉斯海"；那个代表了失落文明的传奇神秘岛屿"亚特兰蒂斯"，则可以翻译成"阿特拉斯岛"。在当代英语中，atlas 指的是地图册。在希腊神话中，阿特拉斯是提坦巨人之一。在"提坦之战"中，他们是奥林匹斯山众神的敌人，因此，当提坦巨人战败之后，大多数巨人都被关进了塔尔塔洛斯。阿特拉斯是个例外。宙斯罚他站在大地的西边，用双肩扛起天空，以阻止他与地母再次拥抱。

Typhon(堤丰)

Does the word "Typhon" look familiar to you? It is very much like the English word "typhoon", isn't it? Yes. Typhon literally means whirlwind, which is the origin of the word typhoon, a tropical storm in the region of the Indian or western Pacific oceans. One version associates Typhon with the son of Gaea and Tartarus. Myth has it that Gaea gave birth to him in anger at the destruction of her offspring, the Giants. Typhon was an immensely powerful monster with one hundred snake heads on his shoulders to emit fire and make every kind of noise. He attempted to overthrow Zeus for the supremacy of the cosmos. The two then fought a cataclysmic battle, which Zeus finally won with the aid of his thunderbolts.

In Greek mythology, there are four monstrous creatures which were taken as offspring of Typhon: Cerberus, the three-headed watchdog of Hades, the multi-headed snake Hydra, the half-woman-half-lion monster Sphinx, and Chimaera, a fire-breathing hybrid creature which was usually depicted as a lion, with the head of a goat arising from its back, and a tail that ends with a snake's head.

Typhon(堤丰)这个词看上去熟悉吗？它很像英语中的typhoon(台风)一词，对吗？没错。"堤丰"的本意就是旋风，是"台风"一词的出处，表示在印度洋或西太平洋地区出现的热带风暴。有关堤丰的一个版本将他看作盖亚和地狱之神塔尔塔罗斯的儿子，盖亚因为失去了那些巨人孩子而在愤怒中生下了堤丰。堤丰是个力大无比的妖怪，肩膀上长着一百颗可以喷火并发出各种噪声的蛇头，他企图和宙斯争当宇宙的主宰，双方进行了一场空前惨烈的战斗，最终宙斯凭借手中的霹雳武器打败了堤丰。

在希腊神话中，据说有四个丑陋的怪物是堤丰的孩子：三头狗刻耳柏洛斯，即冥王哈迪斯的看门狗，九头蛇海德拉，半人半狮的斯芬克司以及能够喷火的混合怪物客迈拉。通常喀迈拉的样子是一头狮子，后背上伸出一只公羊头，尾巴则是一个蛇头。

The Myths 神话故事

Having dethroned his father Uranus, Cronus became invested with supreme power. He married Rhea and they had six children: three sons, Hades (Pluto), Poseidon (Neptune), Zeus (Jupiter), and three daughters, Hestia (Vesta), Demeter (Ceres), and Hera (Juno). However, the curse and prophesy from his father Uranus kept him uneasy all the time. He was afraid that his children might one day rise up against his authority. In order to render the prophecy impossible of fulfilment, Cronus took the excessive precaution of swallowing up all his five children, one by one, immediately after their birth. When it came to Zeus, the sixth and last child, Rhea resolved to try and save this one child at least. She wrapped a stone in baby-clothes and handed it over to the eager father. Thus Zeus was saved, and eventually, as we shall see, became the rebellious one and took the place of his father to become the great national god of the Greeks.

Rhea hid her son Zeus on the island of Crete, where a sacred goat provided the infant with milk, and the nymphs Melissae fed him with honey. Under the watchful care of the nymphs and the priests of Rhea, the child throve rapidly, developing great physical powers, combined with extraordinary wisdom and intelligence. When Rhea thought Zeus was strong enough to challenge his father, she brought Zeus back to the palace. Zeus artfully tricked his father into drinking a potion, which made him vomit immediately. One by one, Zeus' older brothers and sisters were thrown from Cronus' heaving mouth.

Cronus and his Titans were not ready to concede defeat. They made war on Zeus and his siblings. Cronus and his brother-Titans took possession of Mount Othrys, while Zeus, with his brothers and sisters, took his stand on Mount Olympus. Acting on the advice of his mother Rhea, Zeus released the Centimani and the Cyclopes from Tartarus. The hundred-handed ones hurled boulders a hundred at a time against the Titans. The Cyclopes made lightning bolts for Zeus to use as a weapon. They also gave Poseidon a magical trident, with which he could shake the earth and shatter any object. For Hades, the Cyclopes fashioned a helmet that made the wearer invisible. With these powerful weapons and the strength of their new allies, victory smiled on Zeus and the Olympians eventually won the ten-year war against the Titans.

This war was called the Titanomachy, which was so terrible that it nearly destroyed the world. After the war, Old Father Sky became so weak that he was in danger of collapsing into Mother Earth. So Zeus condemned the Titan Atlas to support the sky on his shoulders for eternity. Zeus cast Cronus and the rebellious Titans down into Tartarus. Then he assigned the Centimani to guard the gates of Tartarus for all time. With the entire world open to them after the war, the Olympians chose the summit of Mt. Olympus for their home. Zeus became the undisputed ruler on Olympus. He made his sister Hera his queen, his brother Hades to govern the Lower World, and his brother Poseidon to have full command over the Sea. However, the supremacy of Zeus was recognized in all three kingdoms, in heaven, on earth, and under the earth.

推翻了父亲的王位之后，克罗诺斯成为至高权利的象征，他娶了瑞亚并生下了六个孩子：三子三女。他们分别是哈迪斯（普路托）、波塞冬（尼普顿）、宙斯（朱庇特），赫斯提（维斯太）、得墨忒耳（刻瑞斯）和赫拉（朱诺）。然而，父亲乌拉诺斯留下的诅咒和预言令他始终寝食难安，他害怕自己的孩子有朝一日会奋起反抗他。为了防止预言成真，克罗诺斯采取了极端的防范手段。他在孩子们呱呱坠地之际，就将他们一个个吞进了肚子。轮到第六个，也是最后一个孩子宙斯的时候，瑞亚决心要救下这个孩子。她用婴儿服包裹好一块石头，将它递给了正在焦急等待的父亲。就这样，宙斯得救了，并且我们将会看到，他成为了那个反抗并取代他父亲的人，最终成为所有希腊人的主神。

瑞亚将儿子宙斯藏在克里特岛上，在那里一头圣羊为他提供乳汁，仙女梅丽西给他喂蜂蜜。在仙女和瑞亚的祭司们精心的呵护下，这个孩子迅速长大，拥有强壮的身体和超凡的智慧。当瑞亚觉得宙斯已经足以与他的父亲抗衡之时，便将他带回了王宫。宙斯机智地骗克罗诺斯喝下了一种药水，使得他不停地呕吐。于是一个接一个地，宙斯的哥哥姐姐们从他父亲的口中被吐了出来。

克罗诺斯和他的提坦巨人们不甘心就此失败，他们向宙斯一辈宣战。克罗诺斯一方占据了俄特里斯山，而宙斯及其兄弟姐妹则驻扎在奥林匹斯山上。在母亲瑞亚的建议下，宙斯释放了被囚禁在塔尔塔罗斯的百臂巨人和独眼巨人。百臂巨人能够同时将上百块巨石投向敌人，而独眼巨人则制造闪电给宙斯作为武器。此外，他们还为波塞冬制作了一把可以撼动地球、击碎一切的神奇三叉戟，给哈迪斯做了一顶戴上便可以隐身的头盔。有了这些强大武器和盟友的帮助，胜利的天平开始向宙斯倾斜，奥林匹斯山的众神们终于在十年之后打败了提坦巨人。

这场战争被称为“提坦之战”。由于过于惨烈，它几乎将世界摧毁。战争结束后，天空之父变得极度衰弱，就快坠入大地之母的怀抱。于是，宙斯便罚提坦巨人之一的阿特拉斯用双肩永远扛着天空。宙斯将克罗诺斯和反叛的提坦巨人们都投进了塔尔塔罗斯，随后他命百臂巨人看管塔尔塔罗斯的大门。如今，天下尽归奥林匹斯山众神所有，他们选择奥林匹斯山作为他们的家，宙斯成为无可争议的统治者。他娶了姐姐赫拉为王后，令哥哥哈迪斯掌管冥界，波塞冬统领海洋。当然，宙斯是天空、大地和地下这三界的至高主宰。

Extra 拓展测试

1. What is the name of the below Titan?

   下面这个提坦巨人叫什么名字？

2. In all the above paragraphs, Cronus, or Kronos as a variant spelling, is taken as the Titan father of Zeus. However, there is a Greek God of Time named Chronos, which is frequently confused with Cronus. That is why sometimes Cronus is described as an old man leaning on a scythe or sickle, with an hour-glass in his hand. A story is generally narrated in a chronological order, or time order.

Can you guess what a chronoscope is?

在上述这些段落里,克罗诺斯(Cronus,或者拼作 Kronos),是宙斯的父亲。然而,还有一位名为刻罗诺斯(Chronos)的时间之神,两者经常会被混淆,这也就是为什么有时克罗诺斯会被描述成这样一位老人:倚靠着一把镰刀,手里则拿着一个沙漏。通常一个故事都是按照 chronological order,也就是时间顺序来讲述的。

你能猜到 chronoscope 是什么东西吗?

(1. 答案:阿特拉斯)

(2. 答案:计时器)

CHAPTER 3 The Origin of Man
第三章 人类的起源

Word Knowledge 词汇知识

Humanity(人类)

The word *humanity* may either be defined as human beings collectively or the quality of being humane. In Latin, both *hom-* and *hum-* have the meaning of man or human being. The root *hum* is derived from *humus*, meaning earth or soil, which might suggest the origin of man from the earth. Accordingly, words containing *hum* are often associated with lowly rank or position, such as *humble*, *humiliate* or *humility*. The word *humid* means similar to moist, which could also be connected to the soil.

单词 humanity 既可以作为人类的总称,也可以表示人性或博爱。在拉丁语中,hom- 和 hum-都可以指人,hum 这个词根源自 humus,意思是"土地"或"泥土",这或许暗示了人类的起源是土地,与此相一致的,是含有 hum 的单词常常表示身份或地位低下,例如 humble(谦卑)、humiliate(羞辱)和 humility(谦逊)。humid 一词和"潮湿(moist)"意思相仿,也可以和土壤相联系。

Promethean(普罗米修斯式)

As the creator and benefactor of mankind, Prometheus has become a symbolic and probably one of the most recognized figures in Greek mythology. The modern word Promethean bears out its heritage. Be it a noun or an adjective, the word signifies either being daringly original or creative, in the way that Prometheus helped create civilization, or being defiant of authority or limits, like Prometheus stealing fire from the gods, or suffering on a grand scale, representing the torture inflicted on Prometheus by Zeus.

作为创造并普惠人类的英雄,普罗米修斯已经成为希腊神话中一个具有象征意义且知名度极高的人物。"普罗米修斯式"(Promethean)这个现代词语所包含的内涵都源自这个人物。无论作为名词还是形容词,它要么表示勇敢的创新,如同普罗米修斯帮助人类创造文明;要么表示反抗权威或打破束缚,如同普罗米修斯盗取火种;要么则表示巨大的苦难,如同宙斯对普罗米修斯施加的酷刑。

Pandora(潘多拉)

In Greek mythology, Pandora was the first mortal woman created by Hephaestus on the command of Zeus, and then sent to the human world as a present. Her name meant "all gifts" because she had been endowed with some special gifts by the gods and goddesses, such as a smooth persuasive tongue by Hermes, a dazzling beauty by Aphrodite and a gorgeous robe by Athena, each of which could make her irresistible and harmful to man.

在希腊神话中,潘多拉是赫菲斯托斯奉宙斯的指令造出的第一个女性人类,她被作为礼物带到了人类世界。她的名字意思就是"所有的礼物",因为诸神分别赋予了她特殊的礼物,譬如来自赫耳墨斯的巧舌如簧,来自阿芙洛蒂忒的惊人美貌以及来自雅典娜的华丽长袍。每一件礼物都使得她在男人的眼中无法抗拒又祸害无穷。

The Myths 神话故事

The creation of man from clay is a miraculous birth theme that recurs throughout world religions and mythologies. Just like Nuwa who molded figures from the yellow earth in Chinese mythology, a similar work was done by Prometheus, a Titan who had stood on the side of the Olympians led by Zeus against his father Cronus, in Greek and Roman mythology. As the name of Prometheus meant "forethought", he could see into the future and predicted the final victory of Zeus in the Titanomachy.

However, Prometheus was embittered by Zeus' cruel treatment of banishing his Titan-brothers eternally into the chthonic depth of Tartarus. To defy the supremacy of Zeus, he formed, out of clay, the first man, into whom Athena had breathed a soul. Full of love for the beings he had called into existence, Prometheus determined to elevate their minds and improve their condition in every way. He therefore shaped men to walk on two legs so that while all the other animals turned their faces downward, humans alone would raise their heads to heaven and gaze at the stars. He taught them astronomy, mathematics, the alphabet, medication and so on.

When Prometheus set about making human beings, his brother Epimetheus, whose name means "afterthought", was assigned the task of creating the lower creatures. Due to a lack of wisdom and common sense, Epimetheus gave each species a special gift to survive on the earth, such as strength to the wild beasts, feathers to winged animals, and hard shells to sea creatures, leaving no superior gifts for the human beings to rival other species. Although endowed with intelligence, Prometheus thought that this gift was not enough, so he contrived to steal some sparks from the heaven and gave the torch to his beloved mankind.

Furious at this second defiance, Zeus commanded that Prometheus be chained to a rock on Mount Caucasus, where a ravenous vulture ever came to tear at his liver which ever grew again. His period of ordeal was to be thirty thousand years. Prometheus faced his bitter fate firmly and never showed signs of weakness and submission to Zeus. He was eventually rescued by Heracles, who killed the eagle and set the benefactor of mankind free.

During Prometheus' pain and suffering, men were not left unpunished. Zeus commanded Hephaestus to fashion a woman out of clay. Up to that time, mankind had consisted entirely of males, so Pandora, which means all-gifted, was the first female mortal. She was so named because she had received every attribute necessary to make her charming and irresistible from the gods and goddesses. Then she was conducted to the house of Epimetheus by Hermes, the messenger of the gods. Although he had been warned by his brother not to accept any gift from Zeus, Epimetheus was so fascinated by the beautiful being that he welcomed her to his home and made her his wife.

The couple lived happily for some time. Then misfortune befell the human world. Epimetheus had in his possession a big cask left by Prometheus and had been warned by his brother not to open it in any case. But woman's curiosity could not withstand so great a temptation. One day, when Epimetheus was out, Pandora lifted the lid and out from the cask came strife and war, plague and sickness, theft and violence, grief and sorrow and all the other evils that the human world would henceforward have to experience. Just as Hope was about to escape, Pandora hastily closed the lid, and thus preserved to man that never-failing solace which helps him bear the many ills in life.

泥土造人的说法在世界各地的宗教和神话故事中是一个反复出现的主题,正如中国神话中的女娲造人,在希腊罗马神话中,类似的工作由普罗米修斯来完成。在宙斯率领奥林匹斯山众神与其父亲克罗诺斯对决的战役中，这位提坦巨人站在了宙斯的一边。因为“普罗米修斯”的意思就是“先知”，他能够看见未来，预见到了宙斯会在这场大战中取得最后的胜利。

然而，宙斯将战败的提坦巨人永久关进地狱深渊塔尔塔罗斯的做法让普罗米修斯心生不满。为了对抗宙斯的权威，他从黏土中造出了第一个人，雅典娜吹了一口气，赋予了这个人灵魂。普罗米修斯深爱自己所创造的人类，下决心尽一切可能提升他们的能力。于是，他将人类塑造成两条腿直立行走的物种，当其他动物低头向下的时候，只有人类可以抬头向上、仰望星空，他将天文学、数学、文字、医学等知识传授给了人类。

就在普罗米修斯着手造人的时候，他的弟弟厄庇墨修斯奉命创造其他的生物。“厄庇墨修斯”的意思是“后知”，由于缺乏智慧和常识，他赋予了自己创造的每个物种一种特殊的能力，例如，他赋予野兽巨大的力量，赋予飞禽羽毛，赋予海洋生物硬壳，结果没有任何一种特殊能力留给人类。尽管普罗米修斯给了人类智慧，但他认为这还不足以保证人类的生存，于是他设法从天宫盗来了火种，将火把传给了他心爱的人类。

自己的权威再次被挑战令宙斯恼羞成怒，他下令用铁链把普罗米修斯锁到高加索山的岩石上，在那里，一只贪婪的秃鹰会天天来啄食他的肝脏，而他的肝脏会重新长出来。如此的折磨会延续三万年。面对如此悲惨的命运，普罗米修斯并未低头，他顽强地忍受着，直到最终海格立斯杀死秃鹰，人类的恩人才获救。

就在普罗米修斯受难期间，人类也遭到了宙斯的惩罚。宙斯命令赫菲斯托斯用黏土塑造了一个女人。当时，所有的人类都是男性，因此，潘多拉是第一个女性，她的名字意思是“所有的礼物”。之所以取这样的名字，是因为她接受了来自诸神的各种礼物从而变得异常迷人，令男人们难以抗拒。神的信使赫耳墨斯把她带到了厄庇墨修斯的家。尽管厄庇墨修斯事先得到过哥哥的警告，不要接受宙斯的任何礼物，但是这个美丽的女人实在令人着迷，所以厄庇墨修斯还是让她进了家门，成为自己的妻子。

这对夫妻幸福地生活了一段时间之后，灾难降临了。厄庇墨修斯家里有一只大箱子，是哥哥托他照管的，但是普罗米修斯警告他在任何时候都不能打开那箱子。然而有一天，厄庇墨修斯出门后，好奇心让潘多拉禁不住诱惑而打开了箱盖，从箱子里飞出了纷争、战争、瘟疫、疾病、偷窃、暴力、痛苦、悲伤等各种各样的不祥之物，这些都成了人类所要经历的东西。就在希望即将飞出之际，潘多拉匆忙关上了箱盖，这才为人类保留了一丝能够帮助他们应对苦痛的心灵慰藉。

Extra 拓展测试

1. Which of the following species was probably created by Epimetheus?
下面哪一个物种有可能是厄庇墨修斯创造的？

A

B

2. Now people often use Pandora's box to refer to a process which, once begun, will generate many complicated problems. Here is an example: *The project, which seemed so promising, turned out to be a Pandora's box*. The phrase has in fact become a common noun as Pandora's box shell, pandora shell, or simply pandora, to mean something from the sea. Do you know what it is?

现在人们经常用潘多拉的盒子来指某个一旦开启，就会产生一连串问题的过程。例如：这项看起来前景颇好的工程，结果却成了潘多拉的盒子。事实上，这个词组已经变成了一个普通名词，可以写作 Pandora's box shell，pandora shell 或者就是 pandora，是一种来自海洋的东西，你知道它是什么吗？

（1. 答案：B）

（2. 答案：蛤蜊）

CHAPTER 4 The Ages of Man
第四章 人类的时代

Word Knowledge 词汇知识

Autochthony(土生人)

Just as there were several theories concerning the creation of the world, so were there various accounts on the origin of man. One account attributed the primitive human beings as having sprung from the earth, like wild plants forcing their way through the ground in the early spring of the year. Such a theory is referred to as Autochthony, which consists of two parts: *auto-*, meaning "self", and *chthon*, "earth". The prefix *auto-* is so powerful that there are many words beginning with it, such as *automatic*, *autograph*, *autobiography*, *autonomy*, *automobile* etc.

如同世界的起源有不同版本一样，关于人类的起源也说法不一。有一种说法是原始人是从地里钻出来的，就像早春时节野草破土而出一般。这种"土生人"的说法被称为Autochthony，这个词包括两部分：*auto-*的意思是"自己"，*chthon* 的意思是"土地"。词缀 auto-非常强大，由此开头的词汇很多，如 automatic(自动的)、autograph(亲笔签名)、autobiography(自传)、autonomy(自治)、automobile(汽车)等。

Deucalion(丢卡利翁)

Deucalion and his wife Pyrrha were an old childless couple, kind and pious and contented with life. Having been forewarned by his father Prometheus of the forthcoming flood, he had made himself a huge chest. When the deluge came, the couple took refuge in it and floated for nine days until it touched land again on Mt. Parnassus. Feeling lonely and insecure, the old couple prayed to the gods for help. An oracle instructed them to cast the bones of their mothers about. They were perplexed as to the meaning of the command, but at length both agreed that by the bones of their mothers were meant the stones of the earth. Accordingly they took up stones from the mountain side and started throwing them over their shoulders. Miraculously, from those thrown by Deucalion there sprang up men, and from those thrown by Pyrrha, women. Thus the world was repopulated, and a new life began.

The word *deuce* means something representing or represented by the number two. It is derived from the prefix *deu*- or *duo*-. For instance, *duet* refers to a performance by two singers, instrumentalists or dancers. *Double* means a thing which is twice as large as usual, and to *duplicate*, to multiply by two.

丢卡利翁和他的妻子皮拉是一对善良虔诚的孤寡老人。因为事先得到了父亲普罗米修斯的警告,丢卡利翁做了一只大箱子。当大洪水来临之际,他们躲在箱子里逃过一劫。在漂流了九天九夜之后,他们在帕纳塞斯山重新踏上陆地。出于孤独和恐惧,他们祈求神明的帮助。神谕指示他们将母亲的骨头扔向四周,他们对此迷惑不解,后来终于达成一致,认为母亲就是大地,骨头就是石头。于是,他们捡起山上的石头朝身后扔去。奇迹出现了:丢卡利翁扔出去的石头都变成了男人,皮拉扔出去的石头都变成了女人,整个世界又恢复了人类的欢声笑语。

英语中 deuce 这个词指的是数字二,它起源于 deu-或 duo-这个前缀。例如:duet 的意思是二重唱或二重奏,double 的意思是两倍,而 duplicate 的意思就是乘以二。

Myth of the Metals(金属的神话)

Myth of the metals was an interesting piece recorded by Plato in his famous book *The Republic*, a Socratic dialogue. According to the myth supposedly told by Socrates, people were framed differently, with different metals mixed into their soul: gold for the rulers, silver for the auxiliaries, and brass or iron for the husbandmen and craftsmen. Children were usually made of the same metal as their parents, but if this was not the case the child must either descend or ascend in the social order. If ever a child made of brass or iron was to become a guardian, the State would be destroyed.

金属的神话出自柏拉图的名著《理想国》,记录的是苏格拉底的一段有趣对话。根据这则神话,不同的人类灵魂被赋予了不同的金属:金子给了统治者、银子给了领导者、铜铁给了农民和手艺人。通常来说,孩子身上的金属属性与他们的父母是一致的,假如出现偏差的话,那么这个孩子的社会阶层必定会出现上升或者下降。一旦某个铜铁性质的孩子成了领导者,那么整个国家都会遭殃。

The Myths 神话故事

Some ancient Greeks denied the creation of men by Prometheus. Instead, they thought that Gaea, Mother Earth, bore them spontaneously as the best of her fruits, especially in the soil of Attica. The first man, Alalcomeneus by name, came to this world even before the birth of the Moon, whose descendants became the so-called golden race. Hence there were the myths about the Ages of Man, or the stages or races of human existence on the earth. Two slightly-different accounts survive from ancient Greece and Roman on the degeneration of humanity over time, which is symbolically indicated with metals of successively decreasing value: the Golden Age, the Silver Age, the Bronze Age and the Iron Age.

Gold was the metal of the sun, so the Golden Age was the best of all ages. It was an age when Cronus sat on the throne. People lived in peace and harmony with nature, who, in turn, satisfied all the wants of man in abundance. There was no evil, no fear, no greed or mistrust. People lived to a very old age but with a youthful appearance and eventually died peacefully. At that time, men had no knowledge of navigation and therefore did not explore the larger world.

The Silver Age fell within the rule of Zeus, who broke the eternal spring into four seasons. Consequently, human race began to learn agriculture and architecture, but they no longer worshipped the gods and offered no sacrifices. With a life span of one hundred years, they lived only a short time as grown adults and spent that time in strife with one another. As the metal of the moon, silver has a dimmer luster than gold. However, the race of the Silver Age was not entirely devoid of virtue.

In the Bronze Age, Zeus created human beings out of the ash trees, a hard wood used in spears. Bronze was a metal connected to weapons, so the mankind in this age were hardened and tough, prone to warfare. They dressed up in bronze, armed with weapons of bronze, and lived in houses of bronze. Towards the end of the Bronze Age, human beings became so wicked and lawless that the gods resolved to destroy them all by means of a flood. Deucalion, son of Prometheus, and his wife Pyrrha, on account of their piety, were the only mortals saved.

According to *Works and Days* by Hesiod, there was a historical period called the Age of Heroes after the Bronze Age. The human race in this age were strong, brave and heroic. They became the heroes who fought at Thebes and Troy. Since this is the only one age that does not correspond with any metal, some writers of later times, such as the Roman poet Ovid, tend to exclude it from the lineage of man.

Iron is the hardest and most troublesome metal to work. The Iron

Age was the name Hesiod gave to his own time. The Iron Age was described as one of endless care and grief. All modern men were created by Zeus as evil and selfish without any faith, truth and justice. It was a race of men deserted by the gods, and presumably Zeus would destroy this race one day.

The Ages of Man is a long passage of continuous degeneration, tracing the lives of men as descending from a state of primitive innocence to evil and corruption. Hesiod wove the mystic and the realistic together, creating a blended story based on the ancient tale, which we could learn from and reflect on.

有一些古希腊人否认普罗米修斯造人的传说，认为在混沌之初，地母盖亚便自然而然地诞下了人类，作为其最佳的果腹之物，尤其是在阿提卡地区。而第一位人类名叫阿勒克美尼斯，其出生甚至要早于月亮女神，而他的后代便构成了所谓的黄金一族。于是，也便有了关于人类时代的神话，说的是人类在地球上存在的不同时期或种族变化。关于人类的演变和堕落，从古希腊罗马流传下来的有两个略微不同的版本，它们的共同之处是都象征性地采用了质地迥异的金属来表示不同的时代：黄金时代、白银时代、青铜时代和铁器时代。

黄金代表了太阳，因此，黄金时代是最好的时代。这是克罗诺斯在位时期，人类和大自然和谐相处，大自然用丰富的资源满足着人类的一切需求，没有邪恶、没有恐惧、没有贪婪、没有怀疑。人类不仅寿命很长，还能容颜不老，死亡也异常安详。在那时，人类还不懂航行，对外部世界一无所知。

白银时代是宙斯统治时期，他将永久的春天划分成了四季，人类开始学习耕作和建筑，然而，他们不再崇拜诸神，也不再向诸神献祭。尽管有百年的寿命，他们的成年期却异常短暂，并且都在彼此的倾轧中度过。作为月亮的象征，白银没有黄金那么耀眼。但是，白银时代的人类也并非一无是处。

青铜时代的人类是宙斯从用来制造长矛的梣树上造出来的。青铜是让人联想到武器的金属，所以这个时期的人类粗暴、凶狠、好战，他们身着青铜衣裤、手拿青铜武器、住着青铜房屋。到了青铜时代的后期，人类变得邪恶而不驯，以致诸神决定用一场洪水来将他们全部清除。普罗米修斯的儿子丢卡利翁和他的妻子皮拉因为对神的虔敬，成为唯一活下来的人类。

根据赫西奥德的长诗《工作与时日》，青铜时代之后出现的是英雄时代。这一时期的人类强壮而英勇，他们成了底比斯和特洛伊战争中的英雄。由于这是唯一一个没有和金属相关联的时代，后来的一些作者，如古罗马诗人奥维德，倾向于把它从人类的谱系当中排除掉。

铁是最硬、也是最难加工的金属。铁器时代是赫西奥德本人所处的时代，这是一个充满忧愁痛苦的时代。宙斯赋予所有现代人的是邪恶和自私，没有信仰、没有真理、没有正义，这个时代的人类已经被诸神所抛弃，并且总有一天会被宙斯所灭亡。

人类的时代是一段漫长的、不断堕落的过程，从最初原始的天真烂漫到后期的邪恶腐化，赫西奥德将古代神话与现实世界巧妙结合，创作出了一个混合的故事，以警醒世人不断反思。

Extra 拓展测试

1. Which human age does the following picture probably describe?
下面这幅图描述的有可能是人类的哪一个时代？

2. In ancient Greece, the ash trees were dedicated to the sea god Poseidon. They stand for sacrifices, sensitivity and higher awareness. The association of the ash trees with "Tree of Life" from which humanity sprang comes from Norse mythology. In Scandinavian folklore, the ash tree becomes Yggdrasil, the symbol of immortality and the link between the three levels of the cosmos. Do you know what it is?

在古希腊,梣树是献给海神波塞冬的树,它代表着牺牲、敏感和崇高的意识,而梣树和"生命之树"的联系源自北欧神话,在斯堪的纳维亚的民间故事中,梣树变身为伊格德拉修,是永生的象征,也是连接宇宙中三个世界的纽带。你知道它是什么吗?

(1. 答案:青铜时代)

(2. 答案:世界树)

CHAPTER 5 The Origin of Love
第五章 爱的起源

Word Knowledge 词汇知识

Amor(爱)

Please examine the following words. What do they have in common?

amorist, *amorous*, *amateur*, *amatory*, *amiable*, *amicable* ...

Yes. They are all formed with the Latin root *amor*-, which means love. Amor is the Roman equivalent for Eros, the little mischievous god of love and son of Aphrodite in Greek mythology. Many people may be more familiar with his Roman name Cupid. In fact, the Greek name Eros means love of all kinds, whereas the Roman name Cupid, a variation on "cupido", means desire or sexual lust. By contrast, the name Amor emphasizes the emotional or spiritual integration between people.

请仔细看看下面这些词：amorist, amorous, amateur, amatory, amiable, amicable……它们有什么共同之处吗？没错，他们都含有拉丁词根 amor-，意思是"爱"。阿莫尔(Amor)是希腊神话中淘气的小爱神厄洛斯的罗马名字，他是阿芙洛蒂忒的儿子。许多人可能对他的罗马名丘比特(Cupid)更熟悉。事实上，希腊名厄洛斯的意思是"所有的爱"，而罗马名丘比特源自 cupido 一词，意思是"欲望"或"性欲"。相比而言，阿莫尔这个名字强调的是人与人之间情感或精神的契合。

Lesbian(同性恋女子)

Lesbian now means a female homosexual or a woman who is primarily attracted to other women. The word used to mean the residents of the Isle of Lesbos, a Greek island, where lived a woman poet Sappho in 600 B. C. Although much of her poetry had been destroyed by religious fundamentalists, the few poems of Sappho that remain speak clearly her love and infatuation with women. Being referred to as the tenth Muse by Plato, Sappho is the first lesbian ever documented. Prior to the word lesbian gaining popularity, women who loved other women were often called "sapphic", and their love, defined as "sapphistry".

lesbian一词现在指女同性恋者,或者天生被女人吸引的女性。这个词原本是指住在希腊莱斯博斯岛(Lesbos)上的居民。公元前六百年,岛上曾住着一名女诗人萨福。虽然她的大部分诗作都被宗教原教旨主义者们所焚毁,但是从残存下来的一小部分中仍然可以清楚地看出她对女性的爱和迷恋。被柏拉图称为第十位缪斯女神的萨福,是第一位被记录下来的女同性恋者。在lesbian一词流行之前,女同性恋者常被称为"萨福女",而此种感情则被称为"萨福爱"。

Gay(同性恋男子)

The word gay, derived from the Old French word "*gai*", originally means joyful or carefree, like the famous line in the poem *Daffodils* by William Wordsworth: "A poet could not but be *gay* in such a jocund company." It is around 1920s or 1930s that the word began to have a new meaning. A gay man is not just a man addicted to sexual pleasure, but a homosexual man. It seems that the word homosexual is much too clinical, suggesting a physical disorder, so the word gay is preferred for its association with mirth and freedom. The abstract noun gaiety has largely cleared of the sexual connotation as with the word gay, and keeps its definition related to festive and celebration.

单词 gay 源自法语的 gai，本义是指快乐和无忧，如同英国诗人华兹华斯《致水仙》中的著名诗句："诗人对此殊激昂，独在花中事幽躅"（郭沫若译）。到了 20 世纪二三十年代，这个词开始有了新的含义，gay man 不仅指沉迷性爱欢愉的男人，还可以指男同性恋者。因为 homosexual 一词似乎太像医学术语，给人以机体紊乱的印象，所以更多的人偏爱用 gay 这个让人联想到快乐和自由的词汇。而抽象名词 gaiety 已经基本上将性的含义完全清除了，保留下来的是和节日及庆祝相关联的喜悦心情。

The Myths 神话故事

Have you ever wondered why there are gays and lesbians in the world? Although scientists have been looking into homosexuality from biological or genetic perspective for a long time, so far no one knows exactly what determines an individual's sexual orientation. Interestingly, there is a myth story ever recorded by Plato, the ancient Greek philosopher, in his well-known book *Symposium*, which seems to account perfectly for such a phenomenon.

According to the myth on love, human race at the very beginning fell into three types: the male, the female, and the hermaphrodite, a being which was of half male and half female. Each of these beings was globular in shape, with rounded back and sides, four arms and four legs, two lots of privates and one head, on which there are two faces, both the same, but each face a different direction. They walked erect, forward or backward, whichever they pleased, but when they broke into a run they simply stuck their legs straight out and went whirling round and round like a clown turning cartwheels.

The males were descended from the Sun, the females from the

Earth, and the hermaphrodites from the Moon. The three sexes were so energetic and arrogant that they tried to scale the heights of heaven and set upon the gods. Zeus felt the threat from the humanity and counselled the other gods on Mount Olympus. The gods did not want to blast them out of existence with thunderbolts as they did the giants, but at the same time they could not let them get altogether out of hand. At last, after racking his rains, Zeus offered a solution.

To put an end to such a disturbance by weakening these people without destroying them, Zeus proposed cutting them all in half, thus killing two birds with one stone, for each one would be only half as strong, and there would be twice as many of them, which would serve the purpose of the gods very nicely. They could still walk about, upright, on the two legs, and if they dared make any more trouble with the gods, they would be split up again, consequently having to hop about on one.

Zeus thus cut the human race all in half. After the work of bisection was done, he asked Apollo to heal the whole thing up, such as turning their faces to front, and pulling in the skin all the way round. Since then, each human was left with one face, two arms and two legs, and one lot of private, and more importantly, a desperate yearning for the other half. They asked for nothing better than to be rolled into one again, such a hunger they had never experienced before. This is what we call love, the innate affection, which is always trying to reintegrate one's former nature, to make two into one, and to bridge the gulf between one human being and another.

Those who were slices of the original female type are now attracted by women and become lesbians, while men who are slices of the male are followers of the male, showing their masculinity throughout their boyhood by the way they make friends with men. Some people may call them shameless, but they are wrong because such a man or woman is of an amorous disposition, which is simply shown in public life. Likewise, the halves from the former hermaphrodite sex will naturally be attracted by people of the opposite sex, the seemingly normal kind in the modern society.

你有没有想过为什么世界上会有同性恋者存在？尽管科学家们一直在尝试从生物或基因的角度研究这个问题，但是迄今为止，没有人确切地知道性取向的决定因素。有趣的是，古希腊哲学家柏拉图曾在他著名的《会饮篇》一书中记载过一则神话故事，似乎为这一现象的存在提供了完美的解释。

根据这则神话，人类最初分为三类：男性、女性和双性，一种一半是男性、一半是女性的生物。所有人的身体都是球形的，无论后背还是侧面都是圆的，他们有四只胳膊四条腿、两套生殖器和一个脑袋，上面长着两张一模一样的脸，朝着不同的方向。他们直立行走，可以随心所欲地向前或向后，而一旦跑起来，他们只需伸出自己的腿，便可以像独轮车上的小丑一样向前翻滚。

男性人类来自太阳，女性人类来自大地，双性人类来自月亮。这三种人类精力旺盛且傲慢无比，甚至企图丈量天空，与天神对决。这令宙斯深感不安，于是他与奥林匹斯山的诸神商讨。他们既不想像消灭巨人那样用雷电把人类全部消灭，也不想看到人类肆无忌惮。终于，在绞尽脑汁之后，宙斯提出了一种解决办法。

为了彻底摆脱麻烦，在不消灭人类的前提下削弱他们的力量，宙斯建议将人类全部劈成两半，如此一来，每个人就只有原来一半的力量，但人的数量却会翻倍，能很好地满足天神们的需求，可谓一箭双雕之策。人类依然可以用两条腿直立行走，而如果他们胆敢再给天神添乱的话，就把他们再一分为二，让他们最终不得不单腿蹦跳。

就这样，宙斯将所有的人类都分成了两半。分人的工作完成后，宙斯叫来阿波罗处理善后事宜，诸如把他们的脸转到前面，把伤口用皮肤盖上之类。自此，每个人类都只剩下了一张脸、两只胳膊两条腿和一套生殖器。更为重要的是，他们极度渴望找到自己的另一半，不惜一切地想要重新合二为一，他们以前从未体验过这种渴望。这就是我们所说的爱，一种天生的感情，努力想要为自己找回另一半的自我情绪，在两个人类之间架起桥梁，合二为一。

那些最初属于女性的半身人，如今只对女人感兴趣，成了女同性恋者，而那些原本属于男性的人类，如今便成了男性的追逐者，从少年到成年，他们只和男性交朋友。或许有些人会认为他们不知羞，那就错了！因为这样的男人或女人只不过是将他们心里的爱公之于众罢了。与此同理，那些原本的双性人自然会被异性吸引，因此成了当今社会最常见的情况。

Extra 拓展测试

1. Which type of human race does the following picture describe?
   下面这幅图描绘的是哪一类人？

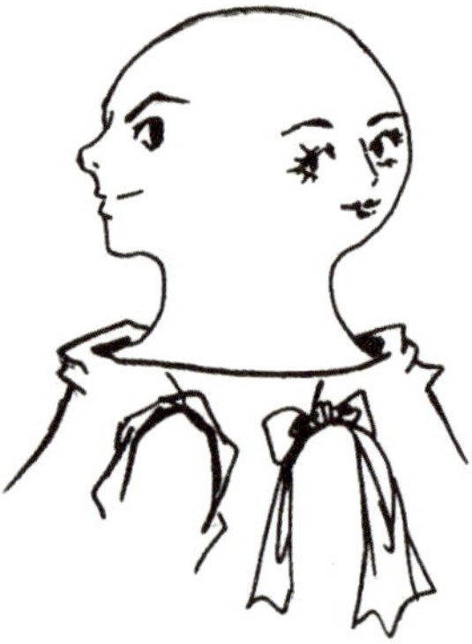

2. The Greek word *mythos* denotes an unverifiable account of story, while the word *logos*, a rational one. Plato, the ancient Greek philosopher and founder of the Academy who was expected to be a logical and reasonable thinker, actually made an abundant use of the ancient myths in his philosophical works. Plato's myths fall roughly into two subjects, those dealing with the origin of the universe and those on morals and the origin and fate of the soul.

   Do you know who is Plato's teacher and his most famous student?

希腊词汇 mythos(神话)的意思是无法证实的故事,而 logos(罗格斯)的意思是合理的故事。作为古希腊哲学家以及学园创始人的柏拉图,本应是一位富于逻辑而理性的思想家,但事实上,在他的哲学著作中运用了大量的神话故事。柏拉图所采用的神话大致分为两个主题:世界的起源和灵魂的真谛及归宿。

你知道柏拉图的老师和最著名的学生分别是谁吗?

(1. 答案:双性人 the hermaphrodite)

(2. 答案:苏格拉底和亚里士多德)

FURTHER READING The Pelasgian Creation Myth
延伸阅读　佩拉斯吉的创世神话

Greek people refer to themselves as Hellenes, and therefore the Greek culture is "Hellenic" in nature. As the son or brother of Deucalion, Hellen was the ancestor of all the Hellenes or Greeks. The original name for Greece is Hellas, from which derived the word "Hellenistic". The Hellenistic period starts from the death of Alexander the Great, and ends with the emergence of the Roman Empire and the defeat of Cleopatra and Mark Antony by Octavian in 31 BC. During this period, Greek cultural influence and power was at its peak, spreading through the Mediterranean and into the Near East and Asia and centering on Alexandria in Egypt and Pergamum in Turkey.

However, before the Hellenistic period, the ancient people who inhabited the coasts and islands of the Aegean Sea and eastern Mediterranean were known as the Pelasgian. The Pelasgian creation myth involves a singular creatrix goddess who dominates humans and predates other deities. According to the myth, Eurynome, whose name means "wide wandering", was the Goddess of All Things. In the very beginning, she rose naked from Chaos, but found nothing substantial for her feet to rest upon. Therefore she divided the sea from the sky, dancing lonely upon its waves.

Catching the north wind at her back and rubbing it between her hands, Eurynome warmed the pneuma and generated the great serpent Ophion. She assumed the form of a dove, brooding on the waves and, in due process of time, laid the Cosmic Egg. At her bidding, Ophion coiled seven times about this egg, until it hatched and split in two. Out tumbled all things that exist, her children: sun, moon, planets, stars, the earth with its mountains and rivers, its trees, herbs, and living creatures.

Eurynome and Ophion made their home upon Mount Olympus, where he vexed her by claiming to be the author of the Universe. Forthwith she bruised his head with her heel, kicked out his teeth, which were then scattered on the earth. Pelasgus, the first man and ancestor of the Pelasgians, sprang up from Ophion's teeth in the soil of Arcadia. Next, the goddess created the seven planetary powers, setting a male and a female Titan over each: Hyperion and Theia for the Sun; Atlas and Phoebe for the Moon; Crius and Dione for the planet Mars; Coeus and Metis for the planet Mercury; Eurymedon and Themis for the planet Jupiter; Oceanus and Tethys for Venus; Cronus and Rhea for Saturn.

希腊人自称“赫楞尼斯”，因此，希腊文化本质上是“赫楞”文化。赫楞是丢卡里翁的儿子或兄弟，也是所有“赫楞尼斯”或希腊人的祖先。希腊原本的名字叫“赫勒斯”，由此衍生出了“Hellenistic（赫勒尼斯的）”一词。赫勒尼斯（希腊）时期从亚历山大大帝去世开始，到公元前31年克娄巴特拉和安东尼被屋大维打败，罗马帝国诞生为止。这一时期，希腊文化的影响力达到了顶峰，以埃及的亚历山大和土耳其的帕加马市为中心，从地中海沿岸延伸至近东和亚洲地区。

然而，在赫勒尼斯时期之前，居住在爱琴海和地中海东部地区的原始居民被称为佩拉斯吉人。在佩拉斯吉的创世神话中，只有一位创世母神，她凌驾于一切神灵和人类之上。传说这位母神欧律诺墨是“万物之神”，她的名字意思是“四处游荡”。在太始之初，她从混沌之中赤条条升起，发现四周并无落脚之地，于是便将天空与海洋分开，独自在浪花间起舞。

欧律诺墨抓来北风作为倚靠，用双手抚摸它，温暖了圣灵并由此创造出了巨蟒厄斐翁。她化身鸽子，孵卧在浪花之上，随着时间的推移，一颗宇宙巨蛋诞生了。在她的命令之下，厄斐翁盘绕巨蛋七次，直至巨蛋一分为二，从中孵化出了他们的后代——世间万物：太阳、月亮、星辰、地球以及地球上的山川、河流、森林、草木和生物。

欧律诺墨和厄斐翁将家安在了奥林匹斯山上，在那里，厄斐翁因为自称宇宙的创造者而惹恼了欧律诺墨，一怒之下，她用脚后跟把他踢得鼻青脸肿、牙齿脱落。那些牙齿散落到大地上，第一个人类佩拉斯戈斯由此诞生，据说他是从落在阿卡狄亚泥土中的莽牙中蹦出来的，他也成了佩拉斯吉人的祖先。接下来，母神又创造了七大星宫，并分别指派一位男性和一位女性提坦巨人来掌管：许珀里翁和忒伊亚负责太阳；阿特拉斯和福柏负责月亮；克利俄斯和狄俄涅负责火星；克厄斯和墨提斯负责水星；欧律墨冬和西弥斯负责木星；俄刻阿诺斯和蒂锡斯负责金星；克罗诺斯和瑞亚负责土星。

Extra 拓展测试

It was Augustus (Octavian) who defeated Cleopatra and Mark Antony and thus turned the Roman Republic into the Roman Empire. Being a legendary figure in history, Cleopatra VII survives in numerous artistic and literary works, both ancient and modern. Apart from her marriage with Mark Antony, she had had a romantic relationship with another Roman politician and military general. Do you know his name?

奥古斯都(屋大维)打败了克娄巴特拉和马克·安东尼，从而将罗马共和国变成了罗马帝国。在历史上，克娄巴特拉七世是一位传奇式的人物，无论是在古代还是现代，她的名字都不断出现在无数的艺术及文学作品当中。除了和马克·安东尼的婚姻之外，她还和另一位罗马政治家、军事家有着一段浪漫史，你知道那是谁吗？

(答案：恺撒大帝)

PART Ⅱ　The Divinities

第二部分
神的谱系

扫一扫,听本部分音频

CHAPTER 1 The Twelve Olympians
第一章 奥林匹斯山的主神

Word Knowledge 词汇知识

Olympian(奥林匹亚)

The word Olympian may refer either to one of the twelve gods and goddesses living on Mount Olympus, or a competitor in the Olympic Games. It could also be used as an adjective to indicate a disaster on an Olympian scale, meaning a tremendous scale. In ancient Greece, there was a plain taken as the chief sanctuary of the god Zeus, where the original Olympic Games were held. Hence the site was named Olympia. Olympic Games may also be replaced by Olympiad, or a period of four years between Olympic Games.

奥林匹亚这个词既可以指奥林匹斯山的十二主神之一,也可以指奥运会的竞技者之一。它还可以作为形容词,用来指影响巨大的灾难。在古希腊,有一块平原被认为是宙斯主要的圣所,也是古代奥运会的举办地。因此,这块地区被称为奥林匹亚。奥运会也可以叫奥林匹亚德,或指两届奥运会之间的四年时间。

Trident(三叉戟)

Trident, the weapon used by the sea god Poseidon, is a three-pronged spear with which earthquakes or tsunamis might be created. In fact, the prefix *tri-* in English simply means three. There are many popular words containing this prefix. For example, trilogy means a group of three related novels, plays and films, such as the film trilogy *The Lord of the Rings*. Tripod, a support for camera, is often used by photographers. In Christianity, God is believed to be a trinity, which means a union of God the father, God the son, God the holy spirit.

海神波塞冬的武器三叉戟是一把三分叉的鱼叉，可以用来引发海啸或地震。事实上，tri-这个前缀在英语中的意思就是“三”，有很多常见词汇都含有这个前缀，例如：trilogy 指的是三部系列小说、剧本或电影，譬如《魔戒》三部曲；tripod 是摄影师们用来支撑相机的三脚架。在基督教中，上帝是三位一体的存在，换言之，是圣父、圣子和圣灵的统一体。

Vulcan(伏尔坎)

Vulcan is the Roman counterpart of the Greek god Hephaestus, god of fire and blacksmith. In some versions of the myth, the fire that Prometheus gave to man was actually stolen from Hephaestus' forge. Hephaestus was believed to have crafted such magnificent equipment as Hermes' winged helmet and sandals, Aphrodite's famed girdle, Achilles' armor, Heracles' bronze clappers and Eros' bow and arrows. The word volcano is derived from Vulcano, a volcanic island in Italy, which was apparently named after Vulcan, the Roman god of fire.

伏尔坎是希腊火神与匠神赫菲斯托斯对应的罗马名字。在一些版本的神话中，普罗米修斯送给人类的火种就是从赫菲斯托斯的打铁炉里偷来的。赫菲斯托斯手艺精湛，制作出了很多奇妙的东西，譬如：赫耳墨斯带翅膀的头盔和飞鞋、阿芙洛蒂忒著名的腰带、阿喀琉斯的铠甲、海格立斯的青铜响板以及厄洛斯的弓箭。火山(volcano)一词源于伏尔坎诺(Vulcano)，显然这座意大利的火山岛正是以火神伏尔坎(Vulcan)命名的。

The Myths 神话故事

The ancient Greeks believed that the home of their gods and goddesses was on the top of Mount Olympus, the high and lofty mountain between Thessaly and Macedon, whose summit, wrapt in clouds and mist, was hidden from the mortal view. Because of their residency atop Mount Olympus, the major deities, twelve in number, were named the Olympians. Six of them, Zeus, Poseidon, Hera, Demeter, Hestia and Aphrodite, were the offspring of the Titans Cronus and Rhea. The rest, Athena, Apollo, Artemis, Ares, Hephaestus and Hermes, were the principal children of Zeus.

Zeus, the great presiding deity of the universe, may be recognized by his rich flowing beard, and the thick masses of hair. Being all-powerful and all-knowing, he could change his shape or the shape of anything else. He generally bears in his uplifted hand a sheaf of thunderbolts and is always accompanied by an eagle. His greatest weakness was his fondness for beautiful women.

As the lord of the seas, Poseidon was the second most powerful god after Zeus. The symbol of his power was the fisherman's fork or trident, by means of which he produced earthquakes and raised up islands from the bottom of the sea. He usually appears standing erect in a graceful shell-chariot, drawn by hippocamps, or seahorses, which swept across without touching the water.

Hera, Zeus' beautiful wife and queen of heaven, was the goddess of marriage and family, and the symbol of a jealous and vengeful wife in many stories. Hera is usually depicted as a solemn and majestic matron on a throne, holding a pomegranate in one hand as an emblem of fertile blood and death, and a scepter surmounted by a cuckoo in the other.

Hera was the mother of Ares, god of war, and Hephaestus, god of fire, yet she disliked both sons, for Ares was too violent and untamed to be lovable, and Hephaestus, too ugly and deformed. Legend has it that rejected by his parents, Hephaestus had been thrown off Mount Olympus and down to earth, resulting in his lameness at birth. To compensate for the poor child, Zeus made Aphrodite, the goddess of love and beauty, his wife.

In contrast to Ares, who often represents the physical or destructive aspect of war, Athena, goddess of wisdom and reason, functions commonly as such intelligent respect as military strategy and generalship. Springing miraculously full grown in armor from Zeus' forehead, Athena was Zeus' favorite child and was allowed to use his thunderbolts.

Artemis and Apollo were twins and children of Zeus and Leto. Therefore, they both represented light and were able to alleviate suffering by curing diseases. Although both skilled in the use of bow and arrow, Artemis surpassed her brother in a far more eminent degree. She was the goddess of chastity, virginity, the hunt, the moon, and the natural environment. Apart from his most important duty as the sun god, Apollo was also the god of music, who would entertain the other Olympians with sweet melodies from his golden harp.

As the youngest Olympian and the son of Zeus and the nymph Maia, Hermes was god of eloquence and patron of merchants. He was well-known as a trickster and the messenger of all the gods. It was his duty to guide the souls of the dead down to the underworld.

Other Olympians worth mentioning are Demeter, goddess of harvest and agriculture, and Hestia, goddess of the fireplace. Demeter, as the wife of Zeus, became also the mother of Persephone, who was tricked into the underworld and became the wife of Hades.

古希腊人相信众神的家在奥林匹斯山上，即塞萨利和马其顿之间那座高大巍峨的山脉，山巅云雾缭绕，凡人的肉眼无法视见。也是因为奥林匹斯山这个住所，十二位主神被统称为奥林匹亚神。其中六个：宙斯、波塞冬、赫拉、得墨忒耳、赫斯提和阿芙洛蒂忒是提坦巨人克罗诺斯和瑞亚的后代。其余六个：雅典娜、阿波罗、阿尔忒弥斯、阿瑞斯、赫菲斯托斯和赫耳墨斯则是宙斯的孩子。

宙斯作为宇宙最高的主宰，拥有长长的茂盛的胡须以及浓密的毛发。他无所不能、无所不知，可以任意变形或变形任何任何东西。在他抬起的手中，通常握着一束闪电，身旁始终环绕着一只老鹰。他最大的弱点就是喜欢拈花惹草。

海神波塞冬是仅次于宙斯的第二大主神，鱼叉，或通常说的三叉戟就是他权力的象征。利用这一武器他可以制造地震，将海底升起变为岛屿。他通常会站在由海马拉着的贝壳战车上呼啸而过。

作为天后和宙斯美丽妻子的赫拉是掌管婚姻和家庭的女神，在许多故事中，她也是妒妇和悍妇的象征。她常常一脸严肃地坐在王位上，左手举着代表生育和死亡的石榴，右手握着一把权杖，权杖的顶端则站着一只布谷鸟。

赫拉是战神阿瑞斯和火神赫菲斯托斯的生母，但是这两个儿子她都不喜欢，因为阿瑞斯太过暴力凶猛，赫菲斯托斯则太过丑陋畸形。传说因为遭到父母嫌弃，婴儿赫菲斯托斯被从奥林匹斯山顶扔了下去，导致他一出生就成了跛子。为了补偿这个可怜的孩子，宙斯将美丽的爱神阿芙洛蒂忒许配给了他。

如果说阿瑞斯代表了战争暴力和毁灭性的一面，那么智慧女神雅典娜则代表着策略和将才等军事战略和领导才能等理性的一面。非常神奇的是，雅典娜是从宙斯的额头里蹦出来的，并且一出生就是全副武装的成人。她是宙斯最心爱的孩子，甚至可以使用父亲的闪电。

阿尔忒弥斯和阿波罗是双胞胎兄妹，是宙斯和勒托的孩子，因此，他们都代表了光明，能够治愈疾病、减轻痛苦。尽管两人都善使弓箭，但阿尔忒弥斯的技艺远超兄长。她是贞洁女神，是狩猎、月亮和自然界的象征，而阿波罗除了主司太阳神之职以外，还是音乐之神，他会用他金制的竖琴为奥林匹斯山的众神们弹奏美妙的旋律。

赫耳墨斯是宙斯和仙女迈亚的儿子，也是十二主神中年龄最小的。他能言善辩，是经商者的保护神。他既是恶作剧精灵，又是众神的使者。他的职能之一就是引导亡魂进入冥界。

十二主神中值得一提的还包括丰收和农业女神得墨忒耳以及女灶神赫斯提。作为宙斯的侧室，得墨忒耳为他生下了珀耳塞福涅，后者被骗入冥界，成了哈迪斯的妻子。

Extra 拓展测试

1. Which of the following is likely to be the trident of Poseidon?
   下面哪一个武器有可能是波塞冬的三叉戟？

A

B

2. Phoebe, Artemis, Diana, Luna, Selene, Hecate ... All the words have one meaning in common: goddess of moon. From the name Luna came such common words as lunar, lunatic, lunarnaut, lunar calendar, lunar eclipse and so on. Selenium, a word derived from Selene, is a chemical element used in making electrical equipment and colored glass. A lack of selenium in human body can lead to illnesses such as depression. Can you guess what selenium is?

   福柏、阿尔忒弥斯、戴安娜、卢娜、塞勒涅、赫卡忒……这些词有一个共同的意愿：月亮女神。从卢娜(Luna)这个名字衍生出的常见名词包括 lunar(月亮的)、lunatic(神经错乱的)、lunarnaut(登月宇航员)、lunar calendar(阴历)、lunar eclipse(月食)等。selenium 一词源自 Selene 这个名字，指一种用来制造电器或有色玻璃的化学物质。人体如果缺少这种物质则会导致疾病。如抑郁症。你能猜到这是一种什么物质吗？

(1. 答案：A)

(2. 答案：硒)

CHAPTER 2 The Family of Zeus
第二章 宙斯的家庭

Word Knowledge 词汇知识

Cornucopia(丰饶角)

It is said that when Zeus was an infant, he was suckled from the horn of a goat. Later, this horn was filled with flowers and fruits and given to Zeus as a present. The filled horn served as a symbol of abundance since then. The word cornucopia, in Greek, means "horn of plenty". Now with the meaning "an inexhaustible store of something", cornucopia is often seen on Thanksgiving Day.

传说在宙斯还是个小婴儿时，他从一只公羊角里吸吮乳汁。后来仙女们就把这只公羊角装满鲜花和水果送给宙斯作为礼物。从此，装满东西的公羊角就成了富饶的标志。cornucopia(丰饶角)这个词在希腊语中的意思就是"装满东西的角"。如今，这个代表"大量、丰盛"的东西常常在感恩节出现。

Metamorphoses(变形记)

Metamorphoses, a Latin epic which retells Greek and Roman myths, was written by the Roman poet Ovid around 8 A.D. As one of the most influential works of western culture, the poem has inspired such authors as Dante Alighieri, Geoffrey Chaucer and William Shakespeare. Metamorphoses is the plural form of the word metamorphosis, which means transformation or shape-shifting. There are many stories in Greek mythology about Zeus who transformed himself repeatedly in order to approach mortal or immortal maidens. In modern English, the prefix *meta-* appears in such words as *metabolism* or *metathesis*, denoting a change of position or condition, and some academic words like *metacognition*, *meta-mathematics*, *meta-analysis*, and so on, meaning higher or across. The word *morphology* now refers to the study of the forms of things

《变形记》是一首重述希腊和罗马神话故事的拉丁语叙事诗，由罗马诗人奥维德创作于公元 8 年左右。作为西方文化中最具影响力的作品之一，这首长诗启发了但丁、乔叟和莎士比亚等作家。metamorphoses 是 metamorphosis 一词的复数形式，意思是“变形”。在希腊神话中，有很多故事讲述的都是宙斯变成各种东西以便接近某个女神或凡人女子。在当代英语中，meta-这个前缀可以构成诸如 metabolism（新陈代谢）或 metathesis（音位变换）这样的词汇，其中 meta-的意思就是改变位置或条件，而在一些学术词汇中，如 metacognition（元认知）、meta-mathematics（元数学）、meta-analysis（元分析）里，meta-是更高或交叉的意思，而 morphology 一词就是“形态学”。

Europa(欧罗芭)

In Greek mythology, Zeus was often seen wooing a mortal maiden under various disguises. Myth has it that if Zeus revealed himself in his true form as king of heaven, the splendor of his glory would cause instant destruction to mortals. Europa, the daughter of Agenor, king of Phoenicia, was one of Zeus' mortal lovers. Charmed with her great beauty, Zeus transformed himself into a white bull, and trotted quietly up to the princess. Unaware of the danger, Europa seated herself on its back playfully. Hardly had she done so than the disguised god bounded away with his lovely burden, and swam across the sea with her to the island of Crete. Such was the origin of the continent Europe. Europe was named after Europa, the mother of Minos, who later became the king of Crete.

在希腊神话中,宙斯在追求人间的美女时,常常会伪装成各种各样的东西,因为据说一旦宙斯露出他宇宙之王的真身,他身上的巨大光芒便会立刻将凡人彻底摧毁。欧罗芭是腓尼基国王阿戈诺耳的女儿,也是宙斯在凡间的情人之一。宙斯被她的惊人美貌所吸引,化身为一头白牛悄悄接近公主。欧罗芭没有意识到其中的危险,顽皮地骑上了牛背。还没等她坐稳,白牛便带着这个可爱的负担飞奔而去,越过爱琴海,来到了克里特岛。这就是欧洲大陆的起源,欧罗芭的儿子弥诺斯后来成了克里特的国王。

The Myths 神话故事

With his golden throne on the highest summit of Mount Olympus, Zeus was respected and awed by all the gods and mortals. All the kings boasted that they were descendants of Zeus. Though he married his own sister Hera, the all-ruling and all-powerful god gave his wife plenty of reasons to be jealous, for Zeus was renowned of his numerous love affairs with both goddesses and mortal maidens. It is generally believed that Zeus had seven immortal wives, whose names were Metis, Themis, Eurynome, Demeter, Mnemosyne, Leto, and Hera.

Metis, Zeus' first wife, was one of the Oceanides or sea nymphs. With supreme wisdom and prudence, she foretold to Zeus that one of their children would dethrone him, which appalled the king. In order to avert the possibility of the prediction being fulfilled, Zeus turned his wife into a fly and swallowed her before any children were born to them. He was too late, for Metis had already conceived a child. Feeling afterwards violent pains in his head, Zeus sent for Hephaestus and ordered him to open it with an ax, which was obeyed. With a loud and martial shout, a beautiful being, clad in armor from head to foot, sprang out from Zeus' forehead. This was Athena, goddess of wisdom and patron of Athens.

As the goddess of justice, law and order, Themis gave birth to six children: the three Horae (Hours) and the three Moirai (Fates). Eurynome, one of the Oceanides, was the mother of the three Graces or Charites. Demeter, the goddess of agriculture, first resisted Zeus, but Zeus violated her in the form of a bull. From their union came a daughter Persephone, the future queen of the Underworld. Mnemosyne, the goddess of memory, was best known as the mother of the nine Muses. Of all the consorts of Zeus, Leto was the one being loved most tenderly, but her lot was far from being a happy one. After a good deal of persecution at Hera's hands, Leto gave birth to Apollo and Artemis, the twin children of Zeus and his most favorite.

Myth has it that Hera, the principal wife of Zeus and queen of heaven, also refused the first proposal of Zeus. Then Zeus transformed himself into a distressed cuckoo. Feeling pity on the little bird, Hera took it inside and held it to her breast to warm it. Zeus revealed himself in his true form and took advantage of her. Ashamed of being exploited, Hera agreed to marry with Zeus. The couple had three children: Ares, the god of war, Hephaestus, the god of fire and forge, and Hebe, the goddess of forever youth.

The union of Zeus with his seven immortal wives empowered him with various faculties, such as wisdom and metamorphosis from Metis, justice and order from Themis, grace and beauty from Eurynome, and prodigious memory from Mnemosyne. In addition to the immortal wives, Zeus was also allied to a number of mortal maidens, from whom descended other minor deities, demigods, heroes, and the like.

在奥林匹斯山最高的山巅,宙斯坐在金色的宝座上接受众神和凡人们的敬仰,所有的国王都自称是宙斯的后代。这个拥有至高无上权力的主神虽然娶了他的姐姐赫拉，却始终让自己的妻子生活在妒忌之中，因为宙斯是出了名的花心，成天拈花惹草。一般认为，他在神界的配偶有七位，分别是墨提斯、西弥斯、欧律诺墨、得墨忒耳、摩涅莫辛涅、勒托和赫拉。

墨提斯是宙斯的第一任妻子，是俄刻阿尼得斯（海洋仙女）之一，拥有超凡的智慧和敏锐，她预言宙斯的孩子有可能会推翻他，令宙斯惊恐不已。为了防止预言成真，宙斯在墨提斯还没有生下任何孩子之前，便把她变成了一只蝇虫吞进了肚子里。但他还是晚了一步，当时墨提斯已经有了身孕。之后宙斯便感到头痛欲裂，他叫来了赫菲斯托斯，命令他用斧子劈开自己的脑袋，火神照着做了。随着一声响亮而有力的吼叫，一个全副武装的美丽身影从宙斯的额头一跃而出。这就是智慧女神雅典娜，雅典的守护神。

西弥斯是代表正义、法律和秩序的女神，她给宙斯生了六个孩子：霍莉（时间）三姐妹和摩伊拉（命运）三姐妹。作为海洋仙女之一的欧律诺墨是美惠三女神的母亲。农业女神得墨忒耳起初对于宙斯是抗拒的，但是宙斯化身成一头公牛侵犯了她，他们的女儿就是后来成为冥界王后的珀尔塞福涅。摩涅莫辛涅是记忆女神，并以身为缪斯女神的母亲而著名。在神界的配偶中，勒托是宙斯最疼爱的一位，但是她的命运却有些不幸。被天后赫拉反复迫害的勒托后来生下了阿波罗和阿尔忒弥斯，一对双胞胎兄妹，也是宙斯最心爱的孩子。

根据神话传说，宙斯的正妻、天后赫拉起初也拒绝了宙斯的求爱，于是宙斯变成了一只受伤的布谷鸟，赫拉怜惜这只小鸟，就把它抱回家，贴在胸口温暖它。宙斯趁机变回原形，占有了她。失去贞洁的赫拉迫于羞耻，答应了宙斯的求婚。这对夫妻有三个孩子：战神阿瑞斯、火神赫菲斯托斯以及青春女神赫柏。

和七位女神的结合赋予了宙斯不同的能力，例如来自墨提斯的智慧和变形能力、来自西弥斯的正义和秩序、来自欧律诺墨的优雅和聪慧、来自摩涅莫辛涅的超凡记忆等。除了神界的配偶外，宙斯和无数凡人女子也有风流韵事，并生下了众多的小神、半神或英雄等后代。

Extra 拓展测试

1. Which goddess wife of Zeus does the following picture probably describe?

下面这幅图描绘的可能是宙斯在神界的哪位妻子？

2. Grace has long been a popular girl's name in western countries, which may be largely due to the association of this word with the Graces, the three minor goddesses of charm and beauty in Roman mythology. As daughters of Zeus and Eurynome, the three lovely sisters, Euphrosyne (Mirth), Aglaia (Splendor), and Thalia (Bloom), were depicted not only as the symbol of perfect beauty and goodness themselves, but also the maiden deities to bestow charm and refinement and joy on people in general.

The word charisma has its origin in Charites, the Greek equivalent of the Graces. Can you guess what charisma means?

在西方社会，"格蕾丝"一直是一个颇受欢迎的女孩名，很重要的原因可能就是这个名字和美惠三女神的联系。在罗马神话中，这三个代表魅力和美丽的小女神，是宙斯和欧律诺墨的女儿，欧佛洛绪涅(欢乐)、阿格拉伊亚(光彩)、塔里亚(花朵)这三姐妹不仅自身就是完美容貌和美德的化身，而且也是能够赋予普通大众魅力和高雅的女神。

单词 charisma 源自希腊美惠女神的对应词汇"卡里忒斯"。你能猜到 charisma 是什么意思吗？

(1. 答案：欧律诺墨)
(2. 答案：神秘的个人魅力)

CHAPTER 3　The Nine Muses

第三章　缪斯女神

Word Knowledge 词汇知识

Muse(缪斯)

Music, *museum*, *muse*, *amuse*, *mosaic* ... What do these words have in common? Yes, they were all originated from the nine Muses in Greek mythology. The original meaning of the word Muses, or Mousai, may either be that of the root '*mosis*', meaning desire or wish, or '*men-*', the mind or to think. In ancient times, the nine Muses were honored by mortals and immortals alike. Plato, the ancient Greek philosopher, built an altar for the nine muses in the library of his famous school, the Academy. The word "museum" actually means shrine or temple to the Muses.

下列单词：music(音乐)、museum(博物馆)、muse(沉默)、amuse(娱乐)、mosaic(马赛克)……有什么共同之处？对，他们都源自希腊神话中的缪斯女神。缪斯这个词最初的意思可能源自表示"希望"或"欲望"的词根 mosis，抑或和 men-这个词根有关，意思是"思想"或"思考"。在古代，上至天神下至凡人，无不对缪斯女神顶礼膜拜。古希腊哲学家柏拉图就曾在他所建立的著名学府——"学园"的图书馆里，为缪斯女神设立了祭坛。英语"museum(博物馆)"一词的意思就是缪斯女神的神殿。

Mnemosyne(摩涅莫辛涅)

Mnemosyne, the mother of the nine Muses, was the Titan goddess of memory and remembrance and the inventress of language and words. Being the daughter of Uranus and Gaea, she was also a goddess of time, representing the rote memorization required to preserve stories of history and the sagas of myth before the introduction of writing. From the name Mnemosyne, we get such modern English words as *memory*, *mnemonic*, *memoir* and so on. The word "mnemonics" is defined as a system or technique of developing the memory. Here is an example: *I tried to think of a mnemonic device so that I could remember the names of the presidents*.

摩涅莫辛涅是缪斯女神的母亲,也是发明了语言和词汇的记忆女神。她是乌拉诺斯和盖亚的女儿,是时间女神,代表了文字发明之前人们对于神话传奇和历史故事的机械记忆。从摩涅莫辛涅(Mnemosyne)这个名字。衍生出了现代英语中的 memory(记忆)、mnemonic(记忆术)和 memoir(备忘录)等这些词。如今,mnemonics 这个词表示某种帮助记忆的体系或方法,例如:我努力想找到一种记忆方法(mnemonic device)来记住那些总统的名字。

Hippocrene(灵泉)

Hippocrene literally means "Fountain of the Horse". According to the myth, there was once a singing contest between the Muses and the Pierides, the daughters of King Pierus, on Mount Helicon. The Muses sang with such extraordinary power that even the mountain raised itself in joyous response. With disbelief, Poseidon sent Pegasus, the white winged horse and child of Medusa, to check the boldness of the mountain in daring to move without his permission. Upon reaching the summit, Pegasus stamped the ground with his hoofs, and out gushed the waters of Hippocrene, which afterwards became the sacred fount to bring forth poetic or artistic inspiration.

The prefix *hippo*- means "horse" in Greek. It could be seen in such words as *hippocampus*, *hippodrome*, *hippology*, *hippomania*, *hippophobia*. The word *hippo* now is understood as the shortened form for *hippopotamus*. In the story of *Harry Potter*, there is a magical creature called *hippogriff*.

Hippocrene(灵泉)一词的本义是"神马之泉"。传说缪斯女神和国王庇厄洛斯的女儿皮厄里得斯曾进行过一场歌唱比赛。期间，缪斯女神的歌声婉转动听，令整座赫利孔山随之起舞。海神波塞冬对于大山未经允许便擅自移动的做法心生不满，派美杜莎的孩子、飞马珀加索斯前去查看。珀加索斯抵达山顶后，马蹄刚一落地，一道泉水便喷涌而出，后来，"神马之泉"便成了诗歌或艺术创作的灵感之泉。

在希腊语中，hippo-的意思是"马"，这个前缀出现在了 hippocampus(海马)、hippodrome(赛马场)、hippology(马学)、hippomania(爱马癖)和 hippophobia(恐马症)等这些词中。如今 hippo 一般作为 hippopotamus(河马)一词的缩略形式。在《哈利波特》的故事中，有一种神奇的生物名叫"鹰头马身有翼兽(hippogriff)"。

Eupheme(欧斐墨)

Instead of saying "Karl Marx has died", Fredrick Engels referred to him as having "peacefully gone to sleep". Euphemism is a rhetorical device in which a mild or indirect word or expression is adopted to substitute for a direct or harsh one. And the word "euphemism" is formed with a prefix *eu*-, meaning "well", and a root *pheme*, "speech". The similarity between Euphemism and Eupheme is quite obvious. In Greek mythology, Eupheme was regarded as the personification of good omen, praise, acclaims and applause. She was a member of the younger Charites or Graces, and the nurse of the nine Muses in the following story.

恩格斯没有说“马克思死了”，而是说他“安详地睡去了”。这里的委婉语是一种修辞手法，表示用间接或温和的词语代替直接或尖锐的话。委婉语（euphemism）一词包含前缀 eu-，意思是“好”，也包含词根 pheme，意思是“话语”。单词 euphemism（委婉语）和 Eupheme（欧斐墨）的相似之处显而易见。在希腊神话中，欧斐墨是吉兆、赞扬和喝彩的代名词。她是美惠女神的后代，在下面的故事中，她则是缪斯女神的抚养者。

The Myths 神话故事

The Muses were the nine daughters of Zeus and Mnemosyne, the goddess of memory. According to the Greek myths, Zeus bewildered Mnemosyne and slept with her for nine consecutive nights. The result of their encounter was the nine Muses, who were similar to everything. Mnemosyne gave the babies to nymph Eupheme and god Apollo, who instilled in them imagination and artistic talents. As followers of god Apollo, the Muses formed his choir and would dance and sing at the banquets of the Olympian gods. As good friends of goddess Athena, they took care of Pegasus, the winged horse, which opened for them by a blow of its hoof the sacred spring of Hippocrene, fountain of poetic inspiration, on Mount Helicon.

Each of the nine Muses was in charge of a particular form of art and was symbolized with a unique item: Calliope, the most honored muse, presided over epic poetry, and is represented with a writing tablet; Clio, the muse of history, had a scroll in her hand; Melpomene, the muse of tragedy, wore a tragic mask, while Thalia, the muse of comedy, a comic mask. Three Muses, Erato, the muse of love poetry, Euterpe, the muse of lyric poetry and Terpsichore, the muse of dance and song, were pictured each bearing a musical instrument, be it a lyre or a flute; Urania, the muse of astronomy, carried a celestial globe; Polyhymnia, the muse of sacred hymns, was crowned with a wreath of laurel.

The Muses were normally sweet and gentle. However, like many other Olympian deities, they would occasionally become fierce or even malicious if anyone dared to challenge their divine powers. One story involves King Pierus of Macedon who named his nine daughters after the Muses, thinking that they were better skilled than the goddesses themselves. The overconfident king and his mortal daughters even entered in a singing contest with the Muses on Mount Helicon. It is said that when the mortal maidens commenced their song, the sky became dark and misty, whereas when the Muses raised their heavenly voices, all nature seemed to rejoice. The mortal singers suffered a total defeat and were transformed by the Muses into singing birds as a punishment and humiliation for them.

There was another singing contest between the Muses and the Sirens, three sea nymphs who used to have beautiful white wings attached to their shoulders. Though sweet and seductive, the Sirens' voices were false and hypnotic which could turn the mariners to sleep and cause shipwrecks. By sharp contrast, the songs of the Muses were loyal and true, which was proved matchless. Like the Pierides, the Sirens paid for their vanity a costly failure with all their feathers being plucked out, and thus being deprived of the power of flying. Their feathers were then made into crowns of victory for the Muses.

Until today, the Muses are the symbols of inspiration and artistic creation. By calling upon and receiving the blessings of the Muses, a poet or dancer or musician can expect to transcend the normal bounds of talent and rise to unimagined level of creative insight. All the ancient writers appeal to the Muses at the beginning of their work. Homer, the Greek epic poet, for instance, asked the Muses both in the *Iliad* and *Odyssey* to help him tell the story in the most proper way. Dante, the great Italian poet, started his classic works *The Divine Comedy* like this: "O Muses, O high invention, aid me now!"

缪斯女神是宙斯和记忆女神摩涅莫辛涅的九个女儿。根据神话传说,宙斯迷恋摩涅莫辛涅的美貌,迷惑了她,和她连续同睡了九个晚上。他们结合的产物就是九个在各方面都非常相似的缪斯女神。摩涅莫辛涅将孩子交给仙女欧斐墨和阿波罗抚养,而正是阿波罗赋予了她们想象与艺术创造的才能。一方面,缪斯女神是阿波罗的随从及其合唱团成员,时常在奥林匹斯山众神的宴会上献歌献舞。另一方面,她们也是女神雅典娜的好友,替她照看飞马珀加索斯,而珀加索斯用马蹄为她们踏开了赫利孔山上的"灵泉",使之成为众多诗歌和艺术创作的灵感之源。

每一位缪斯女神掌管着一个特定的艺术领域,拥有其独特的象征物品:名气最大的缪斯女神卡利俄珀负责英雄史诗,其象征物是写字板;克利俄主管历史,手握卷轴;头戴悲情面具的墨尔波墨涅主司悲剧,与之对应的,则是头戴滑稽面具的塔利亚,她主司喜剧;有三位缪斯女神手里拿着乐器,她们分别是主司爱情诗的埃拉托、主司抒情诗的欧忒耳珀和负责舞蹈及歌唱的特耳西科瑞,她们所持的乐器不是里拉琴就是长笛;掌管天文的乌拉尼亚手里拿着地球仪;主管颂歌的波吕许谟尼亚则头戴月桂花环。

通常来说,缪斯女神都是甜美而温和的,但是,她们偶尔也会像奥林匹斯山的众神那样,变得凶狠甚至邪恶,那就是当有人胆敢挑战她们的神技之时。有一个故事讲的是马其顿国王庇厄洛斯,认为自己的九个女儿赛过缪斯女神,不仅以她们的名字来给女儿取名,还不自量力地让女儿和缪斯女神在赫利孔山上进行歌唱比赛。传说比赛那天,当人类少女敞开歌喉时,天空变得黑暗而阴霾,而当缪斯女神的天籁之声响起的一刻,大自然都呈现出欢乐的景象。凡人歌手不仅惨败而归,而且受到了缪斯女神的惩罚和羞辱,变成了一群会唱歌的鸟儿。

另一场歌唱比赛发生在缪斯女神和塞壬三姐妹之间。塞壬原本是海洋仙女,肩上长着美丽的白色翅膀。尽管她们的嗓音甜美诱惑,但却非常虚假,令人昏昏欲睡,能够导致船只触礁沉没。而缪斯女神的歌声则截然不同,它们真实而动人,无可比拟。最终,像皮厄里得斯的女儿们一样,塞壬三姐妹为她们的虚荣付出了惨重的代价。她们被拔光了所有的羽毛,丧失了飞翔的能力,而那些羽毛则被制成王冠,戴在了缪斯女神的头上。

直至今天,缪斯女神都是灵感和艺术创作的象征。通过呼唤缪斯女神，祈求她们的赐福，诗人、舞蹈家或音乐家们期待能够超越平凡的界限，达到无法企及的艺术高度。古代所有的作家在他们创作之初，都会恳求缪斯女神助其一臂之力。例如，古希腊诗人荷马在创作史诗《伊利亚特》和《奥德赛》时，曾希望缪斯女神能告诉他如何去做。意大利著名诗人但丁，也在其经典作品《神曲》的开头如此写道："啊，诗神缪斯！啊，崇高的才华！现在请来帮助我！"

Extra 拓展测试

1. Which literary or artistic field was the following Muse likely to be responsible for?
   下面这位缪斯女神有可能掌管的是什么领域？

2. After the defeat on Mount Helicon, the Pierides were transformed into magpies, some singing birds, as a punishment. Do you know what kind of birds they are?
   赫利孔山上败给缪斯女神后，作为惩罚，马其顿国王的女儿们被变成了 magpies——一种会唱歌的鸟，你知道这是什么鸟吗？

（1. 答案：历史）
（2. 答案：喜鹊）

CHAPTER 4
The Classification of Nymphs
第四章　仙女的分类

Word Knowledge 词汇知识

Evolution of Nymphs(宁芙的演变)

A nymph is a minor female deity typically associated with a particular location or landform. It is a concept originated from Greek and Roman mythology. Therefore the word is a bit archaic now. In modern times, this beautiful idea of animating all nature in detail reappears under the various local traditions extant in different countries. Thus do the Oceanides and Nereides live again in the mermaids, whist the flowers and meadow nymphs assume the shape of those elves and fairies.

A mermaid now refers to a mythical sea creature with the head and trunk of a woman and the tail of a fish, conventionally depicted as a beautiful maiden with long flowing golden hair. Mermaids can be found in the folklore of many cultures worldwide.

An elf is typically represented as a small, delicate and elusive figure in human form with pointed ears, magical powers and a capricious nature. Elves appear mainly in Germanic mythology and folklore.

The word fairy has its origin in the Latin word *fata*, or "the Fates", the three goddesses who preside over the birth and life of humans. Therefore, a fairy, though also a human-like creature, seems to have the potential or inclination to do good for people. Fairies are often portrayed in literature as "testing" humans to see their worthiness and then meting out either punishment or reward accordingly.

There are two other words that are about creatures similar to a fairy. Like an elf, a pixie is also small and humanlike being with pointed ears, yet it is typically known to be more mischievous than a fairy. Pixies are said to delight in deliberately misleading people. Being the only kind of fairy that has wings to fly, sprites are dazzling in color and about the size of large insects. They are playful and at times obnoxious. One of their favorite pastimes is pestering butterflies. The word sprite comes from the Latin word *spiritus* or *spirit*, meaning "soul" or "ghost". The capitalized word is now known as a soft drink by the Coca-Cola Company.

宁芙是一种地位稍低的小女神，通常和某种位置或地形相关联，宁芙的概念源自希腊罗马神话，因此这个词现在略显古旧。然而，在当代文学中，这种将大自然拟人化的美妙想法又以不同的方式在各个国家重新出现，于是我们看到俄刻阿尼得斯和涅瑞伊得斯变身为美人鱼，那些与鲜花和绿荫相伴的宁芙则演变成了仙女或精灵。

美人鱼现在指一种上半身为少女、下半身为鱼尾的神秘生物，在传统的描述中，她们都拥有美丽的金色长发。在世界各地的民间故事中都能看到美人鱼的存在。

精灵通常的形象是耳朵尖尖、小巧玲珑的人形生物，他们拥有法力、变幻莫测。精灵主要出现在日耳曼民族的神话及民间故事中。

"仙女(fairy)"这个词最早起源于拉丁语中的 fata，也就是掌管人类生死的"命运三女神"。因此，尽管仙女也是人形生物，但她们似乎更倾向于为人类做好事。在文学作品中，我们经常看到仙女们"检验"人类的品格，然后根据检验结果，来决定是该奖赏还是惩罚人类。

另外还有两个和仙女相类似的词汇。如同精灵，皮克希也是一种有尖尖耳朵的人形小生物，但是他们通常要比仙女们更加调皮捣蛋。据说他们以故意误导人类为乐。而作为唯一一种带翅膀的小精灵，斯波莱特的大小与巨大的昆虫差不多，他们闪闪发光、淘气顽皮，偶尔惹人讨厌。他们最大的消遣就是追逐蝴蝶。sprite 这个词的出处是拉丁语的 *spiritus* 或者 *spirit*，意思就是"灵魂"或"鬼魂"。如今，如果大写的话，斯波莱特(Sprite)就是可口可乐公司的著名饮料"雪碧"。

Joint Naming of the Ancient Greeks
(古希腊人的统称命名)

There was a tradition in ancient Greece that deities or people of one family, one clan, or one kind would be put together and referred to with one collective name. Often such a collective name was patronymic in nature, or contained information about the family origin. For example, the word "Titan" describes a kind of older gods with great strength and intelligence. "The Titans" is a joint name for male Titans, while "the Titanides", for the female. The name of "the Oceanides" could easily be associated with "Oceanus", the father of these ocean nymphs. Similarly, "the Pierides" were the nine daughters of King Pierus of Macedon. Although there are many other names, such as the Oreades, the Limoniades, or the Nereides, whose meanings are difficult to interpret, keep in mind that they are simply names of a group with similar characteristics.

古希腊人有一个传统，就是用一个统称来指代同一家、同一族、同一类的神或人，这个统称一般是父系家族的姓氏，或者包含了家族起源的相关信息。例如："提坦"指的是一种拥有强大体力和智力的初代神，"提坦们(the Titans)"是男性提坦巨人的统称，而"提坦尼得斯(the Titanides)"则指女性。"俄刻阿尼得斯(the Oceanides)"这个统称很容易联想到这些大洋仙女的父亲"俄刻阿诺斯(Oceanus)"，同样，"皮厄里得斯(the Pierides)"就是马其顿国王庇厄洛斯(Pierus)的九个女儿。虽然还有很多诸如"俄瑞阿得斯""利墨尼阿得斯""涅瑞伊得斯"这样的名字，意思并不好猜，但是大家只要记住它们就是指拥有类似特征的一组神或人就好了。

The Myths 神话故事

In Greek mythology, the nymphs were beautiful maidens of fairy-like form, presiding over the woods, grottoes, streams, meadows and so on. They fell roughly into three distinct classes: water nymphs, tree nymphs, and mountain nymphs.

Water nymphs are classified into three categories: the Oceanides, the Nereides and the Naiades. Ocean nymphs were daughters of Oceanus and Tethys. Three thousand in number, they were collectively referred to as the Oceanides. Like most sea divinities, they were endowed with the gift of prophecy. The Nereides, the fifty daughters of Nereus and Doris, were nymphs of the Mediterranean Sea. The best known of the Nereides were Thetis, the mother of Achilles, and Galatea, the beloved of Acis. The Naiades were the nymphs of fresh-water springs, lakes, brooks, rivers, and the like. The Naiades were intimately connected in idea with those flowers which were named after them, such as Nymphae, or water-lilies.

There are three important words for nymphs living in the woods: the Dryades, the Hamadryades and the Meliades. The first word is a collective noun generally understood as the spirit of trees. It is also the name for all tree nymphs who partook the distinguishing characteristics of a particular tree to whose life they were wedded. The second, the Hamadryades, is believed to be general word for the trees themselves, or wood nymphs. They would cease to exist when the trees were either felled or withered away and dead. In Greek mythology, for each particular type of tree, there will also be a name related to it, such as the melancholy Birch Nymph, the sturdy Beech Nymph, and the little coy Linden Nymph. The third word, the Meliades, referred to the nymphs who presided over fruit-trees, yet there are other sources claiming them to be the spirits of ash trees.

Mountain nymphs fall roughly into four distinctive types: the Oreades, the Napaeae, the Limoniades, and the Hyades. The first two types of nymphs were both swift in movement and good at chasing games, but they contrast sharply in their disposition. The Oreades, the principal and constant companions of Artemis, were tall and graceful mountain nymphs, acting as bold huntresses. Conversely, the Napaeae were the kind and gentle and shy nymphs of the valleys and glens. They were usually seen hiding behind the leaves while the Oreades were hunting wildly in the mountain. The Limoniades, or meadow nymphs, were usually represented dancing hand in hand in a circle. The Hyades were cloudy divinities, and, from the fact of their being invariably accompanied by rain, are pictured as incessantly weeping.

As the goddess of hunting and wild life, Artemis, the twin sister of Apollo, was said to be always followed by a band of eighty nymphs—twenty Amnisiades and sixty Oceanides. The Amnisiades, the daughters of the river god Amninos, formed the core retinue of Artemis and tended to her deer. The Oceanides, all nine years old in observed appearance, formed the choir of Artemis. In addition, the attendants and companions of the goddess included nymphs of other realms such as some bird-legged nymphs who attended the Stymphalian shrine of Artemis.

在希腊神话中，宁芙指一些类似于仙女的美丽少女，她们掌管着森林、岩洞、河流和草原等地方。她们大致可以分为三类：水宁芙、树宁芙和山宁芙。

水宁芙又可以细分为俄刻阿尼得斯（大洋仙女）、涅瑞伊得斯（海中仙女）、那伊阿得斯（水泉仙女）三类。大洋仙女是俄刻阿诺斯和蒂锡斯的女儿们。据说她们有三千之众，统称为俄刻阿尼得斯。她们像其他的海洋神仙那样，拥有预言能力。涅瑞伊得斯是涅柔斯和多里斯的五十个女儿，主要生活在地中海地区，她们中最著名的是阿喀琉斯的母亲忒提斯以及埃西斯的恋人伽拉忒亚。那伊阿得斯是掌管新鲜泉水、湖泊、小溪、河流等的仙女，她们和生活在周围的花朵密不可分，因此，很多花也以她们来命名，比如睡莲(Nymphae)。

关于生活在森林中的树宁芙，有三个重要的词汇：德律阿得斯（树仙）、哈墨德律阿得斯（木仙）和弥利阿得斯（果树仙女）。第一个词是树宁芙的总称，通常指那些生活在树上的仙女们，她们和某种树木相结合，并拥有此种树木特有的品质。第二个词哈墨德律阿得斯一般理解为树木本身，或称木宁芙，一旦树木枯萎死亡或遭砍伐，她们也便不复存在了。在希腊神话中，每一种特殊的树木都有与其相对应的树宁芙，诸如忧郁的桦树仙女、坚强的柏树仙女、小巧而羞怯的椴树仙女等。第三个词弥利阿得斯是掌管果树的仙女，但是也有人认为她们是梣树仙女。

山宁芙大致可以分为四种不同的类型：俄瑞阿得斯（山中仙女）、那庇伊（幽谷仙女）、利墨尼阿得斯（绿荫仙女）和许阿得斯（云中仙女）。前两种山宁芙都以善于奔跑、行动敏捷为人所知，但是她们却个性迥异。俄瑞阿得斯身材高大优美，是阿尔忒弥斯的主要随从，常以女猎手的形象伴其左右，与之相反，那庇伊则是出没在山间幽谷的仙女，她们善良、温和且害羞。当俄瑞阿得斯在山中狂奔逐鹿的时候，她们便悄悄地躲在树叶后面窥视。绿荫仙女利墨尼阿得斯最常见的形象就是一群手拉手在草地上起舞的少女。作为云中仙女，许阿得斯总是和雨神相伴而行，其典型形象就是流泪的仙女。

阿波罗的双胞胎妹妹阿尔忒弥斯是狩猎女神，也是野生动植物的保护神，传说她的身后总是跟着一大群随从，其中包括八十位宁芙仙女——二十位阿尼西阿得斯（大河仙女）和六十位俄刻阿尼蒂斯（大洋仙女）。阿尼西阿得斯是河神阿尼诺斯的女儿。她们替阿尔忒弥斯照看她的驯鹿，并构成了其侍女的主要组成部分。而六十位大洋仙女则组成了女神的圣乐团，她们的样貌看上去个个都是九岁的女童。此外，阿尔忒弥斯的侍从及朋友还包括一些其他领域的仙女，例如，有一类仙女长着鸟腿，主要负责管理女神的斯廷法罗斯圣殿。

Extra 拓展测试

1. Which of the following is likely to be the home of the Hyades?
下面哪一幅图有可能是许阿得斯的家？

A

B

2. Water nymphs are also a kind of ornamental aquatic plant. Do you know they are?
水宁芙也可以指一种观赏性的水生植物，你知道它们是什么吗？

（1. 答案：B）
（2. 答案：睡莲）

CHAPTER 5 The Deities of Darkness

第五章 神的黑暗系

Word Knowledge 词汇知识

Aether(以太)

Of all the deities in ancient Greek Mythology, those related to darkness and the underworld were certainly the most detested. Although most mortals fear of mentioning their names, such deities as Nyx, Erebus, Achlys, Hades and Persephone are bound to fill people's mind with awe and exhortation so as to force them to be cautious with their earthly undertakings. Whether you like it or not, this particular lineage of Greek deities has contributed a lot of interesting words to the English language. The first divine generation included Erebus, the primordial god of darkness, and Nyx, goddess of night. One of their sons was Aether, the god of pure or upper air. The English word "quintessence" originally means ether, the fifth substance in addition to air, fire, water and earth, which was considered the essence of the universe. Now the meaning has been extended to the most important features or the best example of something.

古希腊神话中,最令人讨厌的恐怕就是那些和黑暗及地狱相关联的神吧。尽管凡人都害怕提起他们的名字,但是正因为有尼克斯、埃里伯斯、艾柯吕斯、哈迪斯、珀尔塞福涅这些神的存在,尘世间的人类才会心怀敬畏与警戒,对自己的言行有所顾忌。不管你喜欢与否,希腊神界中这一另类的分支为英语贡献了许多有趣的词汇。最早的黑暗之神埃里伯斯和黑夜女神尼克斯构成了这一谱系的第一代。他们的一个儿子以太，代表了天堂纯净的空气。英语中 quintessence 这个词就是指“以太”，即空气、火、水、土之外的第五元素，古希腊人认为这是宇宙的精华。如今，该词的意思已经延伸为表示某物的最重要特征或最佳范例了。

Thanatos and Hypnos(萨纳托斯和许普诺斯)

Of the offspring of Erebus and Nyx, there were the twin sons Thanatos and Hypnos. As the god of death, Thanatos became the origin of such words as *thanatology*, *thanatophobia*, *thanatopsis*, *euthanasia*, *athanasy* and so on. Mors, the Roman equivalent of Thanatos, could also account for the reason why the words like *mortal*, *mortality*, *mortality rate* are related to death. As for Hypnos, if you know that he was the Greek god of sleep, don't you think that such words as *hynopsis*, *hypnotic*, *hypnotherapy*, *hypnotize* suddenly become a lot easier than before? Again Somnus, the Roman name of Hypnos, may provide you with clues for the below words: *somnambulant*, *somniloquence*, *somnifacient*, *somnolent*, *insomnia* etc.

在埃里伯斯和尼克斯的后代中，有一对双胞胎兄弟：萨纳托斯和许普诺斯。作为死亡之神的萨纳托斯，是英语中 thanatology(死亡学)、thanatophobia(死亡恐惧症)、thanatopsis(死亡观)、euthanasia(安乐死)、athanasy(不死)这类词的出处。而萨纳托斯的罗马名字叫摩耳斯，这个名字可以解释为什么 mortal(凡人)、mortality(必死的命运)、mortality rate(死亡率)这些词都和死亡有关。至于许普诺斯，如果你知道他是古希腊的睡眠之神，难道你不觉得像 hypnosis(催眠)、hypnotic(催眠剂)、hypnotherapy(催眠疗法)、hypnotize(使进入催眠状态)这样的词一下子变得容易理解了吗？同样，许普诺斯的罗马名索莫纳斯为我们提供了理解下列词汇的线索：somnambulant(梦游者)、somniloquence(梦呓)、somnifacient(安眠药)、somnolent(似睡非睡的)、insomnia(失眠症)。

The Oneroi(欧尼罗伊)

Homer describes the House of Dreams as having two gates, one of which was formed of ivory, while the other, of horn. The ivory gate represents deceptive or false dreams, whereas the horn, which carries the meaning of "fulfil", stands for factual or true dreams. The Oneroi, the gods of dreams, were the sons of Hypnos and the third generation of the night deities. Among them, Morpheus, Phobetor and Phantasos were the most prominent. Morpheus, the principal god, was depicted as a winged youth, bearing in his hand a cluster of poppies. As he steps with noiseless footsteps over the earth, he gently scatters the seeds of this sleep-producing plant over the eyes of weary mortals. If someone is said to be in the arms of Morpheus, we now understand that he or she is sleeping or dreaming.

In Greek, *phobos* means fear, so Phobetor was the god of frightening dreams or nightmares. Related words are *phobia* and *phobic*. Phantasos represented weird dreams. Dreams prompted by him are said to be rich in imaginary and may yield important hints of past, present or future. In fact, the word fantasy is simply a variant spelling of phantasy.

诗人荷马描述的"梦之屋"有两扇大门:一扇象牙门和一扇羊角门。象牙门表示欺骗性的虚假梦境,而羊角有"实现"的意思,因此羊角门代表了客观真实的梦境。睡眠之神欧尼罗伊是许普诺斯的儿子们,也是黑夜之神的第三代。他们中最著名的是摩耳甫斯、福柏托尔和芳塔索斯。摩耳甫斯是主要的睡梦之神,常见的形象是一位带翅膀的年轻人,手中拿着一把罂粟。他悄无声息地来到人间,将这些具有催眠作用的罂粟籽轻轻撒到倦怠的凡人眼皮上,现在,如果我们说有个人"躺在摩耳甫斯的臂弯里",那意思就是说"他/她正在睡觉或做梦。"

希腊语中的 phobos 意思就是"恐惧",因此,福柏托尔掌控的是吓人的梦,他是"噩梦之神"。与他相关的词汇有 phobia(恐惧症)和 phobic(恐惧症的)。芳塔索斯代表的是奇怪的梦。据说由他掌控的梦境极富想象力，能够为过去、现在或将来提供某种暗示。事实上，英语的fantasy(奇幻)一词不过是从phantasy演化来的另一种拼法罢了。

The Myths 神话故事

Hades, the son of Cronus and Rhea, and the youngest brother of Zeus and Poseidon, was the ruler of the dark lower world called Erebus, which was named after his predecessor, and inhabited by the shades or spirits of the dead. The ancient Greek believed that when a mortal ceased to exist, his spirit tenanted the shadowy outline of the human form it had quitted. These shadows or shades would be driven by Hades into his dominions, whose entrance was described as being in the far west beyond the furthermost edge of Oceanus.

In the grim underworld there were four great rivers, three of which had to be crossed by all the shades. These three were Acheron (sorrow), Cocytus (lamentation), and Styx (intense darkness), the sacred stream which formed the boundary of the realms. Myth has it that Charon, the unshaven old boatman, would only ferry over the Styx those whose bodies had received funereal rites on earth, and who had brought with them his indispensable toll, a small coin placed under the tongue of the dead. If these conditions had not been fulfilled, the unhappy shades were left behind to wander up and down the banks for a hundred years as restless spirits.

On the opposite bank of the Styx was the tribunal of Minos, the supreme judge. All shades had to confess fully before him of their actions or deeds on earth, based on which a sentence of happiness or misery would then be pronounced. The tribunal was guarded by the terrible triple-headed dog Cerberus, who permitted all shades to enter, but none to return. After this, the shades were conveyed to two opposite directions, some to the dread judge Rhadamanthus, while others, to the blissful Elysium.

The great judgment-hall of Rhadamanthus was surrounded by the river Phlegethon, the waves of which rolled flames of fire, and lit up these awful realms. There Rhadamanthus declared to each comer the precise torments which awaited him in Tartarus. The wretched sinners were then seized by the Furies, who scourged them with their whips, and hurled them down into the depths of endless torture. The principal sufferers in the gloomy Tartarus were Tityrus, Tantalus, Sisyphus, Ixion, and the Danaids.

Not all shadowy spirits were doomed to suffer in Tartarus. A few favored heroes would be conducted to Elysium, a delightful region filled with all that could charm the senses or please the imagination. After enjoying themselves in Elysium for a thousand years, they were destined to animate other bodies on earth. Before they leave, however, they had to drink from the river Lethe (oblivion), a gentle, silent stream whose waters had the effect of dispelling care, and producing utter forgetfulness of former events.

作为克罗诺斯和瑞亚的儿子,宙斯和波塞冬最小的弟弟,哈迪斯是黑暗冥界的统治者。他所管辖的地区叫埃里伯斯,也是前任管辖者的名字,来到这里的都是亡魂或亡灵。古希腊人相信,一个凡人死后,他的灵魂会借住在模糊的人形躯壳之下。随后,这些亡灵被哈迪斯驱赶至他的领地,其入口据说在西方,在大洋神俄刻阿诺斯疆域的尽头。

在阴森的冥界,有四条大河,其中三条是所有亡魂都必须经过的:阿刻戎河(悲伤)、科赛特斯河(恸哭)以及构成冥土边界的斯堤克斯河(黑暗)。传说,满脸胡须的老船夫卡戎只会把那些在阳间经过正规葬礼仪式的亡魂送过河去,并且这些亡魂的舌头下必须放一枚硬币,当作必须缴纳的过路费。如果有一个条件没有满足,这些亡魂就只能变成冥河畔的孤魂野鬼四处游荡了。

斯堤克斯河的对岸就是大判官弥诺斯的仲裁庭。所有的亡魂都必须在这里彻底坦白自己在阳间的所作所为,大判官再根据他们的供述做出判决。裁决的监督者是那只可怕的三头狗刻耳柏洛斯,它只允许亡魂进入，却从不会让任何亡魂出来。此后，亡魂会分成两路，其中一些去向可怖的判官拉达曼堤斯，还有一些，则进入了极乐之地伊利索姆。

环绕在判官拉达曼堤斯裁判所周围的是佛勒革同河，河里翻涌出的滚烫火焰将这片恐怖的区域点亮。在这里拉达曼堤斯向所有前来的亡魂宣布他们的最终刑期。宣判之后，复仇三女神会立刻上前抓住这些罪恶的亡魂，狠狠地鞭笞他们，再将他们投入塔尔塔罗斯的万丈深渊。在那里接受惩罚的有名罪人包括提提鲁斯、坦塔罗斯、西西弗斯、伊克西翁和达那伊得斯姐妹。

并非所有的亡魂都注定被投入塔尔塔罗斯受罚，有一些受到青睐的英雄们会被带到伊利索姆——一个充满欢乐与美好的极乐世界。在那里，这些幸运的亡灵们可以享受千年，之后，他们可以投胎转世。然而在离开冥界之前，他们必须饮下勒忒河（忘川）水。这条静谧小河的水据说可以驱散烦恼，让人彻底忘记前世的一切。

Extra 拓展测试

1. Which of the following do you think is Cerberus?
你觉得以下哪一个是刻耳柏洛斯？

A

B

2. *The Phantom of the Opera* is a novel written by French writer Gaston Leroux and was first published in 1910. It has become world famous due to its various stage and film adaptations, including a Broadway musical. Can you see the association between the word "phantom" and a Greek myth?

《歌剧魅影》是法国作家加斯顿·勒鲁的小说，出版于1910年。由于小说被改编成了各种各样的舞台剧或电影而享誉全球，其中就包括百老汇的音乐剧。你能看出来“魅影”一词与希腊神话的关系吗？

3. Look at this sentence first: *That country seems to have a plutocracy and it may not always represent the middle class*. Can you guess the meaning of the word "plutocracy"? Here is a clue: Pluto was the Roman equivalent of Hades, god of the underworld, and he was very wealthy.

先来看个句子：That country seems to have a plutocracy and it may not always represent the middle class。你能猜到“plutocracy”是什么意思吗？给你个线索：Pluto是冥王哈迪斯对应的罗马名字，而他富得流油。

(1. 答案：B)

(2. 答案：phantom源自Phantasos或phantasm，意思是“幽灵”)

(3. 答案：意思就是财阀当政，富豪统治)

FURTHER READING Tantalus
延伸阅读 坦塔罗斯

According to the myth, Tantalus was once among the favorite and most intimate mortals of Zeus. It seemed that the rest of the gods were also favorable towards him because he was frequently invited to the table of the deities on Mt. Olympus. However, Tantalus did not prove worthy of all these favors and honors as he committed several crimes and injustices against the gods. First, he stole ambrosia and nectar from Mt. Olympus, thinking that he could take them back to his people to make them immortal. Second, he revealed some important secrets that Zeus had confided in him in person, thus betraying the hospitality and trust of the gods. Third, Tantalus instructed his impious friend Pandareus to steal the favorite pet of Zeus, his golden dog created by Hephaestus, and then refused to return it.

Although the above mentioned crimes were clear proofs of Tantalus being on the wrong track, the gods did not punish him at first, expecting him to realize his own mistakes and correct himself. Unfortunately, Tantalus failed them by committing even worse crimes against them. One day, he invited all the gods of the Olympus to a banquet. But either because he wanted to test their genius or because he did not have enough food, he killed his son Pelops, cooked him, roasting the pieces of his body, and then served him to the gods. The gods, realizing the gruesome nature of the menu, did not touch the offering, except Demeter, who was upset by her daughter's abduction by Hades, ate, absentmindedly, a part of the boy's shoulder.

When it was revealed what had happened, Zeus ordered Clotho, one of the three Fates, to bring Pelops to life again. The missing part of his shoulder was replaced by an ivory piece forged by Hephaestus.

Tantalus was thrown out of Olympus and punished for eternity in Tartarus after death in the company of Ixion, Sisyphus, the Danaids, and others. He was made to stand in a pool of water, right under the branches of a fruit tree. Whenever he reached for the fruit, the branches would go higher and out of reach. Whenever he bent down to get a drink, the water receded before he could get any.

Since the Greek mythology gave us the myth of Tantalus, this name has become the origin of the English verb "tantalize". If someone is tantalized or something is tantalizing, that person must be undergoing similar experience as the hero of the myth, or something desirable is always out of reach. Here is an example: "The prospect of companies parting with some of that cash is tantalizing for stock investors."

传说坦塔罗斯曾是宙斯最喜爱、最亲近的人类之一，而奥林匹斯山其余的神仙似乎对他也颇为友好，时常邀请他参加众神们的宴会。可是，坦塔罗斯却不识抬举，辜负了神仙们的好意，犯下了数桩有违神旨的罪行。首先，他偷了奥林匹斯山的玉液珍馐，想要带回去给他的百姓们，让他们长生不老。其次，他泄露了宙斯私下里告诉他的秘密，辜负了众神对他的信任。再次，他指使自己邪恶的朋友潘得柔斯偷走了宙斯最心爱的宠物，那只由赫菲斯托斯亲手打造的黄金犬，并拒绝归还。

尽管上述罪行已足以证明坦塔罗斯品行不端了，但是众神起初并没有惩罚他，仍然寄希望于他能意识到自己的错误，改过自新。不幸的是，坦塔罗斯非但不改，反而在犯罪的道路上越走越远。这天，他邀请奥林匹斯山的众神参加宴会。不知是想要检验神仙们的智商，还是因为食材不够，他杀了自己的亲生儿子佩洛普斯，将他剁碎煮熟献给众神佐餐，众神识破了这道恐怖菜肴的真相，都没有碰。只有得墨忒耳，当时因为女儿刚被哈迪斯拐走，有些心不在焉，将男孩的一小块肩膀吞下了肚。

真相大白之后，宙斯下令让命运三女神中的克罗托帮助佩洛普斯起死回生，并让赫菲斯托斯用象牙补上了他缺失的肩膀。坦塔罗斯则被逐出奥林匹克斯山，死后被投入塔尔塔罗斯，和伊克西翁、西西弗斯、达那伊得斯姐妹一样，遭受永久的惩罚：他要站在一片池水中，头顶是一棵果树。每当他快要够到果子的时候，树枝就会抬起一点，让他无法吃到。每当他弯腰想喝点水时，水面就会下沉，他也无法喝到。

由于希腊神话中关于坦塔罗斯的故事，如今便有了英语中 tantalize 这个动词。假如我们说某人被 tantalized，或者说某种东西 tantalizing，那就表示这个人正经历着地狱中坦塔罗斯般的痛苦，或者指某种东西“诱人却很难得到”，例如：“对于股票投资者来说，上市公司拿出现金分红是极具诱惑力的。”

Extra 拓展测试

Tantalus is also the name given to a specific type of decanter of drinks. In this case, the stoppers of the bottle are firmly clamped down with the use of a locked metal bar in order to prevent people from stealing the drink. The decanters are clearly visible but the liquor is out of reach without a key. Can you guess where this Tantalus is originated?

Tantalus 也是一种特制的玻璃酒柜的名称。这种柜子里的酒，瓶塞都由一根金属条牢牢锁住，以防有人把酒偷走。酒瓶虽然就在眼前，但是没有钥匙的话，就没法喝到酒。你能猜到这种酒柜源自哪国吗？

（答案：英国）

PART Ⅲ Nature Myths

第三部分

大自然的神话

扫一扫，听本部分音频

CHAPTER 1 The Changing Season
第一章 四季变化的故事

Word Knowledge 词汇知识

Horae(时序女神)

In Greek mythology, Horae, or Horai, were daughters of Zeus and Themis and originally three goddesses of the seasons, Thallo (Spring), Auxo (Summer) and Carpo (Autumn) respectively, and the natural portions of time. For the ancient Greeks, winter was not recognized as a season but a temporary period of death and slumber of nature. In later times, Horae were regarded as a triad of maiden goddesses of order in general and natural justice, their names being Dice (Justice), Eunomia (Order) and Irene (Peace), which could well be attributed to their mother Themis.

A well-known line in *Dead Poets Society*, a 1989 American drama film and box-office success, goes like: "Carpe diem. Seize the day, boys. Make your lives extraordinary", which was voted one of the greatest movie quotes by the American Film Institute. Carpe, a word derived from Carpo, is used to urge people to make the most of their present time, for the future is unforeseen.

在希腊神话中,霍莉(时序女神)是宙斯和西弥斯的三个女儿,名字分别为塔罗(春)、奥克索(夏)和卡波尔(秋),她们最初是季节和时光变化的代表。在古希腊人看来,冬天不是一个季节,而是大自然暂时死亡或休眠的阶段。到了后来,霍莉又被赋予了正义和秩序三女神的含义,她们的名字变成了狄刻(正义)、欧诺弥亚(秩序)和厄瑞涅(和平),让人自然联想到她们的母亲西弥斯。

在1989年发行的好莱坞剧情片《死亡诗社》中有一句非常著名的台词："把握今天，及时行乐，让你的人生不平凡。"后来这句台词入选了美国电影学院最伟大的电影台词之一。这里的carpe一词源自carpo，用来鼓励人们珍惜当下，因为未来是不可预测的。

The Fates(命运三女神)

In Greek mythology, it was a rule of the Fates that whoever consumed food or drink in the underworld was doomed to spend eternity there, which was the exact reason why Persephone was bound to return to Hades after having some seeds of pomegranate offered by him. The Fates, or Moirai in Greek, were daughters of Nyx and three goddesses who preside over the birth and life of humans. Each human was thought of as a spindle, around which the three Fates would spin the thread of human destiny. Clothos was responsible for spinning the thread, Lachesis, for measuring the thread, and Atropos, for cutting the thread. Literally, the word Clothos means spinner, Lachesis, allotter or drawer of lot, and Atropos, inflexible or unturnable.

在希腊神话中，命运女神的规则之一就是任何人一旦在冥界饮食，便永远无法离开那里，这也就是为什么珀尔赛福涅在吃了哈迪斯给她的石榴籽之后，注定还要回到他身边。命运三女神，或希腊语中的摩伊拉，是黑夜女神尼克斯的孩子，掌管着人类的生死和命运。每一个人都像一个纺锤，环绕在上面的纺线握在命运三女神的手中：克洛索主司纺线、拉基西斯主司长度、阿特洛波斯主司割线。"克洛索"一词的本义就是纺线者，"拉基西斯"的意思是分配者或抓阄者，"阿特洛波斯"的意思则是不可逆转。

Demophoon(得摩福翁)

The myth of the abduction of Persephone from her mother Demeter was depicted as in a cycle of three phases: the descent or loss, the search and the ascent, with the last one being the most important. During the search, Demeter travelled once to a place called Eleusis, where she was received with hospitality by the family of Celeus, the king of the country. Though grief-worn and dejected, Demeter agreed to stay and secured her service as nurse to his infant son Demophoon. The young child throve amazingly under the care of Demeter, which aroused the great curiosity of his mother. One night she was impelled to peek at the proceedings and saw her son being placed in the flames. She shrieked aloud in her horror, which forced Demeter to reveal her true self and her failed intention of making the child immortal.

The word Demophoon, or sometimes spelt Demophon, consists of two parts: *demo-*, which means "people" or "populace", and *-phon*, "sound". Demography refers to the study of statistics such as birth, death, income, or the incidence of disease, which illustrate the changing structure of human population.

得墨忒耳的女儿珀尔赛福涅被劫持的神话包括下沉或失去、寻找和上升三个阶段,其中最后一个阶段是最重要的。在得墨忒耳寻找女儿的过程中,她曾来到一个叫作厄琉西斯的地方,在那里她受到了国王刻琉斯一家的热情款待。尽管内心悲伤而沮丧,得墨忒耳还是同意留下来,帮忙照看国王的幼子得摩福翁。在得墨忒耳的精心照料下,小王子迅速长大,这令他的母亲非常好奇。一天夜里,她忍不住偷看了一眼,结果发现儿子被放在火上烤,她吓得大叫起来,叫声打断了得墨忒耳的育儿过程,她不得不露出真容,表明自己这样做原本是想给小王子不死之身。

得摩福翁(Demophoon)有时拼作 Demophon,它包含两部分:demo-的意思是"人"或"人口",-phon 的意思是"声音"。Demography 指描述人口结构变化的统计学,包含出生、死亡、收入和疾病等数据。

The Myths 神话故事

Have you ever wondered why there are four seasons in a year? The ancient Greeks explained this with the myth of Demeter and Persephone. As the daughter of Cronus and Rhea, Demeter was the goddess in charge of harvest and productiveness. Man in his primitive state knew neither how to sow nor how to till the ground. It was Demeter who exerted civilizing influences on man by introducing the knowledge of agriculture and thus put an end to the nomadic life.

Demeter, as the wife of Zeus, became the mother of Persephone, to whom she was so tenderly attached that her whole life was bound up in her. Whenever Demeter came down from Mount Olympus to tend her fields, she brought her young daughter along with her. However, one day whilst Persephone was picking flowers in a meadow, she strayed from her mother's side at the sight of a beautiful narcissus, whose exquisite scent perfumed the air. Just as she stooped down to gather it, the earth suddenly ripped open at her feet. Hades, the grim ruler of the underworld, appeared from its depths, seated in his dazzling chariot drawn by four black horses. Regardless of her tears and fears, Hades swept up the terrified maiden and carried her back down to the gloomy realm, leaving hardly a trace of what happened.

When Demeter became conscious of her loss, she searched frantically everywhere for her beloved daughter. Knowing nowhere to seek for her child, her grief was intense, and the whole world felt the influence of her anguish and dejection. Though the husbandman sowed the grain, and the oxen ploughed the fields, no harvest rewarded their labor. All was barren, dreary and desolation. The world was threatened with famine. Even the gods and goddesses felt the loss of their accustomed honors and sacrifices.

To appease the anger of the mother, Zeus at length sent Hermes, his faithful messenger, to the lower world with a petition to Hades, urgently entreating him to restore Persephone to the arms of her saddened mother. Upon receiving the news, Hades consented to resign Persephone, who joyfully prepared to follow the messenger to the abode of life and light. Then Hades offered Persephone a few seeds of pomegranate, which in her excitement she thoughtlessly swallowed.

Demeter was overjoyed to have her daughter back. However, she realized that Persephone must go back to Hades when she heard about the pomegranate. Pitying the disappointment of Demeter, Zeus succeeded in effecting a promise by inducing Hades to allow Persephone to spend six months of the year with her mother, and the other six, with her grim lord below. With the company of her beautiful daughter, Demeter resumed her long-abandoned dwelling in Olympus and her job in the fields.

This is how the change of seasons came to be. Every year, when it was time for Persephone to return to Hades, Demeter missed her so much that the wind turned cold, the plants died, the birds flew away, and it was winter again. Then when Persephone returned to her mother as Zeus promised, the flowers blossomed, the trees bore fruit, the wheat grew and the whole world sang with joy to welcome the glorious spring time once again.

你是否想过为什么一年会有四季？古希腊的人们用得墨忒耳和珀尔赛福涅的神话对此做了解释。得墨忒耳是克罗诺斯和瑞亚的女儿，是掌管丰收和富饶的女神。原始状态下的人类对播种和耕作一无所知，是得墨忒耳将农业知识传授给他们，从而结束了游牧生活，为人类播下了文明的种子。

得墨忒耳也是宙斯的妻子，他们的女儿珀尔赛福涅不仅是她的掌上明珠，更是她全世界。每次得墨忒耳从奥林匹斯山下来查看农田时，都会带着女儿。然而有一天，当珀尔赛福涅在草地上采摘野花的时候，她看到了一朵美丽的水仙花，被那浓郁的香气所吸引，她离开了母亲的视线。就在她俯下身准备摘花的时候，她脚下的土地突然裂开了，从裂缝中跳出了一辆金灿灿的由四匹黑马牵引着的马车,马车上坐着的就是可怕的地狱之王。不顾她的眼泪和恐惧,哈迪斯一把抓起吓坏的女孩,把她带回了自己黑暗的王国,几乎没有留下一点痕迹。

当得墨忒耳意识到女儿不见了的时候,她开始疯狂地四处寻找。因为没有一点关于孩子的线索,她悲痛欲绝,整个世界都感受到了她的悲伤和沮丧。虽然农夫依然在播种,耕牛依然在犁地,但是他们的劳作不再有收获。一切变得荒芜、阴郁而凄凉,全世界都面临着饥荒的威胁,甚至天上的诸神也失去了他们惯有的供奉。

为了平息这位母亲的怒火,终于,宙斯指派他忠诚的信使赫耳墨斯,到冥界请求哈迪斯放了珀尔赛福涅。接到宙斯的消息,哈迪斯同意放珀尔赛福涅回去,就在后者欢天喜地地准备跟随信使返回光明世界的时候,哈迪斯掏出了几颗石榴籽递给珀尔赛福涅,兴奋中的女孩没有多想,就把它们吞了下去。

女儿的回归让得墨忒耳欣喜若狂。但是,一听说那个石榴的事,她马上意识到女儿还得返回哈迪斯身边去。得墨忒耳的失望让宙斯心生怜悯,他承诺让哈迪斯允许珀尔赛福涅每年六个月和母亲待在一起,其余六个月则陪伴冥王。有了美丽的女儿在身边,得墨忒耳重新回到了奥林匹斯山的住所,开始工作。

这就是四季变化的原因。每年,当珀尔赛福涅去往哈迪斯那里后,得墨忒耳思女心切,风会变冷,植物枯萎,鸟儿南飞,冬天到了。而当珀尔赛福涅回到母亲身边的时候,花儿开放,树儿结果,麦苗生长,整个世界一片欢乐的景象,春天又来了。

Extra 拓展测试

1. Which of the following fruit that Persephone ate bound her to the Underworld?

下面哪种水果使得珀尔赛福涅注定与冥界无法分离?

A

B

2. The myth about the nursing of Demophoon by Demeter says that the goddess gave him no food, but would anoint him daily with ambrosia, and every night laid him secretly in the fire in order to render him immortal. In Latin, the word root *brotos* means mortal and *ambrotos*, immortal. So can you guess what *ambrosia* is?

在得墨忒耳抚育得摩福翁的神话故事里,据说女神无须给婴儿喂任何食物,只是每天用 ambrosia 擦拭他的身体,每晚悄悄地把他放到火里烤,以使他获得永生。在拉丁语中,brotos 这个词根的意思是"凡人",而 ambrotos 的意思是"神人",那么,你能猜到 ambrosia 是什么吗?

3. Ceres was the Roman equivalent of Demeter, the goddess of agriculture. The English word "cereal" is simply derived from Ceres. What does "cereal" mean?

农业女神得墨忒耳的罗马名字叫刻瑞斯(Ceres),英语中 cereal 一词便源自刻瑞斯,那么 cereal 是什么意思呢?

(1. 答案:A)

(2. 答案:能让人长生不老的仙果)

(3. 答案:谷物,麦片)

CHAPTER 2 The Myth of the Sun
第二章 太阳的神话

Word Knowledge 词汇知识

Helios(赫利俄斯)

Many people tend to associate the sun god with Apollo, yet Apollo was generally known as the son of Zeus and Leto. In contrast, the parents of Helios were the Titans Hyperion and Theia, siblings of Cronus or Zeus' father. Therefore, Helios existed much earlier than Apollo, and the word Helios actually has the same meaning with the Latin word *sol*, which indicates the sun itself. The word *Solar*, the adjective form, can be used to form such useful phrases as *the solar system*, *the solar calendar*, *the solar terms*, *solar eclipse*, *solar energy*, and so on.

提到太阳神,很多人会联想到阿波罗,然而大家都知道,阿波罗是宙斯和勒托的儿子,而赫利俄斯的父母是提坦巨人许珀里翁和忒伊亚,宙斯的父亲克罗诺斯的手足。换言之,赫利俄斯的存在要比阿波罗早得多。事实上,赫利俄斯和拉丁语中的 sol 是同一个意思,即太阳本身,其形容词 solar 可以用来构成很多有用的词汇,比如 the solar system(太阳系)、the solar calendar(阳历)、the solar terms(节气)、solar eclipse(日食)和 solar energy(太阳能)等。

Clytie(克吕提厄)

Clytie, an Oceanid or a water nymph, loved the sun god Helios very much but was eventually deserted. Myth has it that Clytie lay herself naked for nine days on the rocks without eating or drinking anything, simply staring at the sun with her hands outstretched towards the sky. The gods were moved at the pathetic sight, and transformed her into a flower, which turns towards the direction of the sun. The flower's name is either *heliotrope* or *turnsole*, both easily understood as the former has the word "Helios" in it and the latter, the "Sol".

水泽仙女克吕提厄深爱着太阳神赫利俄斯,然而最终却被后者所抛弃。传说克吕提厄全身赤裸地躺在岩石上,双手伸向天空,目光凝视着太阳,就这样不吃不喝地坚持了九天九夜。诸神被她的悲情所打动,于是在第九天把她变成了一朵始终朝向太阳的花。这朵花的名字既可以是 heliotrope,也可以是 turnsole,因为前者包含了"赫利俄斯(Helios)"的名字,而后者包含了"太阳(Sol)"。

Eos(厄俄斯)

Eos, the sister of Helios, was the goddess of the Dawn. Like her brother, she too had her own chariot, which she drove across the vast horizon both morning and evening, before and after the sun god. Hence she is the personification of both the rosy morn and twilight. Her palace is placed in the west. The Roman equivalent of Eos is Aurora, which, if written in the lower case, means polar light or northern light. Hesperus, one of her children, was the evening star.

赫利俄斯的妹妹厄俄斯是曙光女神。和哥哥一样,她有自己的战车。每天,她在太阳神之前或之后飞跃地平线,因此,她既是曙光也是暮光的化身。她的宫殿则坐落在西方。厄俄斯的罗马名字叫奥罗拉,如果小写的话，这个词的意思是“极光”。奥罗拉有一个孩子名叫赫斯珀洛斯，即长庚星。

Cycnus(天鹅座)

Cycnus was a devoted friend of Phaethon, the mortal son of the sun god Helios. One version of the Cycnus myth says that it was he who pleaded with Zeus to stop the uncontrollable and rampaging chariot with a thunderbolt, which eventually led to the death of his best friend. With overwhelming grief and a guilty feeling, Cycnus found it impossible to leave his friend to the creatures of the river to feed on, so he dove repeatedly into the river to gather the charred remains of Phaethon. Moved by his selfless display of devotion, Zeus decided to give Cycnus a gift of immortality and transformed him into a glorious swan with an altered name Cygnus. Cygnus is now known as a northern constellation lying on the plane of the Milky Way.

席古拿斯是法厄同的忠实好友，而法厄同是太阳神赫利俄斯的凡人儿子。关于席古拿斯神话的其中一个版本认为，是他请求宙斯用闪电来制止失控狂奔的战车，从而导致了好朋友法厄同的惨死。而他自己也因为极度的悲伤和自责，在法厄同死后，不忍心看见好友的尸体被鱼虾吞食，于是反反复复地潜入水中去搜寻他烧焦的残躯。宙斯被他的真情和无私所打动，决定赐他一个不死之身，将他变成了一只美丽的大鹅，并改名为席格拿斯。如今，席格拿斯代表了银河系中的一颗北方星座：天鹅座。

The Myths 神话故事

In Greek mythology, anything that you took for granted comes to life in a new way. Take the sun that comes up every day for example. The ancient Greeks believed that it was the work of a sun god named

Helios. According to the myth, Helios, the son of the Titans Hyperion and Theia, would rise every morning in the east, preceded by his sister Eos (the Dawn), who, with her rosy fingers, painted the tips of the mountains, and drew aside that misty veil through which her brother was about to appear. In a flame-darting chariot pulled by four fire-breathing steeds, Helios drove across the sky, bringing light into the world. At noon, Helios rode high into the sky, providing the brightest light of the day. As his journey ends, he descended over the western horizon, leaving the earth sunset, and followed closely by his sister Selene (the Moon). Finally he returned to his palace in the east and rested for the next day's journey.

Helios had a mortal son named Phaethon, whose mother was one of the Oceanides. One day when his friend Epaphus showed disbelief over his assertion that the sun god was his father, Phaethon, full of resentment and vanity, made up his mind to find the radiant dwelling of Helios and inquire for himself. Few mortals dared to visit the great palace of the sun god, so when Phaethon presented in front of his father, Helios was very happy to see this good-looking and brave young man. So proud of his mortal son, Helios even told Phaethon that he would give him anything he wanted. The impetuous youth immediately requested permission to drive the chariot of the sun for one day.

Helios tried to dissuade his son from so perilous an undertaking, but Phaethon was determined and presumptuous. Since Helios had given his word, he could not take it back. So that morning it was Phaethon who mounted the solar chariot. Helios gave him all the pointers he could and anointed the face of his son with a sacred balm to enable him to endure the burning flames. The eager youth joyfully snapped the reins and the chariot took off.

At first, everything went smoothly. Phaethon was flushed with a great feeling of power on the magnificent chariot of his father. Then the horses became restive and unmanageable, for they were used to the powerful hand of Helios. Wildly they rushed out of their usual track, now soaring so high as to result in cold polar caps, now descending so low as to set the forests on fire, leaving hot sandy stretches of desert and rumbling volcanoes everywhere. Terrified at the awful devastation he had caused, the inexperienced charioteer dropped the reins from his trembling hands. The scorched earth called on Zeus for help, who then hurled his thunderbolt at the chariot and sent it down into a river.

Phaethon, a mortal being, could not survive the force of a thunderbolt and fell like a shooting star into the river Eridanus, where it was received and buried by the Heliades, the seven nymphs and daughters of Helios. His sisters mourned so long for him that they were transformed by Zeus into poplar trees so that they could stay on the river banks to protect their brother for always. The myth has it that the tears that Heliades shed, falling into the waters, became drops of clear, transparent amber.

在希腊神话中,任何我们习以为常的东西都可以被赋予新的生命。比如我们看到的太阳,在古希腊人的眼里,这是太阳神赫利俄斯的杰作。根据这则神话,赫利俄斯是提坦巨人许珀里翁和忒伊亚的儿子,每天清晨,他从东方升起,跟在妹妹厄俄斯(曙光女神)的身后。妹妹用她玫瑰色的手指将山尖染红,将朦胧的面纱揭开,为哥哥的出发做好准备。随后,赫利俄斯耀眼的马车由四匹喷火的骏马牵引着,从天空中飞驰而过,为世界洒下光明。正午时分,赫利俄斯抵达天空的最高处,日照也达到最强。随着他行程的结束,他渐渐消失在西方的地平线下,留给大地落日的余晖,并将舞台交给妹妹塞勒涅(月亮女神)。最后,他返回自己位于东方的宫殿,为来日的行程养精蓄锐。

赫利俄斯有一个凡人儿子名叫法厄同,其母是海洋仙女俄刻阿尼蒂斯之一。一天,因为朋友厄帕福斯表示不相信他是太阳神的儿子,法厄同下决心要找到赫利俄斯的光明殿,当面确认这件事。由于很少有凡人胆敢拜访太阳神的住所,因此,当法厄同出现在赫利俄斯面前时,这位太阳神父亲非常开心,他为自己有这样一位英俊而勇敢的儿子感到骄傲。于是他告诉法厄同,有任何要求都可以提出来,虚荣的年轻人脱口而出的就是想要驾驶父亲的太阳战车。

赫利俄斯试图打消儿子的这一念头，强调这一工作太过危险，但是法厄同非常坚决，根本听不进去。何况赫利俄斯一言既出，驷马难追。于是，那天早晨，法厄同登上了太阳战车。赫利俄斯反复叮嘱儿子注意事项，并在他的脸上涂上神油，以防他的皮肤被灼伤。跃跃欲试的年轻人一把夺过缰绳，冲了出去。

起初，一切还算顺利，站在战车上的法厄同感觉自己光芒四射。可是过了不久，四匹马便开始焦躁不安、不听指挥了，它们习惯了赫利俄斯有力的臂膀。此刻开始偏离路线，狂冲乱撞，一会儿冲上云霄，导致人间被冻成冰盖，一会儿又跌落地面，引起森林大火，留下连片的沙漠和火山。眼见闯下了大祸，这位毫无经验的车夫彻底吓傻了，他丢下了手里的缰绳。地上的人们向宙斯求救，熊熊的烈火中，宙斯及时赶到，他将闪电投向失控的战车，使之最终沉入了河里。

法厄同以凡人之躯如何能躲过天神的雷劈，他的躯体犹如一颗流星坠落波江，波江的仙女们名叫赫利阿得斯，是赫利俄斯的七个女儿。她们在掩埋了弟弟之后，依然难过得久久不愿离去。于是，宙斯把她们变成了白杨树，这样她们就可以永远守在河岸边，看护着自己的弟弟。据说赫利阿得斯的眼泪落入水中，立刻变成了晶莹剔透的琥珀。

Extra 拓展测试

1. How many differences can you spot in the following two pictures which describe Phaethon riding the Chariot of his father?

   下面这两幅图描绘的都是法厄同驾驶太阳战车的情景，你能找出几处不同？

2. Wanting to drive the awesome Chariot of the sun was one thing, but to actually do it was another. As soon as he took off, Phaethon realized that he had taken on more than he could handle. When the horses felt the weakness of the charioteer, they began to run wild and off-track, causing immense destruction to the world, such as the great desert in Africa and the black skin of the Ethiopian people. Word has it that the chariot even blazed a gash in the skies which supposedly became an important spiral galaxy. Do you know what it is?

想要驾驶帅气的太阳战车是一码事,而实际操作则是另一码事。刚一出发,法厄同便意识到了什么叫作心有余而力不足,而奔驰的骏马也感到了车夫的软弱,开始变得狂野和肆无忌惮,结果给世界带来了巨大的灾难,诸如非洲的大沙漠,埃塞俄比亚人的黑皮肤等。据说战车还在天空划了一道大口子,形成了一个重要的旋转星系,你知道这个星系叫什么名字吗?

(1. 答案:五处)

(2. 答案:银河系)

CHAPTER 3 The Mer Sisters
第三章 海洋姐妹

Word Knowledge 词汇知识

The Mer Sisters(海洋姐妹)

Have you ever watched the Disney movie "Pirates of the Caribbean: On Stranger Tides"? If so, you must have been impressed by the beautiful mermaids who lured the sailors with their enchanting voices. However, such a depiction of mermaids as dangerous creatures is likely to be an adaptation from the Greek myth of the Sirens. Mer, in English, means ocean, so "the mer sisters" refers to all the female creatures living in the ocean, such as the gorgons, the sirens and the mermaids.

The myths of the mer sisters reflect ancient people's fear in the hidden dangers in the unexplored sea. If the gorgons and the sirens were both terrifying creatures from Greek and Roman mythology, the mermaids were more benevolent beings seen in European or many other cultures. Of the many mythological stories on mermaids, the most famous one must be *The Little Mermaid*, a fairy tale by the Danish writer Hans Christian Andersen. In Chinese mythology, mermaids lived in the South Sea. They spent days weaving a beautiful water-proof cloth called Dragon Yarn, which would then be sold on the market, the mirage that mortal people see. As you can see, mermaids are often portrayed as lonely and emotional girls who have great curiosity about life on land.

你看过迪士尼的电影《加勒比海盗 4:惊涛怪浪》吗? 如果看过,那你一定对片中用迷人的歌声诱惑海员的美人鱼印象深刻吧? 然而,这种将美人鱼描绘成危险生物的情节很可能是对希腊神话中塞壬故事的改编。在英语中,mer的意思是"海洋",因此"海洋姐妹"就是指那些生活在海里的雌性生物,例如:戈耳戈、塞壬和美人鱼。

有关海洋姐妹的神话反映了古代人民对海洋中潜在危险的恐惧,如果说戈耳戈和塞壬姐妹是来自希腊罗马神话中可怕的海妖,那么美人鱼则是欧洲或其他文化中更加温和的生物。关于美人鱼最著名的故事当属丹麦作家安徒生的童话《小美人鱼》。在中国神话中,美人鱼生活在南海,她们夜以继日地编织一种美丽的防水布料"蛟绡纱",然后把它们拿到集市上去卖,而那个集市便是凡人看到的"海市蜃楼"。可见,美人鱼的形象常常是孤独而敏感的少女,她们对于陆地生活充满了好奇。

Siren Song(塞壬的歌声)

In Greek mythology, the Sirens were dangerous creatures, who seduce nearby sailors with their enchanting music and singing voices to shipwreck on the rocky coast of their island. In modern English, *siren song* or *siren call* has become a common expression to refer to something that is very appealing and has the power to tempt people, though yielding to the temptation may have unfortunate effects. Here is an example: *The opportunity for fame and fortune is the siren song that has long lured the ambitious to the big city*.

The Sirens were said to have lived on Leukai, the islands on the northwest coast of Crete. Leukai is the Greek word for "white ones" as the prefix *leuko-* or *leuco-* literally means "white". Hence there are such medical words in English as *leukemia*, *leucocyte*, *leucoma*, *leucocytosis*, *leucorrhea*, which are all derived from Greek.

在希腊神话中,塞壬是危险的生物,她们用魅惑的音乐和歌声诱惑附近船只上的水手,导致船只触礁沉没。在现代英语中,"塞壬的歌声"或"塞壬的呼唤"已经成了一种常见词汇,用来指某种强烈的诱惑,一旦陷入其中,便可能造成不幸的后果。例如:名利的诱惑如同塞壬的歌声,将胸怀抱负的人们召唤进这座大城市。

传说塞壬姐妹住在克里特岛西北方向的卢铠岛上。在希腊语中“卢铠”一词的意思是“白色物”，leuko-或 leuco-这个前缀表示的就是“白色”。因此，英语中有许多医疗方面的词汇，如 leukemia（白血病）、leucocyte（白细胞）、leucoma（角膜白斑）、leucocytosis（白细胞增多）、leucorrhea（白带）等，都源自希腊语。

The Harpies(哈比)

The Harpies resembled the Sirens in several respects: First, they were also three in number. Second, they were winged female divinities with the head of a fair-haired maiden and the body of a vulture. However, unlike the Sirens, who had beautiful voices and musical talents, the Harpies could only produce harsh, semi-human screams. The bodies of the Sirens were of human size, which were much bigger than those of the eagle-like Harpies. Besides, the feathers of the Harpies were said to have a foul stench, forming a sharp contrast to the beautiful wings once on the shoulders of the Sirens.

With their rapid flight, the Harpies were employed by the gods to punish those who angered them, often by robbing them of their food, or by carrying them off unaccountably. As the Harpies were viewed as mean and cruel, to "harp" carries such connotation as to keep complaining about something or someone. Here is an example: *My boss keeps harping at me to get the accounting report done today*.

哈比和塞壬有几处相同的地方：首先，哈比也有三位。其次，她们也是带翅膀的女性神，拥有金发少女的面庞和兀鹫的身体。然而，和塞壬的美妙声音及音乐天赋不同的是，她们只能发出半似人声的凄厉叫声。塞壬的身体和人类相仿，这无疑要比老鹰大小的哈比大得多。此外，据说哈比的羽毛有一股难闻的腐臭味，这与长在塞壬肩上的美丽翅膀有着天壤之别。

哈比飞行速度极快，因此众神常借她们来惩罚那些激怒自己的人，比如让哈比突然抢走他们的食物,或者令他们莫名其妙地失踪。由于哈比的刻薄和冷酷,to harp 也包含了这样的意思,用来指不停地抱怨某人或某事。举个例子:老板今天向我喋喋不休地催要财务报表。

The Myths 神话故事

Originally sea nymphs, the Sirens were three mer sisters whose upper part of the body was that of a maid and the lower, that of a sea-bird. They could sing so sweetly that their voices had the power to turn the mariners to sleep and cause shipwrecks. As companions of young Persephone, they used to have beautiful wings attached to their shoulders, which were given by Demeter to help search for her daughter who was abducted. However, being unable to fulfil the task, the Sirens were cursed by Demeter as living only until the mortals who heard their songs were able to pass them by.

According to the myth, the Sirens, due to their vanity and the persuasion of Hera, once challenged the Muses in a singing contest. In sharp contrast to the songs of the Muses which were loyal and true, those of the Sirens were false and seductive, leading to death and destruction of many unfortunate mariners. Therefore, after being defeated by the Muses, the Sirens were plucked all of their feathers as a punishment and a mark of humiliation. Out of their anguish of losing the competition, the Sirens turned white and fell into the sea at Aptera (featherless), where they formed the islands in the bay called Leukai (the white ones).

Though irresistibly alluring, the Sirens' song failed at least twice. One failure took place in the *Argonautica* when Jason took Orpheus as his assistant. Orpheus, being the greatest musician of all time, played his lyre so beautifully that the music drowned out completely the Sirens' voices. Another incident involves Odysseus, who, acting on Circe's advice, took precautions against the Sirens by having himself tied to the mast and stopping the ears of his men with wax before they reached the fatal island.

When the entrancing melody reached the ears of Odysseus, he struggled desperately to free himself and shouted for his men to turn towards the lush and flowery meadows of the singing sisters. But no one paid any heed to him. The sailors kept straight on until they were entirely out of hearing. For once the Sirens had sung in vain. The eldest of the sisters, Parthenope, loved Odysseus so much that she threw herself into the sea after his ships had passed. Another version says that the Sirens were fated to die if someone heard their singing and escaped them. Therefore, after Odysseus passed by them, the Sirens flung themselves into the water and perished.

塞壬是三位海洋姐妹,原本属于海宁芙的她们上半身是少女,下半身是海鸟。她们的歌声如此甜美,能够令听到的水手昏昏欲睡,从而导致海难。她们曾经是珀尔赛福涅的随从,得墨忒耳赋予她们美丽的翅膀,吩咐她们帮助寻找被绑架的女儿。然而,由于塞壬并没有很好地完成任务,于是得墨忒耳诅咒她们,一旦有凡人能够不为她们的歌声所动,她们就必死无疑。

传说在天后赫拉的劝说以及自身虚荣心的驱使之下,塞壬三姐妹曾经不自量力地向缪斯女神发起挑战,比拼谁的歌声更美。而事实证明:缪斯女神的歌声真实动人,塞壬的声音虚假魅惑,只会导致海难和死亡。因此,作为惩罚和耻辱的标记,塞壬姐妹在惨败之后,被缪斯女神拔掉了所有的羽毛,从此再也无法飞翔。巨大的痛苦令塞壬姐妹变得惨白,她们坠入大海的地方叫“埃佩泰拉”(无翅),在那里形成的岛屿叫“卢铠”(白色物)。

尽管塞壬的歌声极具诱惑,令人难以抗拒,但她们至少失败了两次。一次是在《阿尔戈船英雄记》里,伊阿宋请来俄耳甫斯做助手。当这位最伟大的音乐家弹奏起他的里拉琴时,美妙的音乐将塞壬的声音彻底淹没。另一次则涉及奥德修斯,他在女巫喀耳刻的建议下,事先采取了预防措施:在靠近塞壬所在的岛屿之前,他将自己绑在了桅杆上,同时用蜡堵上手下的耳朵。

塞壬魅惑的歌声传进奥德修斯的耳朵时，他拼命挣扎大喊，试图挣脱并奔向那片开满鲜花的富饶绿地，然而没有人理睬他，水手们继续划桨，直至塞壬的声音渐渐消失在远方。塞壬的歌声第一次失效了，大姐帕耳忒诺珀深深地爱上了奥德修斯，眼看着他的船只渐行渐远，心碎之下她投海自尽。另一种说法是，一旦有人听到塞壬的歌声却能不为所动，那么塞壬必死无疑。因此，当奥德修斯的船队离开之后，塞壬姐妹便投入大海，从此不见了踪影。

Extra 拓展测试

1. Siren is seen on the logo of a world-famous American coffeehouse chain, which was said to symbolize the overpoweringly attractive and almost seductive quality of its coffee. Which of the following is the logo of the coffee giant?

   塞壬还是一家世界著名的美国咖啡连锁企业的标志，据说塞壬象征了他们咖啡的诱人香味和品质。你知道下面哪张图是这家咖啡店的标志吗？

A

B

2. The word “siren” now means a device that makes a loud prolonged signal or warning sound. Do you know what it is?

   如今，siren 一词表示一种可以发出长长警报声的装置，你知道是什么吗？

（1. 答案：A）

（2. 答案：汽笛；警笛）

CHAPTER 4 The Myth of the Wind
第四章 风的神话

Word Knowledge 词汇知识

Chloris(花神克洛莉丝)

One version of the Hyacinthus myth says that it was Chloris who first made a flower from the blood of the dying youth, for Chloris was the goddess of flowers and nymph of the happy fields Elysium, the area of the Underworld where the worthy souls lived. Myth has it that Chloris was abducted by Zephyrus who then made her his bride and turned her into a deity known as Flora after they were married. Together they had a son Karpos, the personage of fruits. In addition to Hyacinthus, Chloris transformed a number of mythological figures including Adonis, Attis, Crocus and Narcissus.

The prefix *chloro-* means "green" literally in Greek. Words containing this prefix are mostly seen in chemistry or used for chemical substances, such as *chloric acid*, *chlorine*, *chloride*, *chloroplast* etc. Comparatively speaking, Flora, the Roman name of Chloris, seems easy to be associated with flowers, as "the florist's" now is known as the place where flowers are sold. Being held in the highest estimation by the Romans, a festival, called Floralia, was celebrated in her honour from the 28th of April to the 1st of May, during which people would decorate everything with flowers, and wear them in their hair. At the time of the Roman Empire, each occupied country, including Britain and large parts of Europe, added their own special touches to the festival. Hence it became known as May Day.

关于雅辛托斯的神话故事中有一个版本，说的是克洛莉丝最先是将濒死少年雅辛托斯的血变成了一朵风信子花，因为克洛莉丝是花神，同时也是极乐世界的仙女，出没于有德行的灵魂死后安居的场所。传说仄斐若斯劫持了克洛莉丝，把她变成了自己的新娘，婚后又将她升格为掌管花界的女神。他们的儿子卡尔波什则是水果之神。除了雅辛托斯之外，经由克洛莉丝之手变成鲜花的神话人物还包括阿多尼斯（金盏花）、阿提斯（杏花）、克罗刻斯（番红花）、那喀索斯（水仙花）。

希腊语中 chloro-这个词缀的意思是“绿色”，含有该词缀的单词大多出现在化学中或用来指化学物质，例如：chloric acid（氯酸）、chlorine（氯）、chloride（氯化物）、chloroplast（叶绿素）等。相比而言，克洛莉丝的罗马名芙洛拉更容易让人联想到鲜花。众所周知，英语中的 the florist's 就是花店的意思。由于地位高贵，罗马人有专门纪念芙洛拉的节日，称为“芙洛拉节”，从每年的 4 月 28 日持续到 5 月 1 日。在此期间人们会用鲜花装饰一切，编成花冠戴在头上。罗马帝国统治期间，从不列颠岛到欧洲大部分地区，都会举办带有自身特色的庆祝活动，渐渐地，这个节日便演化成了今天的“五朔节”。

Hyperborea（极北乐土）

The word “hyperborea” consists of two parts: *hyper*, meaning “beyond”, and *borea*, “north wind”. So the word depicts a land beyond the north wind. In Greek myth, the north wind had a home: a cave on Mount Haemus in Thrace, from where Borea sent the cold winds. Ancient Greeks imagined that beyond Borea's realm there lay a paradisiacal land where cold, along with old age and want, was unknown. The inhabitants, the worshippers of Apollo, led long and blissful lives.

There are many words with the prefix “*hyper-*” in modern English. Here is a list of them: *hypertext*, *hyperlink*, *hypermarket*, *hypersonic*, *hyperbole*, *hyperactive*, *hypercritical*, *hyponym*, *hyperopia*, *hyperspace* etc.

单词 hyperborea 由两部分组成：hyper 的意思是“在……之外”borea 的意思是“北风”，因此，这个词所描述的就是一片北风吹不到的乐土。在希腊神话中，北风有一个家：在色雷斯哈伊莫斯山上的一个洞穴里，波瑞阿斯从那里开始将寒冷的北风吹向大地。在古希腊人的想象中，波瑞阿斯的领地之外，还有一片天堂般的乐土，那里没有寒冷、衰老、全无物欲。那里的居民都是阿波罗的崇拜者，他们享受着长寿而幸福的生活。

在当代英语中，有许多包含词缀 hyper-的单词，例如：hypertext（超文本）、hyperlink（超链接）、hypermarket（超大型超市）、hypersonic（超音速的）、hyperbole（夸张）、hyperactive（多动的）、hypercritical（吹毛求疵的）、hyperym（上义词）、hyperopia（远视）、hyperspace（多维空间）等。

The Myths 神话故事

The oldest accounts in Greek mythology refer to Aeolus as the king of the Aeolian Island, to whom Zeus gave the command of the winds, which he kept shut up in a deep cave, and freed at his pleasure, or at the command of the gods. In later times the above belief underwent a change, and the Anemoi were taken as the wind gods who were each ascribed a cardinal direction. Apart from some minor gods, the principal wind gods were Boreas, the north wind, Eurus, the east wind, Notus, the south wind, and Zephyrus, the west wind, among which what is worth mentioning are probably Boreas and Zephyrus.

Boreas and his brother-winds were often imagined as horse-shaped gods in form. An old Greek folk belief was that the winds Boreas and Zephyrus would sweep down upon the mares in early spring and fertilize them in the guise of wind-formed stallions. The horses born from these couplings were the swiftest and finest of their kind. The fabulous horses of King Laomedon of Troy were said to have been sired in this way by Boreas upon the Trojan mares.

Boreas, the son of Astraeus and Eos, deities of the stars and dawn was the god of winter. He swept down from the cold mountains of Thrace, chilling the air with his icy breath. One day, while flying over the river Ilissus, Boreas beheld on the banks Orithyia, the charming daughter of an Athenian king. He carried her off to his home in Thrace and made her his bride. Their children included Khione, goddess of snow, and the Boreades, Zetes and Calais, a pair of winged warriors who journeyed with Jason's Argonaut expedition. The Athenians regarded Boreas as a friendly relative and called for his aid during the Persian Wars.

Being the gentlest of the winds, Zephyrus is known as the messenger of spring. Although mostly as a supporting character, he appeared in several myths, one of which is a love triangle with the wind god rivaling the sun god Apollo for the love of a beautiful teenager named Hyacinthus. Hyacinthus was a very handsome and athletic Spartan prince, who won the hearts of both Zephyrus and Apollo. However, Hyacinthus chose to be the company of Apollo, thus driving Zephyrus mad with jealousy. One day, spying the pair playing a game of discus on a meadow, Zephyrus, in a fit of rage, blew a gust of wind at them, causing the disc to go off-course and strike right on the head of the boy and killing him on the spot. Overwhelmed with grief at the sad end of his young favorite, but being unable to restore him to life, Apollo transformed him into the flower called after him, the Hyacinth.

Apollo was furious with Zephyrus about the death of his beloved, and vowed to punish him. At this moment, Eros showed up to protect the wind god by justifying his act as being committed in the name of love. On the condition of such open defense, the wind god served Eros ever since. Therefore, in the love story between Eros and Psyche, Zephyrus, on the command of Eros, functioned as the transport to carry first Psyche from the mountain top where she was abandoned to the palace in a verdant meadow where the god of love resided. When Psyche felt lonely and homesick, it was also Zephyrus who conducted her two sisters to her fairy-like abode.

在希腊神话最古老的版本中,宙斯将风的管辖权交给了伊俄勒斯。他是伊奥利亚岛的国王,平日里这些风都被关在一个深深的洞穴里,什么时候放它们出来,要看伊俄勒斯的心情,或者诸神的指令。后来,上述故事演变成了关于阿涅摩伊的神话,阿涅摩伊是风神的统称。除了一些小风神之外,四大主要风神包括北风之神波瑞阿斯、东风之神欧洛斯、南风之神诺托斯和西风之神仄斐若斯,其中值得一提的或许是波瑞阿斯和仄斐若斯。

波瑞阿斯和他的风神兄弟们常以飞马的形式出现。古希腊人相信在初春时节,波瑞阿斯和仄斐若斯会席卷马厩,扮演种马的角色为马厩中的母马授精,而此后诞生的小马就是最优良最敏捷的品种。传说特洛伊城的国王拉俄墨冬所拥有的那些精良马匹就是波瑞阿斯和城中的母马交配的产物。

作为星空之神阿斯脱俄斯和曙光女神厄俄斯的儿子,波瑞阿斯是冬季之神。他从色雷斯寒冷的山上吹来,将冰冷的气息传遍大地。一天,当波瑞阿斯从伊里苏斯河上空飞过的时候,他瞥见了河岸上美丽的欧丽泰亚,她是雅典国王的女儿。波瑞阿斯将她带回了自己的住处,变成了自己的新娘。他们的孩子包括冰雪女神开俄尼以及被称为波瑞阿蒂斯的仄忒斯和加莱两兄弟,他们是一对带翅膀的勇士,也是跟随伊阿宋的阿尔戈英雄之一。雅典人将波瑞阿斯视为友邻,在波斯战争中曾请他助一臂之力。

仄斐若斯是风神中最温和的一位,因而成为春天的使者。尽管在大多数神话故事中,仄斐若斯都只是配角,但有一则关于他和太阳神阿波罗争夺美少年雅辛托斯的三角恋故事流传颇广。雅辛托斯是斯巴达的一位王子,相貌英俊、身材健硕,太阳神和风神都对他一见倾心。然而,少年却选择了与阿波罗为伴,这令仄斐若斯恼怒不已。一天,风神窥见情敌和少年在草地上玩掷铁饼的游戏。仄斐若斯心生妒忌,对着他们悄悄吹起一阵风,飞行中的铁饼因此改变了轨迹,正中少年的头部,致其当场殒命。眼看着自己心爱的伙伴惨死面前，自己却无力回天，阿波罗心碎不已，于是，他将仄斐若斯变成了一朵风信子花，名字就叫雅辛托斯。

好友的惨死让阿波罗对仄斐若斯大为光火，发誓要对他进行惩罚。这时，厄洛斯出面替风神说话，认为他是出于爱才那么做的，这一仗义执言的行为让风神从此甘愿效力于小爱神。因此，在厄洛斯和普赛克的爱情故事中，仄斐若斯扮演了交通工具的角色，是他首先将被遗弃在山顶的普赛克带到了厄洛斯绿荫深处的宫殿里。后来当普赛克感觉孤单想家的时候，又是他把美少女的两个姐姐带到了她童话般的住处。

Extra 拓展测试

1. Which of the following do you think is Borea, god of the north wind? 你认为以下哪一幅图是北风之神波瑞阿斯？

A

B

2. Derived from Zephyrus, god of the west wind, the word "zephyr" denotes a soft gentle breeze, a personification of the west wind. Besides, it may also be understood as a very light article of clothing, or anything of fine, soft or light quality. Thus the word "zephyr" is widely used around the globe in the name of a music band, of a computer system, or of a basketball team. Zephyr is also the name of an automobile produced in the United States. Can you guess which automobile company it is from?

单词 zephyr 一词源于西风之神仄斐若斯(Zephyrus)的名字，指"轻柔的微风"，是西风拟人化的表达。此外，它还可以表示"轻薄的织物”或任何柔软、轻薄、精致的东西。因此,zephyr 一词出现在全世界许多地方,它是乐队的名字、电脑系统的名字、篮球队的名字……有一款美国产的汽车也叫这个名字,你能猜到它是哪家汽车公司生产的吗?

(1. 答案:B)

(2. 答案:Ford 福特)

CHAPTER 5
Myth of the Constellation
第五章　星座神话

Word Knowledge 词汇知识

Ursa Major and Ursa Minor(大熊星座和小熊星座)

Ursa Major is a well-known and significant constellation in many cultures. Being one of the oldest constellations in the sky, a great number of tales and legends across the globe associate it with a bear.

In Latin Ursa Major means "Greater she-bear". In Greek, Arktos is the word for "bear". Hence the name Arctic, means bearish and describes the far northern parts of the earth where the Great Bear Constellation dominates the heavens. As a very large constellation, Ursa Major is also known for its famous asterism, or star grouping, the Big Dipper.

Ursa Minor means "little bear" in Latin, but this circumpolar constellation resembles a dipper more than a bear, and is therefore commonly called the Little Dipper. It is much less conspicuous than the Big Dipper, but it contains the most important navigational star in our sky, Polaris, the Pole or the North Star.

在世界许多文化中,大熊星座都是一个重要而著名的星座,同时,它也是最古老的星座之一,许多关于这个星座的传说故事都和"熊"有关。

在拉丁语中,Ursa Major 的意思是"大母熊"。而在希腊语中,指代"熊"的单词是 Arktos,也因为如此,Arctic 一词既可以表示"像熊一样的",也可以表示"地球的北极"。在那里,大熊星座主宰着天空。作为一个大型星座,大熊星座包含一个著名的星群,这一星群俗称"北斗七星"。

虽然在拉丁语中,Ursa Minor 的意思是"小熊",但是这个拱极星座看上去却更像一个小斗,也因此得名"小北斗七星"。相比而言,它没有"北斗七星"容易辨认,但是,它拥有一位重量级成员:天空中那颗最明亮的导航之星——北极星。

Orion(猎户座)

The name of the constellation Orion derives from a Greek myth, which relates to a handsome and muscular mortal hunter. As a son of Poseidon, ruler of all the seas, Orion was comfortable at sea as he was on land. He was able to navigate great distance across the ocean with his head above water the whole time. Everything about Orion was larger than life, including his opinion of himself.

Artemis, the beautiful goddess of the hunt, was impressed by Orion's superb skills in archery and formed a hunting team with him. However, Apollo, the twin brother of Artemis, resented the blossoming friendship between his sister and the boastful Orion. He complained to Gaea, the most ancient of all the gods, about the brag of this young man's daring to kill every animal on the planet. Gaea, who became furious hearing this, decided to dispatch him with a giant fearsome scorpion.

This was indeed no ordinary scorpion, so what Orion could do was to run wildly to avoid being stung by its lethal tail. It was not until he jumped into the sea that he could finally escape from the chaser, yet his fate was doomed. Being a tiny black speck down on the ocean, he was shot dead by Artemis, who was then challenged by Apollo her skills as an archer.

Orion's body was eventually placed into the sky, where Artemis hoped to gaze upon for all eternity. The goddess also put Orion's two favorite hunting dogs, Canis Major and Canis Minor, near him so that his friend wouldn't be alone. As the constellation of Orion sets each night in the west, another constellation can be seen rising in the east. It is the Scorpion, chasing him across the sky.

猎户座的名字源于希腊神话中一位英俊健硕的猎手。作为海神波塞冬的儿子,俄里翁无论在陆地还是海上都如履平地,他可以只把脑袋露出水面,在海里游很长的距离。在俄里翁的生活里,所有的东西都是大一号的,包括他对自己的看法。

俄里翁的射箭技术非常高超,就连狩猎女神阿尔忒弥斯也对他刮目相看,两人时常相约一起狩猎。然而,阿尔忒弥斯的双胞胎哥哥阿波罗却不喜欢这个狂妄自大的年轻人,为了拆散他们,阿波罗来到地母盖亚面前,告诉她说俄里翁吹嘘要杀死地球上所有的动物。盖亚一听大为震怒,决定派一只巨大的蝎子去解决此事。

这不是一只普通的蝎子!为了不被蝎子的尾巴蜇到,俄里翁拼了命地四处奔逃,一直到他跳进海里才终于摆脱了蝎子的追杀。然而,他的命运注定以悲剧结尾。远远看去,他在海上就是一个小黑点,而这个小黑点成了阿波罗和妹妹比拼射箭的目标。阿尔忒弥斯在无意之间杀死了自己的好朋友。

最终,阿尔忒弥斯把俄里翁的尸体升上了天空,希望一抬头就能看见他,同时,为了让好朋友不那么孤单,她把俄里翁最喜欢的两条猎犬变成了大犬座和小犬座陪伴在他左右。每天夜里,当猎户座从西边的天空升起之际,在东边的天上,有另一个星座也会同时出现,那就是依然在追赶他的天蝎座。

The Myths 神话故事

In the charming retinue of Artemis, virgin huntress and goddess of the crescent moon, there was a beautiful nymph called Callisto, the daughter of Lycaon, King of Arcadia. Devoted to the pleasures of the chase, Callisto had made a vow never to marry. However, Zeus, under the form of the huntress goddess, succeeded in obtaining her affection. The almighty god loved her passionately and often sought her company. Before the year was out, she bore him a son, Arcas by name, who later became the eponymous ancestor of the Arcadians.

Zeus' frequent absences from Mount Olympus aroused Hera's suspicion. In time, the vengeful queen discovered the truth and devised an effectual scheme of retaliation. One day, Callisto suddenly found herself changed into a bear, with monstrous bushy jaws and bloodshot eyes, though she remained human in heart. She instantly left her son and went into hiding in the forest.

Fifteen years passed. Little Arcas matured to youthful manhood. He was hunting merrily in the woods one day when a huge grey bear suddenly appeared before him. The young man was terrified at the sight of the grisly bear, and the bear was amazed and overjoyed to recognize her own son in the young hunter. The youth leveled his spear at the slowly approaching bear and was about to pounce it when Zeus intervened to stop the folly. He had not been able to find the whereabouts of his beloved mistress until recently, and had been secretly shielding her from all danger and harm. Now he transformed his son into a little bear. Grabbing both bears by their tails, Zeus hurled them into the safety of the sky, where they still roam close together to this day, known as the constellation of the Great and Little Bear.

Some people say Arcas grew up to become the king of Arcadia and brought agriculture to that wild and rugged country, for which he was immortalized among the stars as Bootes, inventor of the "Wagon", which is the other name for the constellation of the Great Bear.

Later the English linked the constellation to both the Bear and Wagon. They saw it as the wagon of King Arthur, whose Round Table is reflected in the constellations circling the Pole, and whose name comes from the Celtic word for "bear". Legend has it that Arthur is sleeping in a cave with his knights beside him, and will return one day to save his country in its hour of need.

The seven most important stars of the Bear-Wagon (the Big Dipper) are also known as the Seven Sleepers of Ephesus, who lie dreaming in a mountain cave waiting for the resurrection. These seven sleepers, unlike Arthur, are said to have awoken after 300 years and gone down to the local town for provisions, after which they went to sleep once more. In ancient China, the seven stars of the Big Dipper were associated with the celestial palace of the Lord on High, the Star God of Longevity, the heavenly mountain, the paradise of the immortals. The star Sirius, the heavenly wolf, guarded this celestial palace. Today Sirius, which shares the space motion Ursa Major, is regarded as an outlying member of it.

在月神兼狩猎女神阿尔忒弥斯的那群漂亮随从中，有一位美丽的宁芙仙女名叫卡利斯托，是阿卡狄亚国王吕卡翁的女儿。为了享受追猎的游戏，她曾发誓终身不嫁。然而，宙斯化身狩猎女神的样子，成功地赢得了她的芳心。众神之王爱得如此热烈，恨不得一直两厢厮守，还不到一年，她便为宙斯诞下了神子，取名阿尔卡斯，这个孩子长大后便成了阿卡狄亚人的祖先。

由于宙斯时常离开奥林匹斯山去和情人幽会，令赫拉起了疑心。不久，天后便知道了真相，在嫉妒心的驱使下，她开始设计报复。有一天，卡利斯托突然发现自己变成了一头熊，宽大的下颚上长着浓密的兽毛，两只眼睛布满了血丝。虽然她的内心依然如旧，但她还是立刻离开了自己的儿子，躲进了森林深处。

十五年时光一晃而过，小阿尔卡斯长成了英俊的少年。这天，他正在森林里愉快地狩猎时，一只巨大的灰熊突然出现在他面前。少年看见恐怖的灰熊吓坏了，而灰熊认出了少年正是自己的儿子，不由欣喜若狂。眼看灰熊步步逼近，少年拉出长矛，准备出击。正在这时，宙斯及时赶到，阻止了他的鲁莽行为。其实，宙斯一直在寻找他心爱的女人，但是始终没有下落，直到几天前，他才刚刚找到她，并在暗地里保护着她。此刻，他索性把自己的儿子也变成了一只小熊，宙斯一手抓住一只熊的尾巴，把母子俩同时甩上了天空，在那里他们才能得到安宁。今天，你依然能够看见他们母子在天空中漫步，他们的名字叫“大熊星座”和“小熊星座”。

也有人说阿尔卡斯长大后，成了阿卡狄亚的国王，他把农业知识带到了那个荒蛮的国度。因此他才得以获得永生，变成了夜空中的牧夫座，也就是“马车”的发明者，而“马车”其实是大熊星座最重要的七颗星，北斗七星的另一个名字。

后来，英国人将“熊”和“马车”联系到了一起。在他们的眼中，大熊星座是亚瑟王的马车，而他的圆桌就是环绕北极星的那些星座。在凯尔特语中，北极星(the Pole)就是“熊”的意思。传说亚瑟王和他的骑士们睡在一个洞穴里，一旦英国有难，他们还会重新回来拯救祖国。

大熊星座中最重要的七颗星(北斗七星)也被称为“以弗所的七个睡眠者”，他们躺在山洞里睡觉，等待着复活的时机。与亚瑟王不同，据说这七个睡眠者每三百年会醒来一次，到山下的市镇里去寻找补给，之后他们会回到洞里继续睡觉。在中国古代，北斗七星是玉皇大帝的天宫，是长寿之星，是天山所在，是神仙之地。而护卫天宫的天狼星，如今被认为是大熊星座的外围成员，沿着它的轨迹一起运转。

Extra 拓展测试

1. Which of the following is Ursa Major?
下面哪一幅图是大熊星座?

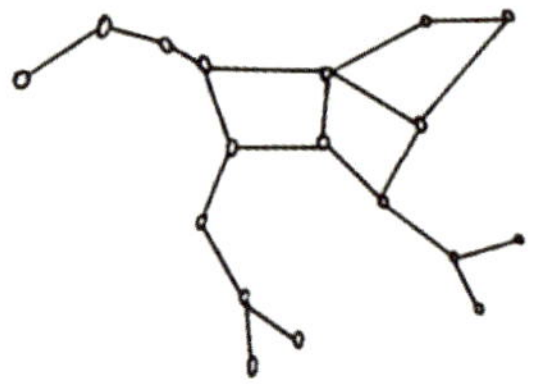

A

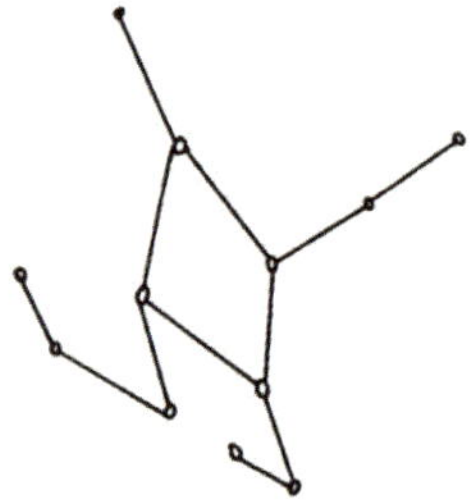

B

2. Canis Major hosts one bright star, which is sometimes taken as a member of Ursa Major. Do you know its name?
大犬座里有一颗很亮的星星，有时也被当作大熊星座的成员，你知道这颗星叫什么名字吗?

(1. 答案：A)
(2. 答案：天狼星 Sirius)

FURTHER READING
The Tragedy of Medusa
延伸阅读 美杜莎的悲剧

In Greek mythology, the Gorgons, Stheno, Ceto, and Medusa, were three hideous-looking sisters with snakes for their hair. Medusa is just one of them and the only one who is mortal. They were the servants of Hades, god of the underworld, who made use of them to terrify and overawe those shades, doomed to be kept in a constant state of unrest as a punishment for their misdeeds. Due to their legendary and powerful gaze which could turn one to stone, the image of Gorgons was very popular in ancient Greece and could be seen on objects and buildings for protection.

Medusa was one of the Gorgons, the three daughters of the sea god Phorcys and the sea goddess Ceto, and the only mortal one. As a priestess of Athena, Medusa was devoted to a life of celibacy. She was originally a very beautiful maiden with golden hair, which caught the eye of Poseidon. Being wooed by the great god of the ocean, she forgot her vows, and became united to him in marriage in the shrine of Athena, which greatly enraged the goddess. Athena sought vengeance by punishing Medusa for this offence in a most terrible manner. Each wavy lock of the beautiful hair was changed into a venomous snake. Her once gentle, love-inspiring eyes now became blood-shot, and her former fair complexion, a loathsome greenish tinge. With the curse of Athena upon her, Medusa would turn into stone whomsoever she gazed upon.

Seeing herself transformed into so repulsive an object, Medusa fled from her home, never to return. According to the myth, the Gorgons were frightful winged monsters, whose bodies were covered with scales, and heads, hissing, wriggling snakes. Their hands were of brass, and their teeth resembled the tusks of a wild boar. Medusa was eventually beheaded by Perseus. As she was pregnant by Poseidon, out from her bloody neck sprang Pegasus, a winged horse, and Chrysaor, a mortal warrior whose name means "he who bears a golden sword". When the blood dripped from Medusa's head onto the plains of Libya, each drop of blood transformed into venomous serpents.

Myth has it that Pegasus, the beautiful winged horse, flew to the top of Mount Olympus, where he was received with delight and admiration by all the immortals. Zeus assigned him a special place in his palace and employed Pegasus to carry his thunder and lightning. Pegasus permitted none but the gods to mount him, except in the case of Bellerophon, the mortal hero whom, at the command of Athena, he carried aloft, in order that he might slay with his sword the Chimera, a fire-breathing monster with a lion's head, a goat's body and a serpent's tail.

The logo of Versace, a famous luxury brand from Italy, has the head of Medusa as its central image, but portraying her as a beautiful woman with golden hair instead, which reminds people of the tragic life of Medusa as the victim of both god Poseidon's lust and goddess Athena's jealousy. According to Gianni Versace, the logo designer and founder of the Versace company, the mythical Medusa is a perfect symbolic figure to represent Gianni's paradox—beautiful but frightening, shocking yet enchanting.

Gorgon fruit is in fact the formal name for a local delicacy in the Yangtze delta in China. The southern Chinese, especially those in the city of Suzhou, love this fruit in season so much that they give it a nickname "hen's head rice", which is indeed a world apart from the western image of snake-haired Gorgons symbolizing anger and evil. So how could the two words be associated with each other? The so-called "hen's head rice" refers actually to the ripe seeds taken from some purple-red water plant, whose shape is a bit ugly like a hen's head, or the head of a Gorgon, but inside it there is the "rice", its pearl-like snow-white kernel. Hence the English equivalent of "hen's head rice" is gorgon fruit.

在希腊神话中，戈耳戈指的是三个长相丑陋的蛇发姐妹：斯忒诺、克托和美杜莎，其中美杜莎是唯一的凡人。她们是冥王哈迪斯的仆人，冥王用她们来恐吓那些生前做了坏事的鬼魂，让他们一刻不得安宁。传说戈耳戈的凝视能够将人变成石头，因此古希腊人喜欢把她们的头像刻在器皿或建筑上。

美杜莎是戈耳戈之一，是海神福耳库斯和海女神刻托的三个女儿中的一个，也是唯一一个凡人。作为雅典娜手下的女祭司，美杜莎曾承诺要永葆贞洁。她原本是一位美丽的金发少女，正是她的美丽吸引了海神波塞冬的目光，在这位大洋之神的诱惑之下，美杜莎忘记了自己的誓言，在雅典娜的神庙里献出了自己的贞操，这使得女神雅典娜大为震怒。为了惩罚美杜莎对自己的背叛，她采用了最可怕的报复方式：将美杜莎的每一缕金发都变成毒蛇，让原本温柔可爱的眼睛布满血丝，曾经白皙的肌肤如今发出瘆人的绿光。在雅典娜的诅咒之下，美杜莎能把她看到的所有人都变成石头。

看到自己变成如此可憎的模样，美杜莎逃离了家乡，从此再也没有回来。根据神话故事，戈耳戈是长着翅膀的怪物，她们的身体上满是鳞片，头上扭曲盘绕着发出"嗞嗞"声的毒蛇，她们的手硬得像黄铜，有野猪般锋利的牙齿。美杜莎最终被珀尔修斯砍了头。因为当时她怀了波塞冬的孩子，从她被砍断的脖子处跃出了飞马珀加索斯以及他的双胞胎弟弟刻律萨俄耳。后者是一名凡人武士，其名字的意思是"佩戴着金剑的人"。据说从美杜莎头上滴下的血落在了利比亚平原上，每一滴血都变成了一条毒蛇。

传说美丽的飞马珀加索斯飞到了奥林匹斯山巅，受到众神的欣赏和喜爱。宙斯特意在自己的宫殿里为他留了一块地方，并让他帮着运载雷电。珀加索斯只允许神骑在他背上，唯一的例外是凡人英雄柏勒罗丰。在雅典娜的授意下，飞马载着他，助他杀死了那个狮头、羊身、蛇尾的喷火女怪喀迈拉。

来自意大利的著名奢侈品牌范思哲，其商标的核心就是美杜莎的头像，不过这个美杜莎却是一位金发美女，唤起了人们对美杜莎悲剧人生的联想，那个遭受海神波塞冬的淫欲和女神雅典娜的嫉妒双重摧残的无辜少女。按照商标设计者和公司创始人詹尼·范思哲的解释，美杜莎身上那些看似矛盾的特征完美地诠释了该品牌的设计理念——美丽得令人震惊，魅惑得令人窒息。

事实上，戈耳戈果（芡实）是中国长三角地区的一种特产。南方人，尤其是苏州人非常喜爱这种时鲜，给它起了个别名“鸡头米”。这个名字和西方人脑海中的蛇发女妖无疑相去甚远，那么这两者究竟是如何联系的呢？所谓的“鸡头米”其实指的是一种紫红色水生植物成熟的果实，这种植物外表有点丑，状似鸡头或戈耳戈的头，但剥开外壳，其内部的颗粒如珍珠般雪白，那就是“米”了，“鸡头米”与英文戈耳戈果的联系由此而来。

Extra 拓展测试

Today, medusas are known as a type of beautiful marine creatures. Do you know what they are?

如今，medusa 这个词代表了一种美丽的海洋生物，你知道它们是什么吗？

（答案：水母）

PART Ⅳ Myths of Love

第四部分

爱的神话

扫一扫,听本部分音频

CHAPTER 1 The Wrath of Hera
第一章 赫拉的怒火

Word Knowledge 词汇知识

Herald(使节)

The word herald is a synonym of messenger. Like Hermes, who was the messenger of all the gods, Iris, the goddess of the rainbow, was the personal messenger of Hera. Iris is usually depicted as a beautiful maiden with wings on her shoulders and a herald's wand in her hand.

使节(herald)这个词和"信使"是同义词,就像众神的使者赫耳墨斯,赫拉的私人信使彩虹女神伊利斯。伊利斯通常被描绘成一位长着翅膀的美丽少女,手持一把信使的节杖。

Heracles(海格立斯)

Heracles was the strongest and most famous hero in Greek mythology. As the son of Zeus and Alcmene, a mortal princess, his name actually means "Glory of Hera". When Alcmene was in labor with Heracles, she was having difficulty giving birth to so big a child. After seven days, she called for help from Lucina, the goddess of childbirth. However, instead of giving her a hand, the midwife tied her legs in knots at the command of Hera. Alcmene struggled in pain and became close to death. At this critical moment, Galanthis, the red-gold haired servant of Alcmene, came over and uncovered to the goddess the scheme of Hera. Thus the baby was saved. But as a punishment,

Galanthis was turned into a weasel.

Worried about Hera's revenge, Alcmene gave her halfgod son up to Athena, who then took the infant to the heavenly queen. Hera did not recognize the mini-mortal enemy and inadvertently nursed him out of pity. The super-strong infant, however, suckled so intensely that Hera pushed him away due to acute pain. Her milk then sprayed across the sky, forming the Milky Way, which we now call the Galaxy because *gala* in Greek simply means milk. The infant, originally named Alcides, was later renamed Heracles after he had acquired supernatural powers from the divine milk of his stepmother.

海格立斯是希腊神话中最强壮、最著名的英雄。作为宙斯和凡人公主阿尔克墨涅的儿子，他的名字实际上有"赫拉的荣耀"之意。当阿尔克墨涅生产的时候，由于胎儿太大，七天七夜都生不下来，于是，她向生育女神鲁西娜求助。然而，女神非但没有帮助她，反而在赫拉的命令下把她的两条腿绑在了一起。阿尔克墨涅在痛苦中挣扎，眼看濒临死亡。关键时刻，她的红发女仆伽兰西斯及时出现，并向鲁西娜揭露了赫拉的阴谋。小婴儿得救了，而作为惩罚，伽兰西斯却被变成了一只黄鼬。

由于担心赫拉的报复，阿尔克墨涅将自己半神的儿子献给了雅典娜，雅典娜把小婴儿抱回家，并请求天后赫拉给孩子喂奶。赫拉没有认出这是情敌的儿子，出于可怜，便同意了。没想到，这婴儿的吮吸力量太大，令赫拉疼痛无比，她一把推开了怀里的婴儿。飞溅出来的乳汁划过天空，变成了天上的银河，现在我们称之为 the Galaxy，因为在希腊语中 *gala* 就是"乳汁"的意思。这个小婴儿从天后的乳汁中获得了超凡的力量，他的名字也从出生时的阿尔喀德斯，变成了后来的海格立斯。

Hebe(赫柏)

Apart from two sons, Ares, the god of war, and Hephaestus, the god of fire, who were either too violent or too ugly, Zeus and Hera had a beautiful daughter Hebe who was known for having the power of bringing eternal youth. On Mount Olympus, Hebe was the cup-bearer who served nectar and ambrosia for gods and goddesses, until she was married to Heracles. The name Hebe in Greek simply means "youth" or "prime of life". Juventus, the Roman equivalent of Hebe, has the similar meaning of "youth", from which derives such words as "juvenile" "rejuvenate" "rejuvenescence", and such phrases as "juvenile court" and "juvenile delinquency".

宙斯和赫拉有两个儿子,战神阿瑞斯和火神赫菲斯托斯,但是除了这两个要么太暴力要么太丑陋的儿子之外,他们还有一个美丽的女儿赫柏,一个能够使人永葆青春的女神。在嫁给海格立斯之前,赫柏在奥林匹斯山的工作是给众神的酒杯里斟满玉液琼浆。她的名字在希腊语中的意思就是"青春"或"最美的年华",她在罗马神话对应的名字是茱文塔斯,同样也有"青春"的含义,由此衍生出了诸如 juvenile(青少年的)、rejuvenate(恢复青春)、rejuvenescence(返老还童)等词和词组 juvenile court(青少年法庭)、juvenile delinquency(青少年犯罪)。

The Myths 神话故事

As the principal wife of Zeus and queen of heaven, Hera appears to be the sublime embodiment of strict matronly virtue, and, on that account, the protectress of purity and married women. Faultless in her fidelity as a wife, she represented the sanctity of the marriage tie and was strongly imbued with hatred of any immorality. She was forever on the run, trying to keep track of Zeus and devise ways of revenge not really upon her husband, but rather upon his hopeless mistresses. Zeus' zest for pretty faces knew no limits, while Hera's persecution of her rivals and their children were relentless. Out of extreme jealousy, Hera once sent the dreadful serpent Python to terrify and torment the beautiful goddess Leto, which compelled Zeus to create Delos, a secret floating island in the

Aegean Sea—the birthplace of Apollo and Artemis.

Apart from the immortal lovers of Zeus, Hera had countless rivals in the mortal world. A proof of the legendary wrath of Hera relates to a beautiful maiden named Io. Zeus was much attached to Io, a priestess of Hera, and had foreseen the jealous intrigues of his wife, so he changed Io into a white cow. Seeing through the deceit, Hera contrived to obtain the animal as a present from Zeus, and placed her under the watchful care of Argus, a monster with one hundred eyes. Fastened to an olive tree, Io had no chance to escape, for the monster never closed more than two eyes at a time.

Zeus, unable to bear the suffering of her mistress, sent Hermes down to kill the monster. With the sound of his magic lyre, Hermes succeeded in putting all the hundred eyes into sleep and thus released Io by slaying Argus. However, Hermes had to flee when he sensed the approach of Hera. The severed head of Argus enraged Hera, who took out all his eyes and stuck them on the tail of a peacock, where they remained up to this day.

In her jealous wrath, Hera sent a gadfly to torment Io, who was driven from land to land, and eventually passed over the strait which divides Europe and Asia. So the strip of water got its name Bosporus, meaning the way of the cow. Zeus pleaded with Hera to leave Io alone and promised that he would never pay Io any more attention. At length Io reached Egypt, where she was allowed to restore her original form. She settled down and gave birth to a son Epaphus, who afterwards became king of Egypt and built the famous city Memphis.

There is another myth of Semele, the beautiful princess of Phoenicia, who was greatly beloved by Zeus but hated by Hera. With jealous malignity, Hera, disguised herself as Semele's old nurse, persuaded the maiden to insist upon Zeus visiting her as he appeared to Hera. Suspecting no treachery, Semele followed the advice. When Zeus revealed himself as the mighty lord of the universe, accompanied by thunder and lightning, Semele was instantly consumed in the flames. At the moment of her perishing, Zeus grabbed from the fire her six-month aborted baby, and sowed it into his thigh. A few months later, Dionysus was born. Dionysus, the god of wine, was also referred to as "the twice-born".

赫拉作为天后和宙斯的正妻,是夫妻美德的崇高象征,也是贞操和妇德的保护神。她对丈夫非常忠诚,因此,作为婚姻纽带的神圣维护者,她痛恨任何形式的背叛。从始至终,她都紧盯着宙斯,尝试用各种方法进行报复,当然不是针对她的丈夫,而是宙斯那些可怜的情妇们。一方面,宙斯猎艳的热情永不停歇,另一方面,赫拉对其情敌及下一代的迫害也永无止境。曾经赫拉出于极度的嫉妒派巨蟒皮同去恐吓和折磨美丽的女神勒托,宙斯迫于无奈,建造了得洛斯,一座位于爱琴海中央的神秘浮岛,那里成了阿波罗和阿尔忒弥斯的出生地。

除了这些神界的情敌外,赫拉在人间也有无数的对手。有一则可以证明赫拉妒火的神话,讲的是一个叫艾奥的少女,她是赫拉身边的女祭司,宙斯对她一往情深,但他预感到了赫拉有可能会出于嫉妒迫害她,于是将艾奥变成了一头白牛。但是,赫拉识破了丈夫的诡计,她设计让宙斯把这头牛作为礼物送给了她。随后,便将白牛绑到一棵橄榄树上,并指派百眼妖怪阿耳戈斯严密看管,由于这妖怪从来不会闭上两只以上的眼睛上睡觉,艾奥毫无逃跑的可能。

宙斯不忍心看着自己的情人遭受折磨,便派赫耳墨斯下凡去杀死那妖怪。赫耳墨斯用他神奇的里拉琴,终于成功地催眠了阿耳戈斯,当那一百只眼睛全部闭上后,他砍下了妖怪的脑袋,释放了艾奥。然而,听到赫拉的脚步声,他不得不先一步离开。看见阿耳戈斯被砍下的脑袋,赫拉怒火中烧,她取下那一百只眼睛,把它们钉到了孔雀的尾巴上,直到今天,那些眼睛依然在那儿。

妒火驱使赫拉又放出了一只牛虻来追逐艾奥,从一个大陆到另一个大陆,可怜的艾奥最终不得不越过横亘在欧洲与亚洲之间的那片海峡,博斯布鲁斯海峡由此得名,它的意思就是"牛的路"。宙斯恳求赫拉饶了艾奥,并保证自己以后再也不去见她了。最后,艾奥逃到了埃及,在那里她终于被允许变回人形,定居下来。她的儿子厄帕福斯后来成了埃及的法老，并修建了著名的孟斐斯城。

另一则神话讲的是腓尼基公主塞默勒，宙斯非常爱她，赫拉非常恨她。妒火中烧的赫拉假扮成塞默勒的老保姆，不怀好意地劝说她去让宙斯显露真身。单纯的少女不知道其中有诈，听从了赫拉的建议。当宇宙之王驾着雷霆战车出现在她面前时，凡人少女瞬间化为灰烬，就在她即将消失的一刻，宙斯从火堆里一把救出了已经六个月的小产婴儿，并把它种在了自己的大腿上。几个月后，狄俄尼索斯降生了。因此，酒神狄俄尼索斯也被称作“二次出生”。

Extra 拓展测试

1. Which of the following picture do you think describes Zeus' mortal lover, Io?
你认为下面那幅图描绘的是宙斯的人类爱人艾奥？

A

B

2. In the myth of Io, Hera sent a gadfly to chase and torment her enemy, which forced Io to wander farther and farther away from Greece. Interestingly, around 4 century B.C., Socrates, the ancient Greek philosopher and teacher of Plato, referred to himself as a "gadfly", a gift bestowed by the gods. According to the words cited by Plato, Socrates believed that all societies needed a "gadfly" to sting the "steed" of state into acknowledging its proper duties and obligations.

在关于艾奥的神话故事中，赫拉放出一只牛虻去追逐和折磨她的情敌，迫使艾奥不得不四处躲藏，背井离乡。有趣的是，在公元前四世纪左右，古希腊哲学家、柏拉图的老师苏格拉底曾自比是一只上帝派来的“牛虻”。根据柏拉图的记载，苏格拉底认为所有社会都需要“牛虻”去叮咬国家这只“骏马”，使之认识到所承担的责任和义务。

3. There is a novel entitled *The Gadfly* written by an Irish writer in 1897. Do you know the name of the writer?
一位爱尔兰作家曾在 1897 年创作过一部小说《牛虻》，你知道这位作家的名字吗？

（1. 答案：B）
（3. 答案：艾捷尔・伏尼契）

CHAPTER 2 The Beauty and the Ugly

第二章 美女与丑夫

Word Knowledge 词汇知识

Harmonia(哈耳摩尼亚)

Harmonia, the goddess of harmony and concord, was the daughter of Aphrodite, the goddess of love, and Ares, the god of war. Harmonia was best known for a fatal necklace, which was forged by Hephaestus in revenge of Aphrodite's infidelity in their marriage. According to legend, the necklace of Harmonia would bring great misfortune to all its wearers or owners. In Roman mythology, the name of Harmonia was Concordia, which embodies the agreement in marriage and society. Apparently, the English words *harmony*, *harmonic minor*, *harmonica* are all derived from the name Harmonia. Such words as *concord*, *concordat*, *Concorde* are also among daily vocabulary.

哈耳摩尼亚是象征和谐与融洽的女神，是爱神阿芙洛蒂忒和战神阿瑞斯的女儿。哈耳摩尼亚以她的项链而出名，这条项链据说是赫菲斯托斯为了报复妻子阿芙洛蒂忒的不忠而专门制作的。传说戴上或拥有这条项链的人，就会厄运缠身。在罗马神话中，哈耳摩尼亚的名字叫肯考狄亚，象征婚姻和社会的和谐。显然，英语中的 harmony(和谐)、harmonic(和声小调)、harmonica(口琴)都源自哈耳摩尼亚这个名字。而 concord(和睦)、concordat(协议)、Concorde(协和式飞机)这些词也属于常用词汇。

Phobos(弗伯斯)

Phobos, the god of fear, was also a child of Aphrodite and Ares. Phobos had a twin brother Deimos, the god of terror, together they accompanied Ares into battle, driving his chariot and spreading trembling fear in his wake. According to the myths, Hephaestus was enraged at the adultery between his wife and Ares, and vowed to take his revenge by cursing any lineage of children resulting from the affair. As a result, most of the offspring of the beautiful goddess seem to have possessed the dark force.

The word phobia, derived from the name Phobos, is now often seen in some compound nouns to mean an extreme or irrational fear of something, such as *hydrophobia*, *acrophobia*, *plane-phobia*, *trypophobia*, *allodoxaphobia*, *socialohobia*, *nostophobia* etc.

恐惧之神弗伯斯也是阿芙洛蒂忒和阿瑞斯的孩子,他还有一个双胞胎弟弟是惊悚之神戴墨斯,兄弟俩随阿瑞斯一起征战沙场,是战争带来的惊恐的化身。根据神话故事,赫菲斯托斯得知妻子和阿瑞斯的私情后,极为震怒,发誓要报复他们,他诅咒两人的后代,最终使得女神的大部分后代都成了黑暗势力的象征。

恐惧症(phobia)这个词源自弗伯斯的名字,现在常用来构成一些复合词,形容对某事或某物极端的或不合情理的害怕,例如:hydrophobia(恐水症)、acrophobia(恐高症)、plane-phobia(恐飞机症)、trypophobia(密集恐惧症)、allodoxaphobia(选择恐惧症)、social-phobia(社交恐惧症)、nostophobia(回家恐惧症)等。

Sub Rosa(玫瑰花下)

The Latin phrase *sub rosa* literally means "under the rose", which could be traced to ancient Greek and Roman mythology. It is said that Aphrodite gave her son Eros a rose after she had an affair with Ares. Eros, then in turn gave the flower to Harpocrates, the god of silence, as a token of gratitude for not betraying the confidence of her mother. Then the rose was dedicated to Aphrodite not only as the symbol of beauty but also as a sign of confidentiality and secrecy. In the western countries, ceilings of dining rooms are sometimes decorated with carvings of roses, or roses may be placed on the table, reportedly to remind the guests that what was said at the table should be kept confidential.

拉丁语中的 sub rosa 字面意思是“玫瑰花下”,这种表达可以追溯到古代希腊和罗马神话。据说阿芙洛蒂忒在和阿瑞斯有了私情之后,给了儿子厄洛斯一朵玫瑰花,厄洛斯则把这朵花转交给了沉默之神哈伯克拉底,作为替母亲保守秘密的谢意。此后,爱神阿芙洛蒂忒的玫瑰花就有了双重含义:一是美的象征,二是保守秘密的符号。在西方国家,人们有时会在餐厅的天花板上刻上玫瑰花的装饰,或者在餐桌上摆上玫瑰花,以悄悄提醒来访的客人们,不要把餐桌上讲的话随便说出去。

The Myths 神话故事

Aphrodite, the goddess of beauty and love, is generally said to have been born out of the foam of the sea, for the word *aphros* in Greek means "foam" and her name is literally interpreted as "foam-born". However, in the *Iliad* by Homer, Aphrodite was described as the daughter of Zeus and Dione, an Oceanid or sea nymph. Whichever version it is, she was a goddess of enchanting and incomparable beauty. So beautiful was she that Zeus feared that the other gods would become violent with each other in their rivalry to possess her. In order to prevent this from happening, Zeus forced Aphrodite to marry Hephaestus, the deformed and humorless god of blacksmith.

There is another story which may account for the marriage between the beauty and the ugly. As a god of fire and all mechanical arts, Hephaestus had resented the cruelty of his parents for hurling him down from heaven, which resulted in his being a cripple all his life. One day, he made a most ingenious throne of gold and presented it to his mother. It was arranged in such a manner that, once seated, Hera found herself unable to move. Although eventually Hephaestus released her from the trap of the magic throne, Hera agreed to the demand of giving Aphrodite's hand to his son.

Hephaestus was overjoyed being bestowed upon the beautiful Aphrodite in marriage. With his skillful craft, he forged for his beautiful bride various jewelry, among which the most well-known was a *strophion*, a saltire-shaped undergarment usually translated as "girdle". This charmed girdle of Aphrodite was said to have the power of making every woman who wore it irresistible to men. Hard as Hephaestus endeavored to win the heart of his beauty, Aphrodite had no affection for her unattractive spouse. She even amused herself by ridiculing his hobbling gait and awkward movements.

A bit of a flirt herself, Aphrodite was never faithful to her husband. On one occasion, Hephaestus heard of a rumor about the affair between his wife and Ares, the god of war. He then secretly fashioned an unbreakable but invisible net of gold chains around his bed. The next day when Aphrodite and Ares met again in bed, they were both trapped by the net. Afterwards, Hephaestus brought all the gods into the bedchamber to laugh at the captured adulterers. However, to his disappointment, those divine witnesses seemed to feel more envious than contemptuous of the war god. Who wouldn't want to sleep with Aphrodite? So when Hephaestus demanded the return of the marriage gifts, Poseidon suggested that Ares should pay for them and he would gladly serve as a guarantor.

Apart from Ares, Aphrodite had a well-known mortal lover Adonis, an astonishingly handsome young man, who had been fostered by Persephone, the queen of the Underworld. As Persephone also loved Adonis dearly and wanted to keep him for herself, Zeus had to settle the dispute between the two goddesses by decreeing that Adonis would spend one third of the year with Aphrodite, one third with Persephone, and the final third with whoever he chose. Adonis chose Aphrodite, and the two remained constantly close with each other.

One day when Adonis was out hunting, he was gored by a wild boar, which was believed to have been sent by the jealous Ares, and bled to death in Aphrodite's arms. His blood mingled with her tears and became the anemone flower. In one version of the story, Aphrodite injured herself on a thorn from a rosebush, and the rose, which had previously been white, was stained red by her blood. The Adonis River, now known as the Abraham River, in Lebanon was said to run red with blood each year during the festival of Adonis.

阿芙洛蒂忒是美与爱的化身，通常认为她诞生于海上的泡沫中，因为 aphros 一词在希腊语中是"泡沫"的意思，所以，她的名字字面意思就是"生于泡沫"。然而，在荷马史诗《伊利亚特》中，阿芙洛蒂忒被描绘成宙斯与俄刻阿尼得，即海洋仙女狄俄涅的女儿。不管是哪个版本，女神无与伦比的美貌都是毋庸置疑的。因为她过于美丽，宙斯担心其他神会为了她而彼此决斗，引起骚乱。为了防患于未然，宙斯强迫阿芙洛蒂忒嫁给了赫菲斯托斯，那个长相畸形而且毫无幽默细胞的锻冶之神。

关于美女与丑夫的婚姻还有另一种解释：因为一生下来就被父母从天庭扔下凡界，从而成了跛子，赫菲斯托斯对父母怨恨不已。有一天，他做了一把非常精巧的金质王座，并把它献给了自己的母亲赫拉，而赫拉发现这把椅子一旦坐上去，就一动都不能动了。尽管最后赫菲斯托斯还是把母亲从神奇宝座的束缚中释放了出来，但是，他却迫使母亲答应了他的要求——把阿芙洛蒂忒嫁给他。

能够娶到美丽的阿芙洛蒂忒作为妻子，赫菲斯托斯内心兴奋而狂喜。他用自己高超的技艺为美丽的新娘制作了各种珠宝首饰，其中最有名的就是一件 X 形的内衣，称作 strophion，一般翻译成"腰带"。据说阿芙洛蒂忒这条神奇的腰带能够让所有穿上它的女人都变得异常迷人，令男人难以抗拒。尽管赫菲斯托斯竭力想要赢得美人的心，但是阿芙洛蒂忒始终无法爱上自己丑陋的伴侣,她甚至嘲笑他的跛足,以模仿他走路的样子为乐。

有些轻浮的阿芙洛蒂忒对于丈夫非常不忠。有一次,赫菲斯托斯听说了她和战神阿瑞斯的绯闻,便悄悄地用金链在床的周围做了一张牢不可破的隐形大网,第二天,当阿芙洛蒂忒和阿瑞斯再次幽会时,两人同时被困在了里面。随后,赫菲斯托斯叫来了所有神仙嘲笑这对奸夫淫妇。然而,令他意想不到的是,那些证人们对于战神的态度似乎羡慕大于鄙视,谁不想和阿芙洛蒂忒同床共枕啊!于是,当赫菲斯托斯提出要妻子归还他送的礼物时,波塞冬建议由阿瑞斯来偿还,而他自己则很乐意充当担保人的角色。

除了阿瑞斯,阿芙洛蒂忒还有一位很有名的凡间情人阿多尼斯。这位帅气逼人的美男子是冥后珀耳塞福涅抚养长大的,因此冥后也对他宠爱有加,不想让他离开自己。不得已,宙斯裁决阿多尼斯每年三分之一的时间陪阿芙洛蒂忒,三分之一的时间陪珀耳塞福涅,剩下三分之一的时间则由他自己决定。阿多尼斯选择了阿芙洛蒂忒,于是,一年有三分之二的时间两人都长相厮守。

一天,阿多尼斯外出打猎,遭遇了野猪的攻击,据说那头野猪是嫉妒的阿瑞斯派来的。眼看自己的情人惨死在怀里,阿芙洛蒂忒伤心不已,他的血混合着她的泪变成了美丽的银莲花。另一种说法是阿芙洛蒂忒在哭泣时弄伤了自己,原本白色的玫瑰花因为沾染了女神的血,从此变成了红色。阿多尼斯河如今被称作亚伯拉罕河,位于黎巴嫩境内。据说每年在阿多尼斯节期间,这条河的河水都会变成血红色。

Extra 拓展测试

1. Which of the following is likely to be the girdle of Aphrodite?
下面哪一个有可能是阿芙洛蒂忒的腰带?

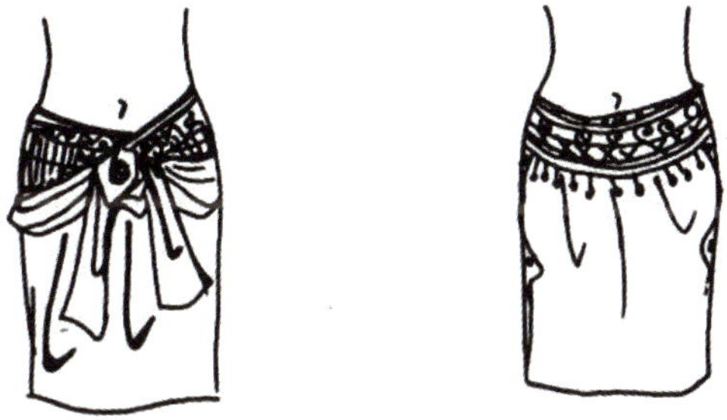

A B

2. Most Chinese readers are more familiar with the Roman name of Aphrodite than her Greek name, probably due to the famous statue Venus of Milo, now kept in Louvre. But do you know that Venus is also the second planet from the sun in the solar system? What is its name in Chinese?

相比阿芙洛蒂忒这个名字,大多数中国读者可能更熟悉的是她的罗马名维纳斯,很大一部分原因在于卢浮宫那尊著名的雕塑《米洛的维纳斯》。但是你知道 Venus 也是太阳系里距离太阳第二近的行星吗? 它的中文是什么?

3. Chinese Kongfu may also be referred to as martial arts. Do you know which Roman god did the word "martial" derive from?
中国功夫也被称为"武术(martial)",那么你知道 martial 一词源自哪一位罗马神名吗?

(1. 答案:A)
(2. 答案:金星)
(3. 答案:马耳斯 Mars,对应希腊战神阿瑞斯 Ares)

CHAPTER 3 Apollo and Daphne
第三章 阿波罗和达芙妮

Word Knowledge 词汇知识

Delphi(特尔斐)

Delphi was considered by the ancient Greeks to be the centre of the world. According to ancient myth, Zeus released two eagles, one from the east, the other, from the west, and caused them to fly toward the centre. They met at the future site of Delphi, where was later housed the Temple of Apollo, the god of prophecy. Legend has it that the oracle at Delphi originally belonged to Gaea, the Mother Earth, and was guarded by the serpent Python. Having slain Python, Apollo founded his own oracle there. In ancient Greece, no cities would be built without first consulting the Delphic Oracle, whose riddling responses to a wide range of questions were delivered by the Pythia, a priestess who sat on a tripod.

Delphi, derived from the Greek word *delphin*, is in fact the origin of the modern word dolphin for the reason that Apollo had instructed people to build the temple under the disguise of a dolphin. The prefix *ora*- of the word oracle means speak, hence oral English, spoken English.

古希腊人认为特尔斐就是世界的中心。根据神话传说，宙斯放出两只老鹰，一只从东，一只自西，飞向世界的中心，结果两只老鹰不约而同落在了特尔斐城，那里后来就建起了预言之神阿波罗的神庙。传说特尔斐神庙最初属于地母女神盖亚，并由巨蟒皮同看守，阿波罗杀死了皮同，取代了盖亚。在古希腊，凡要建城者，必须先来特尔斐神庙领取神谕，坐在三足鼎上的女祭司皮提亚针对五花八门的问题，为人们提供高深莫测答案。

特尔斐一词源自希腊语的 delphin，是现代英语中“海豚(dolphin)”的原形，因为阿波罗曾变成海豚，指导人们修建神庙。神谕(oracle)一词的前缀 ora-意思是“说”，因此，oral English 就是“口头英语”。

Swan(天鹅)

Swan is one of the sacred birds of Apollo. Myth has it that when Apollo was born, swans circled the island of Delos seven times for it was the seventh day of the month. Apollo is often depicted riding a chariot pulled by swans, which are not only symbols of grace and beauty, but also associations with love, music and poetry. There is a belief among ancient Greeks that swans, having been mute most of their lifetime, would sing beautiful songs just before they die. Hence the swan song has become a metaphorical phrase to mean a final gesture, effort, or performance given before one's death or retirement.

天鹅是阿波罗的圣鸟。传说阿波罗降生时，因为恰巧是那个月的第七天，天鹅绕着浮岛得洛斯盘旋了七圈。阿波罗常常被描绘成驾驶着天鹅牵引的战车，这些圣鸟不仅是优雅和美丽的象征，也代表了爱情、音乐及诗歌。在古希腊，人们相信天鹅一生大部分时间都是沉默的，只有在临死前才会吟唱凄美的歌曲，因此，“天鹅之歌”如今成了一种比喻，用来指某人临死或退休前的告别演出。

Crow(乌鸦)

Myth has it that Apollo had a white raven, which he would leave at home to guard his beloved wife Coronis when he was away. One day, this bird messenger flew to him with the intelligence that his wife, already pregnant with Asclepius, had transferred her affection to a youth of Haemonia. Apollo, burning with rage, instantly destroyed her with one of his death-bringing darts. Later, feeling bitterly remorseful and venting his anger on the bird for its negligence, he flung a curse upon the raven so furious that it scorched its feathers from pure white to intense black. Hence all ravens and crows become black.

根据神话传说,阿波罗有一只白色的渡鸦,每当他离开家时,他会把渡鸦留在家里看护他的妻子刻洛尼斯。一天,这只渡鸦飞来报信,告诉阿波罗说他那已经身怀六甲的妻子移情别恋,爱上了海墨尼亚国的一位年轻人。盛怒之下,阿波罗立刻抽出他那致命的箭头射杀了自己的妻子。然而不久之后,他便痛悔不已,并迁怒于渡鸦的失职。太阳神发出了猛烈的诅咒,渡鸦的羽毛瞬间被烧焦。从此之后,所有的渡鸦或乌鸦就都变成黑色的了。

Know thyself!(了解你自己!)

According to the myth, Apollo preached moderation in all things, so the phrases "Know thyself!" and "Nothing in excess!" were always on his lips. As one of the Delphic maxims, "Know thyself" or "Know yourself!" had inspired many famous Greek philosophers, including Socrates, who later expounded upon it and taught us as follows: The unexamined life is not worth living.

根据神话传说,阿波罗教导人们在做任何事情时都应适度,因此,"了解你自己"和"不要过度"这样的话常挂在他嘴边。而"了解你自己"这句话作为特尔斐格言之一,也启发了许多希腊著名的哲学家,其中就包括苏格拉底。他后来将此格言发扬光大,提出了这样一句至理名言:浑浑噩噩的人生不值得过。

Apollo, the god of light, prophecy, music, poetry, arts and science, is by far the most widely worshipped among the Olympians, and the only one whose Greek and Roman name are identical. As the son of Zeus and Leto, Apollo became identified with the sun god Helios, while his twin sister Artemis was similarly equated with Selene, the Titan goddess of the moon. They were both adept at using bows and arrows. According to the myth, Apollo killed Python, the terrible serpent, with a bow and arrows only four days after his birth.

However, Apollo and Artemis were not the only immortal archers. Eros, the winged love god and son of Aphrodite, was also seen frequently playing with his bow and arrows to intervene in the affairs of gods and mortals. One day, Apollo happened to see Eros bending his bow. Proud of his own superior strength and skill, Apollo laughed at the efforts of the little god, saying that such a powerful weapon should be left for a man worthy to use it. Eros replied angrily that his arrow was to conquer the heart instead of the world.

Eros drew from his quiver two darts of different workmanship: one of gold, which had the effect of inspiring love; the other, of lead, which created aversion. Taking aim at Apollo, he pierced his breast with the golden shaft, whilst the leaden one he discharged into the bosom of a beautiful nymph Daphne. Apollo fell instantly in love with Daphne, whom, however, fled from him like a hunted deer at his approach.

Out of repulsion, Daphne made the best of her legs, running through rough fields and pathless woods, but the passionate sun god pressed hard upon her. As he ran, he called out to her to slow down, but Daphne never cared so much as to throw one glance backward. At length, almost faint with fatigue, Daphne cried to her father Peneus, the river god, for assistance. Her plea was answered immediately. Just as Apollo threw out his arms to embrace her, she found herself glued to the ground, a layer of soft bark growing over her fair skin, and her hair transformed into foliage. She was turned into a laurel tree.

Apollo was heart-broken at the loss of Daphne. To show his undying love for the nymph, he decided that the laurel would be his favorite tree. With his powers of eternal youth and immortality, Apollo rendered Daphne ever green. For this reason, the leaves of the laurel trees do not decay. In ancient Greece, the laurel was used to form a crown or wreath of honor and renown for deathless poets and poetry. Thus the most accomplished poet always desires to be made a poet laureate.

As a representation of eternal youth and the perfection of all that is graceful and refined, Apollo rarely seems to have been happy in his love. Although he married Coronis, a nymph of Larissa, he killed his wife in a fit of rage and out of groundless suspicion. Coronis left an infant son named Asclepius, who afterwards became god of medicine, yet even this dear child was destroyed by Zeus' thunderbolts because of his extraordinary powers of restoring the dead to life.

阿波罗作为光明、预言、音乐、诗歌、艺术和科学的象征，可以说是奥林匹斯山诸神中最受崇拜的一位，也是唯一一位在希腊和罗马语中拥有相同姓名的神。他是宙斯和勒托的儿子，地位相当于太阳神赫利俄斯，而他的妹妹阿尔忒弥斯则相当于月亮女神塞勒涅。他们都善使弓箭，据说阿波罗刚出生四天，就用弓箭射死了巨蟒皮同。

不过，阿波罗和阿耳尔忒斯并不是神界仅有的弓箭手。阿芙洛蒂忒的儿子厄洛斯，那个带翅膀的小爱神也常常用弓箭在天堂或人间搞些恶作剧。有一天，阿波罗碰巧看见厄洛斯在弯弓，于是嘲笑他力气太小，告诉他说这种危险的武器还是留给我们这些大人们吧。厄洛斯生气地回答说，他的箭不是用来征服世界，而是用来征服人心的。

厄洛斯从他的箭囊中抽出了两支不同的箭：一支金头的箭用来播下爱的种子，另一支铅头的箭则用来引发厌恶。他瞄准阿波罗的胸口射出了那支金箭，而将那支铅头箭射向了一位美丽的仙女达芙妮。中箭的阿波罗立刻爱上了达芙妮，而后者却像一只受惊的小鹿，一见阿波罗，掉头就跑。

出于反感，达芙妮拼命逃跑，她跨过田野、穿过森林，而热情的太阳神却在后面紧追不舍。他边跑边喊，希望他心爱的人能停下来，但达芙妮却连头也不愿回一下。最后，精疲力竭的达芙妮不得不大声呼喊，请求她父亲河神皮里奥斯的帮助，河神立刻做出了回应。就在阿波罗快要把达芙妮拥入怀中之际，少女的双脚突然扎入土壤，一层柔软的树皮遮盖了她白皙的肌肤，她的发丝渐渐被树叶所取代，达芙妮变成了一棵月桂树。

失去爱人的阿波罗心碎不已，为了表示他对达芙妮的爱永远不变，他决定把月桂当成自己最心爱的树。借助自己的神力，阿波罗让达芙妮成为常青树。正因如此，月桂树叶永远不会枯萎。在古代希腊，人们把月桂做成王冠或花环的样子，戴在那些不朽的诗人头上作为荣誉的象征，那些最杰出的诗人都希望自己有一天能成为"桂冠诗人"。

虽然阿波罗自己是永恒青春和完美的化身，但是他的情路却似乎异常坎坷。尽管他后来娶了勒里撒的仙女刻洛尼斯，他却出于毫无根据的怀疑，在盛怒之下杀死了自己的妻子。刻洛尼斯留下的遗孤就是后来成为医药之神的阿斯克勒庇俄斯，而这个心爱的儿子也因为拥有起死回生的超凡能力，最终被宙斯的雷电劈死了。

Extra 拓展测试

1. How many differences can you spot in the following two pictures?
   找不同。你能找到几处？

2. Laurel wreaths represent victory and status. If someone says he or she sits or rests on his or her laurels, can you guess what the actual meaning is?

既然月桂树冠代表胜利和地位，那么如果我们说“某人坐在他/她的月桂上”，你能猜到这是什么意思吗？

（1. 答案：四处）

（2. 答案：吃老本）

CHAPTER 4 Hero and Leander
第四章 海洛和利安得

Word Knowledge 词汇知识

Hero(海洛)

Although a tragic story, the myth about Hero and Leander has inspired artists and writers and adoring fans for thousands of years. Dante, for example, in his *Purgatorio*, the second part of the *Divine Comedy*, compares a beautiful woman across a stream to Leander straining to see Hero across the Hellespont. William Shakespeare, in his *Two Gentlemen of Verona*, namedropped the two gentlemen to Hero and Leander in a little witty banter in scene one. Among the numerous poets and artists who have ever created works on the basis of this tale are such big names as Lord Byron, John Keats, Lord Tennyson, Rubens, Turner, Rossetti, and so on.

The word "hero" has an extremely important position in Greek mythology. First, it is the name for one of the five Ages of Man by Hesiod. Second, stories of heroes have formed a fascinating part of ancient Greek mythology. These daring god-like mortals, usually with some special gifts, could face down monsters, defeat enemies, and right injustices, setting them high above the race of mankind. The classic myths of such heroes include those of Heracles, Theseus, Perseus, Jason, Achilles, and so on.

In modern English, hero is literally defined as a person who is admired for doing something brave or good, but it could also be used to refer to the principal character in a play or movie or story. Hero-worship, either a noun or a verb, depicts a great admiration for someone whom is considered extremely beautiful or intelligent, as in the following example: *Unfortunately, in many IT cultures, hero-worship is the norm.*

尽管海洛和利安得的神话故事是则悲剧，但在数千年的岁月长河中，它却为无数的艺术家、作家和爱好者们提供了创作的灵感。例如，但丁在《神曲》的第二部分《炼狱》中，就将一名渡河的美女比作是努力游向海洛的利安得。莎士比亚在《维洛那二绅士》的第一幕中，借用海洛和利安得来打趣两位绅士，手法机智巧妙。而在无数曾经以这一故事为主题创作过诗歌或绘画作品的艺术家中，可以听到诸如拜伦、济慈、丁尼生、鲁本斯、特纳和罗塞蒂等如雷贯耳的名字。

在希腊神话中，"英雄"一词有着异常重要的地位：首先，它是古希腊诗人赫西奥德所划分的五个人类时代之一；其次，英雄故事构成了古希腊神话中激动人心的一部分。那些像神一样大胆的凡人勇士往往天赋异禀，能够降妖除魔、匡扶正义，其超出常人的能力也使他们与常人不同，其中最经典的神话故事包括英雄海格立斯、忒修斯、珀耳修斯、伊阿宋、阿喀琉斯等。

英语中的 hero 一词本义表示因为勇敢或善事而受人尊敬的人物，但它也可以指小说、戏剧或电影中的主角。hero-worship 既可以作名词，也可以作动词，描述的是对某个异常美丽或聪明的人的极度喜爱。例如："不幸的是，在许多信息技术文化中，英雄崇拜仍是常态。"

Pyramus and Thisbe(皮拉摩斯和提斯柏)

Some people tend to associate the tragedy of Romeo and Juliet with the myth of Hero and Leander. It is true that William Shakespeare has been greatly influenced by Greek mythology, but the allusion should be made to another myth, also a tragic story about Pyramus and Thisbe.

In the city of Babylon lived two lovers, Pyramus and Thisbe, who were forbidden to wed due to the hostility between their parents. Every day they whispered sweet nothings through a crack in the wall that separates their houses. They made an appointment to meet under a mulberry tree and Thisbe arrived first. Upon seeing a lioness with a mouth bloody from a recent kill, she screamed and fled, leaving behind her veil. A little while later, Pyramus showed up. He was horrified at the sight of a lioness ripping apart the veil which had been stained with blood. Assuming that his beloved must have been devoured, the heart-broken Pyramus killed himself with his own sword. His blood splashed on the white mulberry fruits, turning them dark. When Thisbe returned, and saw the dead body of Pyramus, she stabbed herself with the same sword. Since then, the formerly white berries of mulberry tree have forever become stained red with the blood of these tragic lovers.

有些人倾向于把罗密欧与朱丽叶的悲剧和海洛与利安得的神话相联系。的确,莎士比亚深受希腊神话的影响,但是罗密欧与朱丽叶的故事暗指的其实是另外一个神话故事,一个关于皮拉摩斯和提斯柏的悲剧故事。

在巴比伦城里住着一对恋人:皮拉摩斯和提斯柏。由于父母间的敌对,他们被严格禁止交往,每天只能通过墙壁上的一道缝隙互述衷肠。他们相约在一棵桑树下见面,提斯柏先到了。但是,一头张着血盆大口的母狮子正在树下徘徊,她吓得大叫一声,立刻跑开,面纱被树枝挂落到地上。不久,皮拉摩斯出现了,他惊恐不已地看到一头母狮正在撕扯恋人的面纱,上面还沾着血迹。他断定提斯柏被狮子吃掉了,于是用自己手中的剑自刎而死,他的血溅到了桑树果子上,白色的果子变成了暗红色。当再次返回的提斯柏目睹恋人的尸体后,她拔出恋人的剑刺向了自己。从此以后,桑树上原本白色的果子都因为这对悲剧恋人的血而永远地变成了暗红色。

The Myths 神话故事

The Hellespont was a narrow strait that links the Mediterranean Sea and the Black Sea. On one side of the strait in Abydos, there lived a brave and handsome youth by the name of Leander, while on the other side in Sestos, a beautiful maiden Hero lived alone in a tower by the Thracian shore. Though a priestess of Aphrodite, goddess of love, Hero was a virgin whose parents had been so overprotective of her that they allowed only an old nurse to accompany their daughter every day.

One day, at a big festival in Sestos celebrating Aphrodite and Adonis, Leander spotted Hero and it was love at first sight. Shimmying over to Hero, Leander, in the softest voice, spoke to her ear, "You are a priestess of Aphrodite. Surely the goddess of love wouldn't approve a virgin." "Wow, I never thought of that," said Hero. Though she was dedicated from childhood to the service of the goddess and forbidden to nurse any idea of love and marriage, nothing could extinguish the flames of love now.

Realizing that her parents would never let her marry a guy from a foreign city, Hero decided to meet Leander in secret every night. Since there was no ferry at that time, Leander had to swim across the strait at the close of each day, sometimes braving high winds and dangerous waters. A torch flickering from the tower beckoned him and guided him. It was a light of love held by Hero. So long as the light was burning, he had no problem conquering the wild sea.

Their trysts lasted through a warm summer, during which they had a blissful time together. However, with the change of season and the approaching of cold winter, the currents in the Hellespont became totally out of control in a stormy night. The tossing tide was lashed into foams and shrieking sea-birds foreboded more ill than good. Hero almost wished that her lover would not come.

But Leander was not to be daunted. Neither could he stand the idea of not seeing his lover. Peering the wavering torch from the distant tower, he plunged into the raging waters. On and on he struggled. Huge billows towered over his head. But he rose up from their threatening depths. Suddenly the gale blew out Hero's light. Leander got completely turned around in the dark. He felt his breath failing him and he was soon swallowed by the waves.

After waiting anxiously and worriedly for a whole night, Hero eventually spotted her lover's mangled body washed ashore at dawn. Overwhelmed with unbearable pain and grief, without much hesitation, she hurled herself from the top of the tower into the rough sea to meet him in death.

赫勒斯滂是连接地中海和黑海的一道狭窄海峡。在海峡一边的阿拜多斯城里，住着一位勇敢而英俊的青年名叫利安得，而在海峡另一边的塞斯托斯，在色雷斯海边的一座灯塔里住着一位美丽的少女海洛。虽然她是爱神阿芙洛蒂忒的女祭司，但在父母的过度保护下，依然保持着处子之身，每天只有一位老保姆陪伴在其左右。

这天，在塞斯托斯举行了一场盛大的庆典，这是阿芙洛蒂忒和阿多尼斯的节日，利安得与海洛在庆典上不期而遇，并一见钟情。小伙子靠近姑娘，用温柔的声音对她耳语道："你是阿芙洛蒂忒的女祭司，爱神肯定不希望你是处女。""哇，我从来没想过这点呢！"尽管从儿时起海洛便一直为女神服务，并承诺禁欲、摒弃情爱的非分之想，然而，此刻爱情的火苗业已燃起，谁又能阻挡得了呢？

海洛意识到父母绝不会允许她嫁给一个外来的年轻人，于是她决定每天夜里与利安得私下会面。因为那时没有渡船，利安得不得不在夜深人静之际，迎着不时出现的惊涛骇浪，游过海峡来与她相会。灯塔上那忽明忽暗的灯光召唤着他、引导着他，那是海洛手中的爱之光，只要有那缕光的存在，他就能战胜海上的一切艰难险阻。

这样的幽会持续了整整一个夏天，这是这对情侣最快乐的时光。然而，随着季节的变换，寒冷的冬天日益临近。在一个风雨交加的夜晚，赫勒斯滂的海水变得咆哮狰狞，滔天的巨浪卷起翻滚的泡沫，惊恐的海鸟预示着凶多吉少。海洛甚至祈祷爱人这晚能够放弃前来的计划。

可是，利安得并没有被恶劣的天气所吓倒，他也无法忍受对爱人的相思之苦。当他隐约瞥见远处灯塔的光亮之后，便纵身跃入汹涌的海水中。他拼命地游啊游，海上的巨浪一次又一次地没过他的头顶，他挣扎着一次又一次地将头伸出水面。突然，狂风吹灭了海洛手中的油灯，黑暗中的利安得彻底失去方向，开始在原地打转，渐渐地，他变得体力不支，一个浪头打来，便再也没能起来。

海洛在焦虑与担心中等待了整整一个晚上，黎明时分，她终于发现在岸边的礁石上，有一具血肉模糊的尸体，那正是她的心上人。伤心欲绝的姑娘并没有多少迟疑，便从灯塔的顶端纵身跃下，她要到阴间与他长相厮守。

Extra 拓展测试

1. Here is a picture of Hero. Could you draw a lamp or torch in her hand?

   下面这幅图画的是海洛，你能在她的手上画上一盏油灯或火炬吗？

2. According to an ancient legend, the Hellespont was named after a girl Helle. Together with her brother Phrixus, she was about to be killed as a human sacrifice, when a ram with golden fleece appeared and rescued them miraculously. The ram took them on its back, and

flew from Greece to the north. Although warned not to look down while the ram was flying, the curious Helle peeked at the vast expanse of water below and then lost her grip and fell into the sea. Hence the strait where she was said to have dropped is known as Hellespont, the Sea of Helle.

The Hellespont is now known as the Dardanelles. Do you know which country it is in?

根据神话传说，赫勒斯滂是以一个名叫赫勒的女孩命名的。就在她和哥哥佛里克索斯作为活人祭品即将被处死之际，一头长着金毛的公羊神奇地出现，救了他们，并驮着他们离开希腊，向北飞去。尽管他们得到警告，说在羊背上时千万不要向下看，但是好奇的赫勒还是忍不住偷偷向下瞥了一眼，于是，便失去重心，落入了海里。此后，她坠落的那片海峡便被称作“赫勒斯滂”，意思就是“赫勒的海”。

赫勒斯滂如今的名字叫作达达尼尔海峡，你知道它在哪个国家境内吗？

（2. 答案：土耳其）

CHAPTER 5 Jason and Medea
第五章 伊阿宋和美狄亚

Word Knowledge 词汇知识

The Argonauts(阿尔戈英雄)

One of the most fascinating stories of ancient Greek mythology is the story of the Argonauts and the Quest for the Golden Fleece, in which Jason was certainly the leading character. The Argonauts, meaning literally "sailors in the ship Argo" in Greek, refer to a group of heroes who accompanied Jason on board the ship Argo to retrieve the golden fleece, a symbol of authority and kingship. The suffix *-naut* in Greek means "sailor", which was then evolved into the reference to "driver" or "operator", as in such words as *astronaut*, *aquanaut*, *taikonaut*, and the like.

阿尔戈英雄和寻找金羊毛的故事是古希腊神话中最激动人心的故事之一,而伊阿宋无疑是这个故事的主角。在希腊语中,the Argonauts的字面意思是"阿尔戈船上的水手们",也就是跟随伊阿宋乘坐阿尔戈船去寻找象征王权与威望的金羊毛的勇士们。-naut 这个后缀在希腊语中的意思是"水手",后来,进一步演化成"驾驶员"或"操作员",因此便有了astronaut(宇航员)、aquanaut(潜水员)、taikonnaut(太空员)这样的词。

Maternal Filicide(谋杀亲子)

The love story between Jason and Medea is in fact a tragedy, which ends with Medea killing her own children to avenge her husband's betrayal. In the earliest version of the myth, Jason and Medea's children were killed by a crowd of Corinthians angry at Medea's behavior. It was Euripides, the famous Greek dramatist, who re-sculpted the story in his play to bring out the nastiest aspects of human relationships, especially within the family. Euripides made Medea breach a fundamental taboo: the bond between mother and child, and the assumption of unconditional maternal love.

Mother wilfully killing children has a particular horror, but it is a sad fact that maternal filicide is not as rare as we might like to think. As you can see, the word "filicide" refers to the killing of one's son or daughter, for the Latin root *filius* means "son" and *filia*, "daughter", and the suffix, *-cide*, "kill". You might know the word "suicide", which is defined as the action of killing oneself intentionally. Likewise, there are such words as *homicide*, *regicide*, *matricide*, *genocide*, and *pesticide*, meaning respectively murder, the action of killing a king, something for killing insects and pests.

事实上，伊阿宋和美狄亚的爱情故事是一出悲剧，结局就是美狄亚为了报复丈夫的背叛，亲手杀死了自己的孩子。在最早的神话传说中，伊阿宋和美狄亚的孩子是被一群愤怒的科林斯人杀死的。后来，古希腊著名的戏剧家欧里匹得斯对这个故事进行了再创作，挖掘出了人际关系，尤其是家庭关系中最不堪的一面。在欧里匹得斯的笔下，美狄亚打破了一个最基本的禁忌：那就是母子间的亲情纽带，或者母爱是无条件的假设。

美狄亚执意杀死自己亲生的孩子显然是一种骇人的行为，然而，令人难过的是，这种生母弑子的行为却并非我们所期望那样仅仅是个案。显然，这里的 filicide 一词指的是杀死亲生子女的行为，在拉丁语中 filius 就是“儿子”，filia 就是“女儿”，而后缀-cide 意思就是“杀”。或许你知道 suicide 一词，指的是有意识的自杀行为，以此类推，homicide、regicide、matricide、genocide、pesticide 分别表示“杀人”“弑君”“弑母”“种族灭绝”“杀虫剂”。

The Myths 神话故事

In Greek mythology, Jason was a hero who was best known as the leader of the Argonautic Expedition in the quest of retrieving the Golden Fleece from the land of Colchis. Being a prince by birth, Jason was in fact brought up by the Centaur Chiron for safe-keeping after his father Aeson, the king of Iolcus, was overthrown by his half-brother Pelias. As a wise and noble-hearted centaur, Chiron taught Jason everything from deadly arts of hunting and archery to the delicate arts of music and healing. When Jason came of age, Chiron told him the secret of his birth and let him return to Iolcus to claim what was rightfully his.

When Jason stood in front of Pelias, asking for the throne as his birthright, his half-uncle was terrified. However, the crafty Pelias pretended to agree that he would give up the kingdom if Jason could prove him worthy of it. The one condition he gave was that Jason must bring the golden fleece back from Colchis. He saw this as an impossible mission and was sure that his nephew would never come back alive from it. Thus came the famous expedition of the Argonauts, who were named after Argos, the boat they had boarded, and were made up of fifty heroes of Greece, including Hercules and Orpheus.

After many trials and tribulations, Jason and the Argonauts eventually reached the kingdom of Colchis, where they were welcomed by King Aeetes. The golden fleece was in the possession of the king, gifted to him by Phrixus, prince of Boeotia, who arrived there on a flying golden ram. However, Aeetes was not prepared to yield the golden fleece to the young heroes, so he demanded the heroes to accomplish some tasks, each of which would mean an end to their lives.

It was a good plan. What Aeetes didn't know, however, was that his daughter Medea had fallen head over heels in love with Jason. Being a priestess of Hecate, Medea was skilled in sorcery and charms known only to the wicked and the wise. Before Jason set about to sow a field with dragon's teeth, Medea made a salve for Jason to protect him temporarily from the fire-breathing oxen ploughing the field. She also instructed Jason to throw a stone at the warriors springing from the soil so that they would turn on each other, launch into battle, and eventually kill each other.

With the help of Medea, Jason survived his first task. The second task assigned by King Aeetes was to take the golden fleece hanging on the tree guarded by the fierce warship-like dragon. Again, Medea brewed a drug which would put the monster to sleep and gave it to Jason. After Jason retrieved the golden fleece, both Jason and Medea left together with Argos and the Argonauts. Knowing that her father would follow them, Medea captured her brother and killed him, spreading his pieces across the ocean so that her father would have to search for all the pieces of his son, providing them with the necessary time to escape.

When Jason returned safe and sound with the golden fleece to his home country, he found his father Aeson at a very old age. He asked Medea to transfer some of his life to his father. By infusing Aeson's blood with magical herbs, Medea gave a few more years to Jason's father without removing them from the son. Pelias' daughters, amazed at the miracle the sorceress had worked, asked her to rejuvenate their father as well. Pretending to consent, Medea tricked them into cutting Pelias into pieces so that she could apply her magical potion on him. Thus the usurper died at the hands of his own children.

Sickened at her cruelty, Jason sought solace in his new attachment—princess Glauce and the beautiful daughter of Creon, king of Corinth. Feeling deserted, Medea sent her rival a wedding-gift, a robe imbued with a deadly poison, in which the bride died a miserable death forthwith. Maddened at the loss of her husband's love, Medea next put to death the three children she had born to Jason. Before she fled in her chariot, she left Jason a note warning him to beware of the Argo. In utter bitterness and frustration, Jason passed a forlorn and useless life. Every day he went to sit in the shade of the old ship Argo and recollect those good old days of its honor and glory. In the end he was crushed to death by the falling stern of the ship.

希腊神话中,伊阿宋作为一名探险英雄而闻名,是他率领阿尔戈号的勇士们从科尔基斯的土地上找回了金羊毛。虽然生来就是王子身份,伊阿宋却是在半人马喀戎的抚养下长大的,因为他的父亲,伊奥克斯的国王埃宋被自己同母异父的弟弟珀利阿斯篡夺了王位。作为最具智慧和仁心的半人马,喀戎既教会了小王子弯弓搭箭的卓越本领,又传授给他音乐医药的精湛技艺。待伊阿宋成年之后,喀戎将他的身世秘密告诉了他,并送他返回伊奥克斯去替父申冤。

当伊阿宋出现在珀利阿斯面前,要求叔叔交出王位的时候,篡位的国王震惊不已。然而,珀利阿斯非常狡猾,他假装同意让出王位,前提是伊阿宋能够证明自己有能力当好国王。他要求伊阿宋去科尔基斯寻找金羊毛。珀利阿斯相信这是一项无法完成的使命,他的侄子必死无疑。于是便有了著名的阿尔戈英雄们,他们的名字源自他们所乘坐的那艘阿戈尔号快船,船上共有50名希腊勇士,其中包括大力神海格立斯以及精通音律的俄耳甫斯。

历经无数的磨难和考验,伊阿宋和阿戈尔号的英雄们最终抵达了科尔基斯国,国王埃厄忒斯对他们的到来表示欢迎。所谓金羊毛,其实是皮奥夏国的王子佛里克索斯留给国王的礼物,因为他来到这里时正骑着一头会飞的金绵羊。然而,埃厄忒斯并不愿轻易地交出金羊毛,所以,他也要求这些希腊勇士们去完成几项足以致命的任务。

虽然埃厄忒斯计划得很好,但他却不知道自己的女儿美狄亚已经被伊阿宋迷得神魂颠倒了。美狄亚是赫卡忒的女祭司,精通巫术、善使迷药。在伊阿宋准备去地里播种龙牙之际,美狄亚为他制作了一种药膏,涂在身上可以保护皮肤不被犁地的喷火牛灼伤。她还示意伊阿宋向泥土里冒出来的兵俑扔石头，如此，这些兵俑就会转而互相打斗、自相残杀了。

有了美狄亚的暗中帮助，伊阿宋完成了第一项不可完成的任务。国王埃厄忒斯交给他的第二项任务就是从可怖的、如舰艇般庞大的恶龙眼皮底下取回金羊毛。这一次，美狄亚为伊阿宋配制了一剂迷药，能够令巨龙昏睡不醒。伊阿宋成功地取到了金羊毛，并和美狄亚一起乘上了返程的阿尔戈号。美狄亚料到父亲一定会追上来，于是她杀死了自己的胞弟，并将他的尸体分成数块撒入大海。眼睁睁看着自己儿子的尸骨被丢入大海，埃厄忒斯怎能不停下来寻找？如此，私奔的情侣便有了足够的时间。

伊阿宋平安地回到了自己的祖国，但是，此时他的父亲埃宋已经垂垂老矣。伊阿宋请求美狄亚能否把他的生命分一点给他的父亲。美狄亚并没有这样做，而是将神奇的草药注入埃宋的血液之中，为他延续了若干年的时光。看到女祭司神奇的法力，珀利阿斯的女儿们也希望美狄亚能帮她们的父亲恢复青春。美狄亚佯装应允，骗她们说必须将珀利阿斯剁成肉酱，她才好施展魔法。就这样，篡位者最终惨死于亲生子女之手。

美狄亚的残酷令伊阿宋心生厌恶，渐渐地，他开始在别处寻求安慰。他的新欢就是科林斯国王克瑞翁的女儿，美丽的格劳刻公主。美狄亚感觉自己被抛弃了，于是在丈夫的新婚之夜，她制作了一件婚纱送给情敌。可怜的新娘刚穿上这件浸满毒液的婚纱，便一命呜呼了。失去丈夫的爱令美狄亚彻底丧失了理智，她随后亲手杀死了自己和伊阿宋所生的三个孩子。驾车离去之际，她警告丈夫留心阿尔戈号。此后，伊阿宋变得一蹶不振，在无尽的痛苦自责中，生活得孤苦凄凉。每天，他都会来到那艘阿尔戈号船旁，坐在阴暗的角落里，回忆那些荣耀美好的旧日时光。一天，船尾突然倒塌，将他砸倒在下面，再也没能起来。

Extra 拓展测试

1. Which of the following is likely to be the centaur Chiron?
   下面哪一幅图有可能是半人马喀戎？

A

B

2. The word argonaut has become a common noun in English to refer to a small floating octopus. Can you guess what it is?
如今 argonaut 一词已经成了英语中的一个普通名词,用来指一种漂浮在海里的小章鱼,你能猜到它是什么吗?

(1. 答案:A)
(2. 答案:舡鱼)

FURTHER READING
The God of Medicine
延伸阅读　医神的故事

Asclepius, the god of medicine, was the son of Apollo and Coronis, who was killed for being unfaithful to her husband. When he was young, Asclepius was sent to Chiron, the wise centaur, who raised him and instructed him in the art of medicine. Myth has it that one day Asclepius saved a sacred snake, who, in return for the kindness rendered, licked Asclepius' ears clean and taught him secret knowledge of healing and resurrection. Hence the image of Asclepius was generally recognizable by his beard and the rod of Asclepius, a snake-entwined staff, which remains a symbol of medicine today.

When Asclepius came of age, his powers were so extraordinary that he surpassed both Chiron and his father Apollo. He could not only cure the sick, but could even restore the dead to life. According to the myth, Asclepius would cure people of their illness in their dreams. So those who sought help from the god would pay a homage to Asclepion, a healing sanctuary and holy temple for worshipping Asclepius, and spend a night there. There were approximately 320 Asclepions in ancient Greece, which became known as the first hospitals in the history of western civilization.

With the protection of Asclepius, fewer people died than before, which displeased Hades, god of the Underworld. At last, he came to Zeus, complaining about the rapid decease in the number of shades being conducted to his realm. Fearing that the influx of human beings would result in imbalance of population and possible defiance against the gods, the great ruler of Olympus killed Asclepius with one of his thunderbolts. The loss of his highly gifted son so enraged Apollo that, being unable to vent his anger on Zeus, he destroyed the Cyclops, who had forged the fatal thunderbolts. For this offence, Zeus suspended Apollo from the night sky and commanded him to serve Admetus, king of Thessaly, for a year. As for Asclepius, Zeus placed his body among the stars as the constellation Ophiuchus, the Serpent Holder. Another version stated that he was later resurrected as a god by Zeus on condition that he would never again revive the dead without approval.

Asclepius was married to Epione, the goddess of soothing of pain. The couple had five daughters and three sons. Among the daughters, there were Hygieia, the goddess of health, cleanness and sanitation, and Panacea, the goddess of universal remedy. Hygienia was in charge of the prevention of sickness and the continuation of good health. Her name became the source of the English word "hygiene". The bowl of Hygienia, a cup or chalice with a snake twined around its stem and poised above it, has been widely used as a symbol of pharmacy. The word "panacea", as a common noun, simply means a remedy for all diseases, or a cure-all.

医药之神阿斯克勒庇俄斯是阿波罗和刻洛尼斯的儿子,阿波罗因为怀疑妻子出轨而杀了刻洛尼斯。阿斯克勒庇俄斯很小的时候,阿波罗便把他托付给智慧的半人马喀戎照管,喀戎不仅抚养他长大,还教给他医药之术。传说,有一天阿斯克勒庇俄斯救了一条蛇的命,出于感恩回报,那条灵蛇舔干净他的双耳之后,将起死回生之术悄悄告诉了他。因此,阿斯克勒庇俄斯的形象通常就是一位长着胡须的男人,手持一根由蛇盘绕的神杖,这根神杖至今仍然是医学的标志。

阿斯克勒庇俄斯成年后,其医术的高明甚至超越了他的老师喀戎和父亲阿波罗,他不仅能驱除病魔,还能起死回生。传说阿斯克勒庇俄斯常常在人们的睡梦之中为他们治疗,因此,那些祈求医神帮助的人就会来到专门供奉他的神庙或圣所,虔诚地祷告,并在那里睡上一晚。在古希腊有近320座供奉医神阿斯克勒庇俄斯的神庙,这些地方就成了西方文明中最早的医院。

由于有了阿斯克勒庇俄斯的保护,病死的人越来越少,这令冥王哈迪斯颇为不满。终于，他找到宙斯，埋怨阿斯克勒庇俄斯使得自己地界的人口迅速减少。宙斯也担心这种情况会导致凡间人口的失衡，进而对众神的权威构成威胁。于是，他用闪电劈死了阿斯克勒庇俄斯。天才儿子的惨死激怒了阿波罗，但他不敢把怒火发泄到宙斯身上，于是转而迁怒于帮助宙斯制造闪电的独眼巨人们。他杀死了所有的独眼巨人，结果被宙斯逐出夜晚的天空，打入凡间，在塞萨利国王阿德墨托斯手下服苦役一年。至于阿斯克勒庇俄斯，宙斯将他的身体升上天空，变成了蛇夫星座。还有一种说法是，宙斯后来将他复活成了神，条件是他在未经允许的情况下，永远不可以再施起死回生之术。

阿斯克勒庇俄斯的妻子是抚慰女神厄庇俄涅。他们有五个女儿和三个儿子。在他们的女儿中，许癸厄亚是健康、清洁和卫生女神，潘娜西亚是全能治疗女神。许癸厄亚主要负责疾病预防和健康维护，她的名字就是英语单词 hygiene（卫生）的出处。许癸厄亚之碗是一个茶杯或酒杯，上面盘绕着一条蛇，蛇尾在杯子的底座，蛇头在杯子的上方。如今，它已成了许多药房的标志。而 panacea 现在已成为一个常见名词，意思就是包治百病的灵丹妙药，或曰“万灵药”。

Extra 拓展测试

The rod of Asclepius is seen on the flag of a specialized agency of the United Nations. Do you know the name of this international organization?

阿斯克勒庇俄斯的蛇杖是联合国一个专属机构旗帜上的图案，你知道这个国际机构的名称吗？

（答案：世界卫生组织）

PART Ⅴ Myths of Human Nature

第五部分
人性的神话

扫一扫,听本部分音频

CHAPTER 1 The Myth of Narcissus
第一章 自恋的故事

Word Knowledge 词汇知识

Narcissus(水仙花)

Have you ever heard of a sad story between Narcissus and Echo? In the myth Narcissus was a young man distinguished for his beauty. One day when he saw his own reflection in a pool, Narcissus fell immediately in love with his own image. Consumed with strong self-love, he died eventually and was transformed into a flower that bears his name. The word narcissus now has the connotation of being vain and self-obsessed. The origin of the word might be traced back to Greek *narkissos*, meaning "numbness", with reference to its narcotic effects. The story may have derived from the ancient Greek superstition that it was unlucky or even fatal to see one's own reflection.

The term narcissism denotes an excessive degree of self-esteem or self-involvement, a condition that is usually a form of emotional immaturity. Nowadays, many people are so addicted to their smartphones that they are constantly updating their statuses and posting selfies to glorify themselves. Don't you think they are becoming narcissistic?

你听说过那喀索斯和厄科的悲伤故事吗？在这则神话里，那喀索斯是一位美少年。一天，他看见了自己在池塘中的倒影，并立刻爱上了那个影子。因为强烈的自恋，他最终憔悴而死，并变成了一朵以他的名字命名的水仙花。于是单词 narcissus 如今就有了虚荣、自恋的含义。这个词的出处可以追溯到希腊语中的 narkissos,意思是"麻木",指的是麻醉催眠的效果。这可能是由于在古希腊有一种迷信,认为看见自己的倒影是很不吉利甚至致命的。

自恋意味着极度的自大或过分关注自我,通常是一种情感不成熟的表现。如今,许多人手机上瘾,终日不停地更新状态或发自拍照炫耀自我,难道你不觉得这就是一种自恋的表现吗?

Echo(回声)

Echo refers to an aural effect of repetitive sound caused by the reflection of sound waves from a surface back to the listener. It is a word originated from a Greek myth, which yet has several variations. The most popular one is certainly the tragedy between Echo and Narcissus, in which the poor mountain nymph suffered from an unrequited love and gradually pined away, leaving only her voice repeating every sound uttered in the hills and dales.

There is another love story between Echo and Pan, the god of wild and shepherd, in which Echo was a nymph who could sing and dance beautifully. But she scorned the love of any man, including Pan, who was so furious at being turned down and instructed his followers to kill her. Echo was torn into pieces and spread all over the earth. Here are some useful words and expressions related to echo: *echolocation*, *echo sounder*, *echo chamber*, *echo effect*, *echoism*.

回声是一种声音效果,表现为声波从某一表面重复反射回听者。这个词源自希腊神话,不过这则神话有几个不同的版本,其中流传最广的无疑是厄科和那喀索斯的悲剧故事。故事中山宁芙一厢情愿的爱情,导致其日渐憔悴,最终香消玉殒,成为山谷中的回声。

关于厄科还有另一个版本的神话,讲述了她和畜牧之神潘的故事。这个故事中的厄科是一位能歌善舞的仙女,但她鄙视所有男人的爱。包括潘神的爱。她的拒绝令后者勃然大怒,指使他的手下去杀了厄科。可怜的姑娘被撕成了碎片，尸骨散落各地。以下是一些和回声相关的词汇：echolocation（回声定位）、echo sounder（回声探测器）、echo chamber（回声室）、echo effect（回声效应）、echoism（回声法）。

Nympho（花痴）

In the myth of Narcissus and Echo, the nymph had an uncontrollable deep affection in the beautiful youth, from which came such words as nymphomaniac and nymphet. Although the word "nymphomaniac", or nympho as its short form, may mean a woman who is obsessed with good-looking men, the word has strong sexual connotation. So use with care.

在那喀索斯和厄科的故事中，仙女厄科无法自拔地深深爱着那个美男子，由此衍生出了包括 nymphomaniac（花痴）和 nymphet（性感少女）在内的词汇。虽然 nymphomaniac 或者它的缩写形式 nympho，可以表示一个痴迷美男子的女性，但是它还隐含着性欲强烈的意思，用时要小心。

Nemesis（内密西斯）

"Nemesis, winged balancer of life, dark-faced goddess, daughter of Justice." This was how she was depicted by an ancient poet in the early second century AD. Being an offspring of Nyx or Oceanus, Nemesis, whose name means "to give what is due", was originally a Nymph goddess and the distributor of fortune, neither good nor bad. But with time passing by, she appeared gradually as the avenger of crime and the punisher of hubris. The word "nemesis" is now defined as punishment or defeat that is deserved and cannot be avoided. The Roman counterpart of Nemesis was Fortuna, from which derived such English words as *fortune*, *unfortunate*, *misfortune*, *fortuneteller*, and so on.

“内密西斯，生命的平衡者，带翅膀的黑面女神，正义的女儿。”这是公元2世纪初一位古希腊诗人对内密西斯的描述。内密西斯名字的意思是“给其应得的”。作为夜女神尼克斯或大洋神俄刻阿诺斯的孩子，她最初只是一位负责时运分配的小仙女，无所谓好运还是坏运。然而，随着时间的推移，她渐渐变成了惩治犯罪与狂妄行为的复仇女神。小写的内密西斯(nemesis)如今表示应得的或不可避免的惩罚或失败。内密西斯对应的罗马名字叫福耳图那(Fortuna)，英语中的fortune(时运/财富)、unfortunate(不幸的)、misfortune(厄运)、fortuneteller(算命先生)等词皆源于此。

The Myths 神话故事

Narcissus was the son of the river god Cephissus and the nymph Liriope. Worried about his extraordinary beauty, his parents consulted a blind seer and was told that the child would have a long life, provided that he never saw his own face. Therefore, his parents removed all the shining objects from home so that the child would not catch sight of his own reflection. With tender care and protection from his parents, Narcissus grew up as a vain teenager who avoided all company.

Echo, a beautiful mountain nymph, was known as a chatterbox. Myth has it that Hera came upon Echo and enquired of her about her husband's whereabouts. Instead of answering Hera's questions, Echo kept talking about something else, which exhausted the goddess' patience. So Hera cursed Echo, “You shall forfeit the use of that tongue with which you have cheated me, except for that one purpose you are so fond of—repeating. You shall repeat the last word you hear.” From then on, the poor Echo could only repeat the last word someone else says.

One day, Echo caught sight of a handsome youth, Narcissus who was sixteen then. Enamored of him at once, Echo followed him, waiting patiently for a chance to speak to him. At last, Narcissus, sensed himself being followed, shouted, "Who's here?" Echo replied, "Here." Echo showed herself and, joyfully gliding towards him, she stretched out her loving arms. To her dismay, however, the young man roughly brushed her aside and went by without so much as a glance at her.

Overwhelmed with shame and humiliation, Echo went away to hide herself in the darkness of the woods. Her body became skinny with grief until it faded away and her bones gradually turned to rocks, till, at length, nothing remained of her except her voice, which gave back, with unerring fidelity, the last sound that was uttered in the hills and dales.

The rejection of Echo's love drew upon Narcissus the vengeance of Nemesis, goddess of revenge, who decided to make the cruel young man see his own face. There came one day when Narcissus was tired and thirsty from hunting, he came upon a clear spring and bent down to drink. A beautiful image appeared in the water, which he thought must be some water-spirit. Then the infatuated youth became desperate, staring and staying day and night at the stream. Before long he died, never suspecting that his lover was none other than his own image. The gods took pity on the fair corpse and turned it into a flower bearing his name. The pale flower is still found near the river banks, leaning towards its own reflection in the water.

那喀索斯是河神刻菲索斯和仙女利里俄珀所生的儿子。因为担心他的惊人美貌会带来不幸,他的父母咨询了一位盲人先知,结果被告知:这孩子将长命百岁,前提是他永远都看不到自己的脸。为了防止儿子看到他自己的样子,那喀索斯的父母将家里一切能够反光的东西全部清除了。在父母的精心呵护下,那喀索斯渐渐长大,他骄傲自负,将所有人都拒之门外。

美丽的山宁芙厄科是个天生的话匣子。传说赫拉遇见了厄科，向她打听她丈夫宙斯的下落，为了帮忙遮掩厄科没有回答赫拉的提问，而是东拉西扯地说别的，令赫拉失去了耐心。于是，赫拉诅咒厄科说："你敢骗我，从今往后，你的舌头将失去应有的功能，唯一能做的就是重复，重复你听到的最后一个词！"从那天起，可怜的厄科就只能重复她所听到的别人说过的最后一个词。

一天，厄科看见一位英俊的少年——年方十六的那喀索斯，对他一见倾心，便悄悄地跟着他，期待能有机会和他说话。那喀索斯意识到了有人在跟着他，于是他大喊一声："是谁在那儿？"厄科回答："那儿。"按捺不住激动的心情，她走了出来，向他伸出手去，主动示爱。然而令她惊愕的是，那年轻人粗暴地拂袖而去，看也没有看她一眼。

巨大的悲伤和羞愧令厄科无地自容，她躲进了黑暗的森林，日渐消瘦，慢慢地，她的身体变得皮包骨头，骨头又变成了岩石，直至最终彻底消失，剩下的只有她的声音，依然在山谷中执着地重复着她所听到的最后一个词。

然而，由于拒绝了仙女厄科的爱，那喀索斯触怒了复仇女神内密西斯，她决定要让这个冷酷的年轻人看到他自己的倒影。于是有一天，打猎归来的那喀索斯又累又渴的时候，他恰巧看到了一条清澈的小溪，就在他弯下腰去准备喝水时，一张美丽的面孔出现在水中。"这一定是某位水之仙女吧！"他想。于是，这位被迷得神魂颠倒的年轻人开始整日整夜地盯着水看，很快便忧郁而死，并且到死都不知道自己爱上的其实就是自己的影子。众神心生怜悯，便将这位美少年的躯壳变成了一朵水仙花。这种苍白的花朵至今还开在河岸边，倾向自己的倒影。

Extra 拓展测试

1. Which of the following do you think is Nemesis, the goddess of revenge?
   你认为以下哪一幅图是复仇女神内密西斯？

A

B

2. There is a well-known oil painting called *Metamorphosis of Narcissus* by a famous Spanish surrealist painter. Do you know the name of the painter?

一位著名的西班牙超现实主义画家曾画过一幅非常有名的油画叫《那喀索斯的变形》,你知道这位画家的名字吗?

(1. 答案:A)

(2. 答案:达利)

CHAPTER 2 Pygmalion
第二章 皮格马利翁

Word Knowledge 词汇知识

Galatea(伽拉忒亚)

The name Galatea originally means "she who is milk-white" in Latin. The best known Galatea is certainly the ivory statue crafted by Pygmalion, which has influenced many writers and artists in the western world. Apart from this popular myth, however, there is another love story between Galatea and Acis in Greek mythology.

As the fairest and most beloved of the 50 Nereids, Galatea was in deep love with Acis, the son of Pan and the river nymph Symaethis. However, Acis had a fierce rival in love, the Sicilian Cyclops Polyphemus who also lost his heart to the girl. One day, upon seeing Acis and Galatea locked in an embrace, Polyphemus killed Acis with a boulder in a fit of jealous rage. To protect her lover from being hurt further, Galatea turned Acis into a river spirit as immortal as herself. The destructive passion of Polyphemus came to nothing.

Polyphemus is the son of Poseidon and a men-eating giant, whose only eye was blinded by Odysseus according to Homer's *Odyssey*. His name means "abounding in songs and legends". In the myth about Perseus, there was a king named Polydectes, which means "he who receives many". So the prefix *poly-*, denoting "much" or "many", is a productive element in the formation of English words, such as *polygamy*, *polysemy*, *polytechnic*, *polyclinic*, *polyethnic*, polyarchy, *polygon*, *polylogue*, and so on.

在拉丁语中,伽拉忒亚这个名字的意思是"牛奶般洁白的女子"。最为人熟知的伽拉忒亚无疑是皮格马利翁所创作的那尊象牙雕塑,那则故事影响了西方世界无数的作家和艺术家。事实上,除了这则广为流传的神话之外,在希腊神话中,还有另一个关于伽拉忒亚和埃西斯的爱情故事。

在海神的五十个女儿涅瑞伊德中,伽拉忒亚是最美丽、最得宠的那个。她深爱着潘神和河仙西莫提斯的儿子埃西斯。然而埃西斯有一个可怕的情敌:西西里的独眼巨人波吕斐摩斯。一天,波吕斐摩斯看到埃西斯正在拥抱自己深爱的女人伽拉忒亚,不由妒火中烧,他搬起一块巨石,砸死了埃西斯。为了保护爱人免受进一步的伤害,伽拉忒亚将埃西斯变成了不死的河魂,狂暴的波吕斐摩斯最终一无所获。

波吕斐摩斯既是波塞冬的儿子,也是吃人的巨人。在荷马史诗《奥德赛》中,奥德修斯戳瞎了他的独眼。他名字的意思是"众多的歌曲和传奇",而在珀尔修斯的神话故事中,有一个国王名叫波吕得克忒斯,意思是"得到很多的人"。可见,在英语构词法中,表示"多"的 poly-是很多词的前缀,例如:polygamy(一夫多妻)、polysemy(一词多义)、polytechnic(多种工艺的)、polyclinic(综合性医院)、polyethnic(多民族的)、polyarchy(多头政治)、polygon(多边形)、polylogue(多边会谈)等等。

Pygmalion Effect(皮格马利翁效应)

Derived from the Greek myth of Pygmalion, the Pygmalion effect refers to such a phenomenon whereby higher expectations lead to an increase in performance. If you think something will happen, you may unconsciously make it happen through your actions or inaction. As a type of self-fulfilling prophecy, the Pygmalion effect not only has relevance to effective talent managing, but also is a very important concept in educational psychology. This is because your belief in your students or employees tends to boost their self-efficacy. Self-efficacy is a person's belief in his or her ability to perform the actions necessary for success.

皮格马利翁效应源自希腊神话中皮格马利翁的故事，指的是这样一种现象：更高的期望值可以带来更好的表现。假如你希望某事发生，你就会有意无意地使之发生。作为一种自我实现的预言，皮格马利翁效应不仅适用于人才管理，也是教育心理学中的重要概念。原因在于你对学生或雇员的期望有助于提升他们的自我效能，而自我效能则是一个人对自身能力的信心，这是成功的必备要素。

The Myths 神话故事

In Greek mythology, the Propoetides are the daughters of Propoetus from the city of Amathus on the island of Cyprus. Myth has it that the Propoetides dared to deny the divine status of Aphrodite, which enraged the goddess greatly. As a consequence of the divine anger, the Propoetides became the first to prostitute their bodies and their reputations in public. Losing all sense of shame, the Propoetides lost the power to blush, as the blood hardened in their cheeks, and only a small change turned them into hard flints.

In Cyprus, there was a talented sculptor named Pygmalion who witnessed the Propoetides prostituting themselves in wretched shame, and since then, lost all interest in women and avoided their company completely. Such disappointment also drove him to create a woman of his own. With consummate skill, he carved a woman with exquisite beauty out of snow-white ivory, which no woman of the world could rival. Such a flawless and realistic masterpiece the statue was, that Pygmalion, who had professed his disdain of all females, named it Galatea with which he fell deeply in love.

Inflamed with love and admiration for his own creation, Pygmalion gazed, embraced and felt it every day. Softest tones were used each time he spoke to her. Every time he caressed it with loving hands, he felt the touch so real that he feared he would bruise her by his eager pressing. He brought it gifts that he thought girls would enjoy, such as pebbles, shells, birds, and fragrant flowers. He dressed it in fine clothing, and put rings on her fingers, necklaces around her neck and pendants on her ears. Naming her the consort of his couch, he laid her on a luxurious bed with her head on the most soft and downy pillows, trusting she could feel.

Such a passion could not go unnoticed by the goddess of love, Aphrodite, who took pity on the young man. In time, when there was Aphrodite's festival day, and Pygmalion went to her temple to sacrifice a heifer at the altar, praying quietly for a bride who would be the living likeness of his ivory girl, Aphrodite gave him a sign that her divinity favored his plea: as the offering burned on the temple, three times the flame leaped high and brightly in the air.

Pygmalion went home, wondering what to make of the manifestation he had seen. When he entered his studio, he went directly to the ivory statue, his mind oscillating between doubt and joy. As he embraced and kissed his image-maid, she seemed to gather some warmth from his lips. Again he kissed her and felt her breast; the ivory seemed to soften at the touch, and its firm texture yielded to his hand, as honey-wax on Mount Hymettus turns to many shapes when handled in the sun, and surely softens from each gentle touch. Fearing he may be mistaken, again and again with a lover's ardor he touches the object of his hopes. It was indeed alive!

Slowly it dawned on Pygmalion that the animation of his sculpture was the result of his prayer to goddess Aphrodite who knew his desire. At last, the votary of Aphrodite found words to thank the goddess. Pygmalion humbled himself at the goddess' feet. Aphrodite blessed the nuptials she had formed, and this union between Pygmalion and Galatea produced a son named Paphos, from whom the city of Paphos in Cyprus (this city was sacred to Aphrodite), received its name.

在希腊神话中，普罗珀艾提蒂斯是普罗珀艾忒斯的几个女儿，她们来自位于塞浦路斯岛上的阿玛瑟斯城。传说由于普罗珀艾提蒂斯胆敢藐视阿芙洛蒂忒的地位，致使女神大为震怒，导致普罗珀艾提蒂斯沦为公众眼中名副其实的娼妓。由于失去了廉耻，她们甚至不知道什么叫害羞脸红，她们面颊下的血液完全凝固了，哪怕一丝微小的改变都可能将她们化为火石。

在塞浦路斯，住着一位天才雕塑家皮格马利翁，他目睹了普罗珀艾提蒂斯既可耻又可悲的娼妓生活，从而失去了对所有女人的兴趣，对她们避而远之。与此同时，这种对俗世女子的失望也促使他开始创作一个属于他自己的女人。凭借着高超精湛的技艺，他用雪白的象牙雕刻出了一尊无与伦比的女性雕像，它是如此的完美与真实，以至于皮格马利翁也被自己的杰作深深打动，为它取名伽拉忒亚。这位对女性曾明确表示出厌恶之情的艺术家，深深地爱上了自己的作品。

每天，爱火焚身的皮格马利翁都会久久地凝视这尊雕像，紧紧地拥抱它，轻轻地抚摸它，对着它轻言细语。他的指尖充满了柔情蜜意，每一次，当他触碰到它的身体的时候，那种感觉都异常真实，以至于他生怕自己一不留神就会伤到它。他为它准备了各式各样的礼物：鹅卵石、贝壳、小鸟、鲜花……一切他觉得女孩子喜欢的东西。他为它穿上美丽的衣裙，戴上戒指、项链、耳坠；他称它为枕边的爱人，为它备好奢华的婚床，将它的头放置在最柔软的羽绒枕头上，他相信这一切它都能感觉得到。

如此浓情蜜意又怎能逃过爱神阿芙洛蒂忒的眼睛，她对这位年轻人心生怜悯。正巧，爱神的节日到了，皮格马利翁来到阿芙洛蒂忒的神庙前，在祭坛上虔诚地奉上了自己的祭品：一头白色的小母牛。同时，他在心里暗暗祈祷，希望爱神能够赐予他一位和自己的象牙雕塑一般美丽的女子。他的请求果真得到了阿芙洛蒂忒的回应：随着祭品在神庙中被焚烧，他清楚地看到有三次火苗蹿上了天空。

皮格马利翁回到家里，暗自思忖衬庙里所见究竟代表了什么。他走进自己的工作室，径直来到那尊象牙雕塑前，心里既忐忑又兴奋。他抱住自己的雕塑爱人，开始亲吻它，它的嘴唇似乎有了一丝温度。他又亲了它一下，并轻抚它的胸部。这一次，象牙爱人似乎变得柔软起来。随着他的指尖滑过它的身体，原本僵硬的肌理犹如伊米托斯山的蜜蜡，在阳光的照耀下开始碎裂脱落，并且在他的抚摸下变得越来越柔软。他害怕这一切只是错觉，于是一遍遍用爱的抚摸去试探他的爱人，它的的确确是活了！

渐渐地，皮格马利翁意识到，他的雕塑之所以能够获得生命，是因为爱神阿芙洛蒂忒听到了他的祈祷，满足了他的心愿。于是，这位阿芙洛蒂忒的崇拜者决定向女神当面致谢。他再次来到神庙，拜倒在女神面前，阿芙洛蒂忒祝福两位新人喜结连理。皮格马利翁和伽拉忒亚结合生下了儿子帕福斯，塞浦路斯的帕福斯城便是以他的名字命名的（这座城市也是阿芙洛蒂忒之城）。

Extra 拓展测试

1. Which of the following is likely to be the sacrifice offered by Pygmalion to Aphrodite?

   下面哪一个有可能是皮格马利翁献给阿芙洛蒂忒的祭品？

A

B

2. Have you ever watched the American musical film *My Fair Lady* in which Audrey Hepburn stars? Do you know the film is in fact an adaptation of a play entitled *Pygmalion*? Do you know who wrote this play?

   你看过奥黛丽·赫本主演的美国音乐剧电影《窈窕淑女》吗？你知道这部电影改编自一部名为《皮格马利翁》的戏剧吗？你知道这部戏剧是谁写的吗？

3. As a variant of the Pygmalion myth, there is a well-known story about a wooden puppet, which has been transformed into a real boy. Do you know the name of the wooden puppet?

作为皮格马利翁故事的一个变体,还有一个广为流传的故事讲的是一个小木偶,后来变成了一个真正的男孩,你知道那个木偶叫什么名字吗?

(1. 答案:B)

(2. 答案:萧伯纳)

(3. 答案:匹诺曹)

CHAPTER 3 The Midas Touch
第三章 点金手

Word Knowledge 词汇知识

The Midas Touch(点金手)

King Midas is popularly known for his ability of turning everything he touched into gold, which was then referred to as the Midas touch or the golden touch. Although the moral of the myth seems to warn people of the disastrous effects brought by greed, the phrase itself is void of such connotation. In modern English it simply means an uncanny ability for making money in every venture. Here is an example: *John put the company's stock prices through the roof thanks to his Midas touch and great business sense*.

国王迈达斯之所以广为人知,是因为他曾拥有一项特殊的能力:所有他触摸过的东西都会变成金子,这种能力被称为"迈达斯之手"或"点金手"。尽管神话故事本身的寓意似乎在告诫人们贪婪带来的恶果,但这一表达本身却并没有这样的意思。在当代英语中,"点金手"仅指在任何投资领域都能赚钱的神奇能力,例如:约翰有点石成金的能力和敏锐的商业头脑,让公司的股价一路大涨。

Donkey's Ears(驴耳朵)

The donkey's ears of King Midas was a punishment and humiliation given by Apollo. One day, there was a musical contest between Apollo and Pan, the god of woods, with Tmolus, the god of the mountain, acting as the judge. To the surprise and dissatisfaction of no one present, Tmolus declared Apollo the winner, but Midas, who just happened to be passing by from there, foolishly interfered, claiming that the decision was not right.

Apollo had just one explanation for this disagreement: "Boy, that man must have the ears of an ass." To add insult to injury, Apollo transformed Midas' human ears into a pair of long, grey hairy ears of a donkey. To hide those long ears from sight, Midas henceforward wore a specific kind of royal turban in all the four seasons of the year.

However, it was impossible for him to hide the secret from his barber, who had to swear an oath of absolute secrecy, one which he was unable to bear. So, to get rid of his terrible burden, the barber dug a hole on a riverside one night, and whispered into it, "King Midas has ass' ears." Filling the hole up carefully afterwards, the barber tiptoed away from it.

In time, some reeds grew on top of this spot and the moment the first breeze ruffled them, they started murmuring Midas' secret to the whole world: "King Midas has ass' ears ... King Midas has ass' ears ... "

In English, both "donkey" and "ass" have derogatory or insulting meaning. They are generally used to mean someone who is obstinate, stupid or silly. Interestingly, "donkey's ears" has now become an idiom as in the following example: *I'm so bored; I've been doing this job for donkey's ears!* Can you guess what it means? In fact, the word "ear" is homophonic to "year". Word has it that donkeys tend to plod along slowly. They take a long time to complete a task or journey. Therefore, a donkey's year takes a long time to elapse.

国王迈达斯的驴耳朵是阿波罗给他的惩罚和羞辱。一天，阿波罗和牧神潘举行了一场音乐比赛，请山神特摩洛斯做评委。不出意料，特摩洛斯宣布阿波罗获胜。然而，就在这时，迈达斯碰巧经过这里，他愚蠢地插话，说比赛结果错误。

对于这种反对的声音，阿波罗给出的解释就是："呵呵，那个人一定长了一对驴耳朵！"雪上加霜的是，阿波罗果真把迈达斯的耳朵变成了一对长长的、毛茸茸的驴耳朵。此后，为了防止他人窥见自己的耳朵，迈达斯一年四季都戴着特殊的皇家包头巾。

然而，如何才能让他的理发师保守秘密呢？尽管理发师发誓绝不会说出去，但是这个秘密显然成了可怕的负担。一天夜里，理发师跑到河边，挖了一个地洞，对着洞中悄悄说道："迈达斯国王有对驴耳朵。"说完，他小心翼翼地把洞口填上，蹑手蹑脚地离开了。

过了一些日子，从那个洞口处长出了一些芦苇，第一缕微风吹过的时候，这些芦苇开始喃喃自语，将迈达斯的秘密昭告天下："迈达斯国王有对驴耳朵……迈达斯国王有对驴耳朵……"

英语中的 donkey 和 ass 都含有贬义或侮辱的意思，通常用来指顽固不化、愚蠢至极的人。有意思的是，"donkey's ears(驴耳朵)"如今已经成了一个惯用语，例如：I'm so bored; I've been doing this job for donkey's ears! 你能猜到这是什么意思吗？事实上，这里的 ear 与 year 谐音。据说，毛驴干起活来非常缓慢，完成一项工作或一段旅程往往需要很长时间，因此，a donkey's year 自然就指漫长的时间了。

The Myths 神话故事

Midas was the king of Phygia in Asia Minor. He had everything a king could wish for, abundant wealth, a big castle, and a beautiful daughter. Even though he was very rich, Midas thought that his greatest happiness was provided by gold. His avarice was such that he used to spend his days counting his golden coins! Occasionally he would cover his body with gold objects, as if he wanted to bath in them. Money was his obsession.

One day, Dionysus, the god of wine and revelry, passed through the kingdom of Midas. One of his companions and his tutor, a satyr named Silenus, being in an intoxicated condition, lost his way and strayed into the rose-garden of the monarch, where he was found by some of the king's attendants. He was then bound with roses and conducted to the presence of the royal master.

Midas treated him with the greatest hospitability. After entertaining for ten days, he was sent back to Dionysus, who was greatly pleased with the king's good-will. As a token of gratitude, the god of wine offered to grant Midas any favour he chose to demand. The avaricious king, whose wealth was already boundless, asked the god for the gift of turning everything he touched into gold. That the god did give him then and there, and Midas took his leave, secretly overjoyed.

The next day, Midas woke up eager to see if his wish would come true. He extended his arm touching a table, which immediately turned into gold. Going into his garden, he snapped a branch from a tree, and the twig shone forth a golden hue. Then he picked up a stone, and instantly it glittered between his fingers. The great transforming power filled his heart with joyful pride. He kept on running in his madness all over his palace until he got exhausted and thirsty.

Sitting at the breakfast table, Midas picked up a grape without thinking. But before he could put it into his mouth, the grape became gold. When he was about to drink, his favorite wine trickled from his jaws as fluid gold. Even the wine cup turned itself into gold in his grip. The same happened with a slice of bread and a glass of water. Suddenly, he started to sense fear. Right at that moment, his beloved daughter entered the room. When Midas hugged her, she was transformed into a gold statue!

The king was astonished and horrified. The substance that he used to have desired so greedily had now become the curse of his existence. The despairing king at last turned to the wine god for help. Kneeling down before Dionysus, he implored that the merciful god to rid him of the golden touch, which had now became a fatal gift. Dionysus, pitying his unhappy plight, smiled and told him to go and bathe in the river Pactolus. Hurling his body into the grateful little stream, the king laved himself thoroughly and was cured. From this time forth the sands of the river Pactolus are golden-colored to this very day.

When he returned home, everything Midas had touched came back to normal. Embracing his daughter in full happiness, Midas decided to share his great fortune with his people. From then on, Midas became a better ruler who was generous and grateful for all goods of his life. His kingdom prospered.

迈达斯是位于小亚细亚的弗里西亚国王，他拥有国王所拥有的一切：滚滚的财富、巨大的城堡和美丽的女儿。尽管他非常有钱，但还是认为黄金能给自己带来最大的快乐。他是如此贪得无厌，以至于每天都要数他的金币，有时，他还会把金子盖在身上，仿佛沐浴在金海之中。金钱令他着迷。

这天，酒神狄俄尼索斯从迈达斯的王国经过。他的一个酒友兼师父，半羊人塞列努斯因为酒后迷路，误入了王室的玫瑰花园。国王的仆人发现了他，用玫瑰的枝条将他捆绑起来，带到国王面前。

迈达斯以最友好的方式款待了赛列努斯，并留他在王宫里住了十天。狄俄尼索斯看到自己的老师平安归来后，对于国王的友善赞赏不已，作为回报，酒神提出可以满足迈达斯提出的任何愿望。尽管已经拥有了无数的财富，但是贪婪的国王却依然希望拥有点石成金之手。酒神立刻应允了他的愿望，迈达斯暗自窃喜，告辞回家。

第二天，迈达斯一睁开眼，便迫不及待地想要验证自己的能力。他伸出手去触摸一张桌子，桌子瞬间变成了金桌；他走进花园，从树上摘下一根树枝，那枝丫在他的手中变得金光闪闪；他捡起一块石头，转眼之间，握在手里的东西成了一块沉甸甸的金石。他为自己这种非凡的能力感到骄傲和欣喜，开始在王宫上下不停地疯狂试验，直到筋疲力尽、饥渴难耐。

迈达斯来到早餐桌旁，不经意地摘下一颗葡萄，还没等他把葡萄送进嘴里，那葡萄就变成了金子；他端起杯子想喝两口，他最爱的葡萄酒就在他的唇边变成了流淌的金水，就连手中的酒杯也自动地变为金杯。一片面包、一杯水……类似的事情还在不断地发生……突然间，迈达斯开始感到恐惧。就在这时，他心爱的女儿走进了房间，而他的拥抱却将她变成了一尊黄金雕塑！

迈达斯既震惊又害怕，他曾经如此渴望的东西如今成了祸根。终于，绝望中的国王向酒神寻求帮助。他在狄俄尼索斯面前双膝跪地，恳请酒神能收回他的点金之手，因为这已经成了一种致命的能力。酒神对他的不幸深表同情，微笑着示意他去帕克托洛斯河洗一洗。迈达斯如获至宝，跳进那条小溪，把全身上下彻底清洗了一遍。据说此后，帕克托洛斯河的沙子便是金黄色的了。

迈达斯回到家里，看到曾经变成金子的东西都恢复了原状，他欣喜地把女儿揽入怀中，决定从此以后将自己的财富分享给他的人民。此后，迈达斯成了一位慷慨大度的好国王，他开始知足常乐，而他的王国也日渐繁荣。

Extra 拓展测试

1. Which of the following is likely to be the turban worn by King Midas to hide his donkey's ears?

   以下哪一张图可能是国王迈达斯用来掩盖驴耳朵的帽子？

A

B

2. With its profitable connotation, the word "Midas" has been adopted widely throughout the world. For example, Midas Inc. is an American chain of automotive service centers headquartered in Florida. The slogan of the company is "Trust the Midas touch".

   The hand of Midas is an item or equipment which could be bought to accelerate the speed or help bring about gold in a popular multi-player online game. Do you know the name of the video game?

由于有盈利的含义，Midas 这个词在全世界被广泛使用。例如，迈达斯公司就是美国一家连锁汽车维修公司的名字，总部位于佛罗里达州，而该公司的口号是“相信迈达斯之手”。

“迈达斯之手”是一款颇受欢迎的大型线上多玩家游戏中的装备，付钱购买后能够帮助玩家加快速度或带来金币，你知道这款游戏的名字吗？

（1. 答案：B）

（2. 答案：魔兽争霸）

CHAPTER 4 The Messenger of Gods
第四章 众神的使者

Word Knowledge 词汇知识

Touchstone(试金石)

According to the myth, on the very first day when he was born, Hermes stole some cattle from his half-brother Apollo, but the theft had been witnessed by an old shepherd named Battus. Frightened at being discovered, Hermes bribed him with the finest cow in the herd not to betray him, and the old man agreed. But out of distrust and uncertainty, Hermes pretended to go away first and then returned to test the confidence of Battus in the disguise of Admetus, the owner of the cattle. He promised to offer Battus two of his best oxen if he would disclose the author of the theft. The ruse succeeded, for the old man could not resist the tempting bait and gave the desired information. As a punishment for the treachery, Hermes changed him into a lump of touchstone with his divine power.

Touchstone literally means a stone used to test the fineness of gold alloys, but now metaphorically it often refers to a standard or criterion by which the validity or merit of something is judged or recognized.

传说赫耳墨斯出生的第一天，他就从阿波罗那儿偷了一些牛，但是，一位老牧羊人巴图斯目睹了他的偷窃行为。因为担心被揭穿，赫耳墨斯便用最好的牛来贿赂老人，让他不要说出去，老人同意了。赫耳墨斯依然不放心，他佯装离开，然后变身为牛的主人阿德墨托斯后重新返回。他向巴图斯承诺，假如他能告诉自己窃贼的名字，就送给他两头牛。他的诡计得逞了，老头经不住诱惑，说出了实情。于是，赫耳墨斯使出神力把巴图斯变成了一块试金石，作为对他违背诺言的惩罚。

试金石的本义是用来测试金矿石纯度的石头，如今，这个词常引申为能够衡量或判断某物可靠性或品质的标准。

Caduceus(神使之杖)

Known as the swift-footed messenger and ambassador of all the gods, Hermes is usually depicted as wearing Petasus, a winged silver cap, and Talaria, a pair of winged sandals. But his main symbol was Caduceus, a winged herald's wand or staff with two snakes twisting around it, which is sometimes confused with another wand possessed by Asclepius, the god of healing. With only one snake and no wings attached to it, the staff of Asclepius was generally associated with medical care, which is why it is now in the centre of the flag of World Health Organization.

赫耳墨斯是众神的信使和外交官，他行走如风。在通常的描述中，都是头戴银色的宽边有翼帽，脚穿一双有翼鞋，但他最主要的标志还是神使之杖。这是一把带翅膀的节杖，上面盘绕着两条蛇。这把节杖经常会和另一把混淆，那就是医药之神阿斯刻勒庇俄斯的节杖。后者没有翅膀，上面盘绕的只有一条蛇，常常和医疗相联系，因此这把节杖成了世界卫生组织旗帜的核心。

Hermaphroditus(赫墨芙洛狄忒斯)

Hermaphroditus, whose name was a compound of his parents' names, was the son of Hermes and Aphrodite. One day, at the age of fifteen, when he was traveling in the woods, he encountered the nymph Salmacis, who fell immediately in love with this handsome boy. After a futile attempt to seduce him, Salmacis pretended to walk away. Then when Hermaphroditus was about to take a bath in the empty waters, she sprang out from behind a tree and jumped into the pool. Despite his struggle, she entwined her arms around him and held tight. To avoid his escaping, the nymph called out to the gods that they should never part. Her wish was granted and their bodies blended into one form, "a creature of both sexes". Since then, anyone who bathed in that pool would be similarly transformed. Now the word "hermaphrodites" simply means one person, animal or plant possessing physical traits of both male and female sexes. In modern English, there are many blending words that are formed in this way, such as *Brexit*, *Eurabia*, *frenemy*, *bromance* etc.

赫墨芙洛狄忒斯是赫耳墨斯和阿芙洛蒂忒的儿子,他的名字就是他父母名字的组合。在他十五岁时,有一天他在森林里遇见了水仙女萨耳玛西斯,后者对这位美少年一见倾心,并试图诱惑他。在遭到拒绝后,萨耳玛西斯先假装走开。随后,正当赫墨芙洛狄忒准备在水中沐浴时,她突然从树后跑出来,跃入了池塘中。水仙女的手臂紧紧环绕住他的身体,他挣扎着想要逃脱,而她则大叫着死也不要和他分开。诸神听到她的叫声后,将他们的身体合二为一,成就了一种"雌雄同体的生物"。从那以后,凡是在那片池塘中沐浴过的生物都会变成此类物种。现在,hermaphrodites这个词就用来指"拥有雌雄两种性征的人或动植物"。在当代英语中,有很多类似的拼缀词,例如:Brexit(英国脱欧)、Eurabia(欧拉伯)、frenemy(敌友)、bromance(兄弟情)等。

The Myths 神话故事

Hermes was the son of Zeus and Maia, the oldest and most beautiful of the seven daughters of Atlas. As a newborn, he was remarkably precocious. Myth has it that only several hours after his birth, he crept stealthily out of his cradle in order to steal some oxen attended by his brother Apollo. Half way on his expedition, however, he found a tortoise and killed it. Stretching seven strings across the empty shell, he invented the first lyre, upon which he began to play immediately with exquisite skill. Having enjoyed himself for some time, he resumed his journey and arrived at his destination at sunset.

Succeeding in separating fifty oxen from his brother's herd, the little thief pulled the hoofs out of the cows' feet and reattached them in the reverse order so that the cattle seemed to be walking backwards rather than forwards. To escape detection, he also covered his own bare feet with two oversized sandals made of myrtle twigs. Feeling hungry, he killed two of the oxen. Then the ingenious infant was said to have invented a fire-stick, with which he lit a cooking fire so that he could enjoy some roasted beef. After that, he returned to his birthplace and clambered into his cot, cooing innocently.

Apollo, with his all-seeing power, soon discovered the little rogue. He complained to Maia of her son's conduct, and angrily aroused the pretended sleeper. The child denied all knowledge of it. In fact, he played his part so well that he even inquired in the most naïve manner what sort of animal cows were. Apollo threatened to throw the babe into Tartarus if he would not confess the truth, but in vain. At last, the furious elder brother seized the babe in his arms and took him to be judged by their almighty father Zeus.

Having listened to the charge made by Apollo, Zeus sternly desired Hermes to say where he had hidden the cattle. The baby, who was still in swaddling clothes, looked up bravely into his father's face and replied, "Now, do I look capable of driving away a herd of cattle? I, who was only born yesterday, and whose feet are much too soft and tender to tread in rough places? Until this moment, I lay in sweet sleep on my mother's bosom, and have never ever crossed the threshold of our dwelling." While saying this, the child looked so solemn and innocent that Zeus could not refrain from smiling at his cleverness and cunning.

Eventually Hermes admitted his guilt. To reconcile with his brother, he gave his lyre to Apollo as a gift. In exchange, Apollo presented Hermes with the Caduceus, a golden wand surmounted by wings. Hearing that the wand possessed the power of uniting in love, all beings divided by hate, Hermes wished to prove the truth of this assertion. He threw it down between two snakes which were fighting. Miraculously, the angry combatants clasped each other in a loving embrace, curling round the staff, remained ever after permanently attached to it. The wand has since become the symbol and sign of Hermes, who henceforth became the god of herdsmen, whilst Apollo devoted himself enthusiastically to the art of music. Recognizing what cunning and speed were needed to accomplish the cattle theft, Zeus made Hermes the messenger of gods.

赫耳墨斯是宙斯和迈亚的儿子，迈亚是阿特拉斯的长女，也是他七个女儿中最美的那个。出生伊始，赫耳墨斯就惊人地早熟。据说他刚生下来没几个小时，就悄悄地爬出摇篮，打算去偷哥哥阿波罗放牧的牛。半路上，他发现了一只乌龟，杀了它，用掏空了内脏的乌龟壳做了第一把七弦的里拉琴，并且立刻就非常娴熟地弹奏了起来。这样自娱自乐了一阵后，他又继续赶路，并在黄昏时分抵达了目的地。

在成功地牵出了五十头牛之后，这个小窃贼先是拔下了牛蹄，然后再反方向把它们装回去，这样一来，牛儿们就似乎在向后走，而不是向前走了。为了躲避追踪，他还用桃木树枝做了一双大鞋子套在自己的光脚丫上。因为肚子饿，他杀了两头牛。然后，这个天才小婴儿竟然还发明了取火棍，并用它生了火，享受了一顿烤牛肉大餐。在此之后，他回到了出生的地方，费力地爬回自己的小床，重新变回一个懵懂的婴儿。

拥有千里眼的阿波罗很快便发现了这个小贼的所作所为，他来到迈亚面前告状，并生气地把床上那个假装睡觉的家伙拎了起来。小婴儿矢口否认，事实上，他太会演戏了，竟然满脸天真地问哥哥："牛是什么东西啊？"阿波罗威胁他如果不讲真话，就把他打入塔尔塔罗斯的地牢，但依旧无果。最后，无计可施的哥哥只好抓着他的胳膊，把他拖到至高无上的宇宙之神宙斯那里去评理。

宙斯听了阿波罗的陈述后，厉声质问赫耳墨斯把牛藏在哪儿了。只见那个依然裹着婴儿服的孩子毫不怯懦，直视父亲的目光，大声说："你看我像是能偷牛的人吗？我这么个昨天才刚出生的小婴儿，这么柔嫩的小脚丫怎么可能在那么粗糙的地面上奔跑？我明明一直都躺在妈妈的怀里乖乖地睡觉，连大门都没跨出过半步。"说这话时，这个小机灵鬼一脸的天真和严肃，宙斯也不由得被逗乐了。

赫耳墨斯最终承认了自己的偷窃行为。为了和哥哥和好，他把自己做的里拉琴送给阿波罗作为礼物，哥哥则把神使之杖送给他作为交换。这是一根带有翅膀的金质节杖。听说这根节杖可以让因仇恨而分开的情侣重新团聚，赫耳墨斯想要测试一下。他朝着两条正在打架的蛇挥了一下节杖，奇迹发生了：两个原本的仇家猛地拥抱在了一起，并且盘绕在节杖上，从此不再离开。此后，这根节杖就成了赫耳墨斯的标志，他也成了牧人的守护神，阿波罗则更多地专注于音乐艺术。联想到赫耳墨斯在偷牛事件中所表现出的速度和计谋，宙斯便任命他为神的使者。

Extra 拓展测试

1. Which of the following is likely to be the wand of Hermes?
   下面哪一把节杖有可能是赫耳墨斯的？

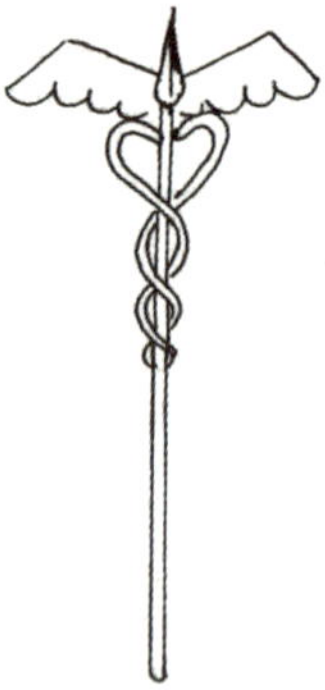

A

B

2. The Roman equivalent of Hermes is Mercury, which is one of the planets in our solar system. Besides, Hermes is known as the brand name of a French high-fashion luxury goods manufacturer. Do you know its Chinese name?

赫耳墨斯在罗马神话中对应的名字叫墨丘利,他也是太阳系的行星之一。此外,Hermes还是法国一个著名的高阶奢侈品牌制造商的名字,你知道它的中文是什么吗?

(1. 答案:A)

(2. 答案:爱马仕)

CHAPTER 5 The Tragedy of Oedipus
第五章 俄狄浦斯的悲剧

Word Knowledge 词汇知识

Oedipus Complex(恋母情结)

Oedipus, in Greek mythology, is the king of Thebes who unwittingly killed his father and married his mother. The popular story we know today is mainly from the three Theban plays by Sophocles, a Greek dramatist in 400 B. C. Drama was an important part of Greek culture. The three tragedies by Sophocles, *Oedipus Rex* (*Oedipus the King*), *Oedipus at Colonus*, and *Antigone*, are notable for their complexity of plot, depth of characterization, and two enduring themes of Greek myth and drama: the flawed nature of humanity and an individual's role in the course of destiny in a harsh universe.

The myth of Oedipus has not only inspired many artists and playwrights, but also researchers and psychologists. Oedipus complex, for example, is a concept of psychoanalytic theory put forward by Sigmund Freud, an Austrian psychoanalyst. The term is used to designate a son's feeling of love toward his mother and of jealousy and hate toward his father, though those were not emotions that motivated Oedipus' actions or determined his character in any ancient version of the story.

In contrast to Oedipus complex, there is Electra complex introduced by Carl Jung, a Swiss psychologist in 1913. However, Sigmund Freud deprecated the term.

在希腊神话中,底比斯国王俄狄浦斯无意间杀死了自己的父亲,娶了自己的母亲。这个流传颇广的故事主要源于公元前400年，古希腊戏剧家索福克勒斯创作的三部底比斯戏剧。戏剧是希腊文化的重要组成部分，索福克勒斯的这三部悲剧：《俄狄浦斯王》《俄狄浦斯在科罗诺斯》和《安提戈涅》，都以情节复杂、人物刻画深刻而出名。同时，引人注目的还有贯穿希腊神话和戏剧的两大主题：人性的缺陷以及个人在严酷世界中的命运。

俄狄浦斯的故事不但为大批的艺术家和戏剧家提供了创作的灵感，同时，也引起了研究人员和心理学家的兴趣。例如，俄狄浦斯情结（恋母情结）是奥地利精神分析学家弗洛伊德提出的一个概念，用来指儿子对母亲的爱恋和对父亲的仇视，尽管此种情感与神话故事中俄狄浦斯的悲剧行为并无关联。

与俄狄浦斯情结相对应的是“伊莱克特拉情结（恋父情结）”，是由瑞士心理学家荣格在1913年提出的。然而，弗洛伊德并不认可这个概念。

Sphinx(斯芬克司)

When it comes to Sphinx, most Chinese would think of the stone statue in Egypt, but do you know that the Egyptian sphinx has the face of a man rather than a woman? Besides, unlike the treacherous and merciless monster in Greek myth, the Egyptian sphinx appears to be benevolent, though with ferocious strength, too.

Though the word "sphinx" originally means "squeeze" or "tighten up" in ancient Greek, it is now understood as something perplexing due to the riddle in the Oedipus story, such as: 1) *The question was a like the Sphinx's riddle to me*. 2) *I've always found her rather sphinx-like*.

提到斯芬克司，大多数中国人都会想到埃及的狮身人面像，可是你知道埃及的斯芬克司拥有的是一张男人脸而不是女人脸吗？此外，埃及的斯芬克司尽管也很凶猛，但和希腊神话中冷酷可怕的怪物相比显得更慈善。

“斯芬克司”这个词最初在古希腊语中的意思是“挤压”或“收紧”，而现在由于俄狄浦斯的故事，它主要指"令人困惑的东西"，例如："这个问题对我来说如同斯芬克司的谜语。""我总觉得她很像斯芬克司（令人捉摸不透）。"

The Myths 神话故事

Ancient Greeks had the tradition of consulting the oracle at Delphi, the temple of Apollo, for their future or important decisions. Laius, king of Thebes, wanted to know if his wife Jocasta would bear him any children. As he himself had married his cousin Jocasta, which was certainly a defiance of the gods, he was warned that he should avoid having children, or he might be killed by his son born of that union.

In due course of time a son was born. In an attempt to avoid the unavoidable, Laius ordered him exposed on a nearby mountain, with an iron pin driven through his ankle. The slave, who had been given the job of abandoning the baby in the wilderness, took pity on the infant and gave him to a kind shepherd, who passed him on to Polybus and Merope, the childless royal couple of Corinth. The child was then named Oedipus, meaning swollen foot, and brought up as the prince and heir of the kingdom Corinth.

The prince had never suspected that the king was not his biological father, until one day he received an insulting hint respecting his parentage. Deeply troubled, Oedipus went to Delphi to inquire about his birth. The oracle, as often, didn't reply directly, but told him that he must never set foot on his native soil, for he was destined to kill his father and marry his mother. The horrified young man then chose never to return to Corinth, which he took to be the country of his birth, and set out on the road to Thebes.

When Oedipus arrived at a crossroad, he saw a chariot coming clattering up towards him, the driver and passenger unconcerned for the young wanderer with whom they shared the narrow road. To avoid being crushed, Oedipus leapt aside onto the rough shoulder, but then he sprinted alongside the chariot, shouting angrily and grabbing for the driver. At this, the passenger, an elderly man with cold eyes, struck him hard on the head with a whip. In an instant, quick-tempered Oedipus pulled the man from the back of the chariot and killed him for the insult. Little did Oedipus know that the man was his true father, King Laius.

Some time later, Oedipus reached Thebes where he found the city afflicted by Sphinx—a monstrous creature with the face of a woman, the body of a lion, and the wings of an eagle. It had blocked the gates to the city and set about terrorizing all who sought exit or entry by demanding the answer to a riddle it had learnt from the Muses: "What goes on four legs at dawn, two legs at midday, and three legs in the evening?" The beast proceeded to devour all who failed to give the right answer.

After King Laius died, Creon, Queen Jocasta's brother, was acting as regent. He was desperate enough to offer the throne of Thebes and his sister's hand in marriage to anyone who could rid the land of the riddling pest. Oedipus, confident in his wits, boldly confronted the Sphinx at the mouth of its cliff-top cave. "'Man' is the answer," he said. "As an infant, he crawls; as an adult he walks on two legs; and in the evening of his life he supports himself with a cane." In anguish surprise at the abrupt end to its deadly game, the Sphinx hurled itself with a blood-curdling howl off the precipice. Oedipus gained the throne and married Jocasta.

Ignorance can be bliss. For many years, Thebes and Oedipus thrived. Out of his incestuous wedlock with Jocasta came four unnatural children. Then a plague struck. No family was spared, and not a day went by without new deaths. Rumor soon gained currency that the curse would not be removed until the murderer of the former king Laius was driven out of the country. An old blind seer was summoned. To his astonishment and exasperation, Oedipus himself was condemned as the wanted murderer.

At this point, Polybus died, and a messenger arrived from Corinth, offering the now-vacant throne to Oedipus. Being mindful of the prophecy, and thought that Polybus and Merope were his parents, Oedipus refused. The messenger, in all innocence and an intention of comforting him, then revealed that they were not his biological parents. Bit by bit, the truth finally became known, like a snowball turning finally into a devastating avalanche. Jocasta hanged herself in horror at her incest, and on discovering her lifeless body, still warm and swaying, Oedipus blinded himself with a brooch torn from her robe.

古希腊人在事关未来或遇到重要决策的时候,都有到特尔斐的阿波罗神庙祈求神谕的传统。底比斯国王拉伊俄斯想知道自己的妻子伊俄卡斯特是否会生一儿半女。由于伊俄卡斯特是他的表妹,这一乱伦的婚姻无疑是对众神的藐视,因此,神谕警告他最好不要有孩子,否则他会被自己的儿子杀死。

不久之后,他们有了一个男孩。为了防止神谕变成现实,拉伊俄斯下令将婴儿扔到附近的荒郊野岭,并用一根铁针穿过婴儿的脚踝,以阻止他逃跑。奉命执行任务的奴仆不忍心就这样把他丢在那里,于是把这个可怜的孩子交给了一位好心的牧羊人。后者恰巧是科林斯国王的仆人,而国王珀吕波斯和王后美罗珀膝下无子,正好需要一个继承人。他们给孩子起名俄狄浦斯,意思是“肿起的脚”,把他当成自己的儿子抚养长大。

小王子对于自己的身世从未有过怀疑,直到有一天,因为与人发生口角,他听到了一些不该听到的话。那些话令俄狄浦斯忧心忡忡,于是他来到特尔斐寻求神谕。和以往一样,神谕没有给出明确的答案,而是告诉他永远不要踏足他的出生地,否则的话,他注定会杀死自己的父亲,迎娶自己的母亲。这道神谕令俄狄浦斯惊恐不已。由于把科林斯当成了自己的出生地,他决定离开这里,前往底比斯。

俄狄浦斯走到一个十字路口,看见一辆马车正朝他飞驰而来,车夫和车上的客人似乎并没有看见迎面走来的年轻人。由于那条路实在太窄，为了不被撞到，俄狄浦斯只好跳到了坑洼的路肩上。紧跟着，他追上前去，气愤地质问车夫并试图抓住他。这时，坐在车上的老者冷冷地抽出一根鞭子，一下打在他的头上。年轻气盛的俄狄浦斯怎能受得了这样的侮辱，他冲上去一把把老人拉下车，并杀了他。俄狄浦斯并不知道，这个人正是国王拉伊俄斯，他的亲生父亲。

不久，俄狄浦斯到达了底比斯。那时，城里正因为斯芬克司而人心惶惶。这是一个长着狮子身、女人面、老鹰翼的怪物。它把守着城门，凡是进出城门的人都必须猜一个谜语。这个谜语是它从缪斯女神那儿学来的，说的是："什么东西在早晨有四条腿，中午有两条腿，晚上有三条腿？"所有答错或答不出来的人都会被这怪物吃掉。

拉伊俄斯死后，王后伊俄卡斯特的弟弟克瑞翁成了摄政王。当时，他迫不及待地想要找到一个人能解开谜语，挽救城邦，因此承诺一旦有人能做到，他会将王位拱手相让，并将王后嫁给他。俄狄浦斯相信自己有这个能力，他来到斯芬克司位于悬崖顶端的洞穴口，大声说道："答案是'人'，因为婴儿用四肢来爬，成年人两条腿走路，暮年时则再加一根拐杖。"斯芬克司没有想到这场致命的游戏这么快便戛然而止。伴随着一声令人毛骨悚然的凄厉长嚎，恼羞成怒的怪物从峭壁的顶端直坠而下。俄狄浦斯登上了王位，迎娶了伊俄卡斯特。

无知是福。在接下来的许多年里，俄狄浦斯生活幸福，底比斯城繁荣兴旺，他与伊俄卡斯特的不伦婚姻为他带来了四个孩子。之后，一场瘟疫爆发，家家户户几无幸免，每天都有人病死。城中开始流言四起，认为只有把谋杀老国王拉伊俄斯的人驱逐出去，才可能天下太平。俄狄浦斯找来了一位盲人先知，然而，令他大惊失色的是，先知指责他就是那个刽子手。

此时，恰有科林斯的使者求见，告诉他国王珀吕波斯去世了，希望俄狄浦斯回去继承王位。俄狄浦斯对于之前的神谕依然心存芥蒂，认为珀吕波斯和美罗珀就是他的亲生父母，于是拒绝了这番好意。使者为了安慰他，无意之间透露珀吕波斯夫妇只是他的养父母的事实。一点一点地，真相终于大白，一个小小的雪球最终变成了一场雪崩。伊俄卡斯特在惊恐中上吊自尽。俄狄浦斯发现她时，一切为时已晚。俄狄浦斯抱着她尚有余温的尸体，拔下她衣服上的胸针，戳瞎了自己的眼睛。

Extra 拓展测试

1. Which of the following do you think is the Sphinx?
   以下哪一幅图是斯芬克司?

A

B

2. Sphinx, like many other proper nouns in Greek mythology, has now become a common noun, but, interestingly, it has several meanings which are a world apart from each other. For example, it may be a stout-bodied moth, or a baboon native to Ethiopia in sub-Sahara Africa. There is also a breed of cat with sphinx as its name. Do you know what it looks like?

   如同希腊神话中的许多专有名词一样,斯芬克司这个名字如今也成了一个普通名词。然而有意思的是,它有好几个截然不同的意思。例如:它可以是一只胖胖的飞蛾,也可以是非洲埃塞俄比亚地区的一种狒狒。此外,它还是一种猫的名字,你知道斯芬克司猫长什么样吗?

(1. 答案:B)

(2. 答案:这是一种无毛的、家犬似的猫。)

FURTHER READING
Damon and Pythias
延伸阅读　生死之交

Like the story of the Sword of Damocles, the myth about Damon and Pythias was also told by Cicero, the Roman statesman, orator and philosopher. According to the myth, Damon and Pythias had been best friends since childhood. They grew up in Syracuse, an important city in Sicily, and both became the followers of the Greek philosopher Pythagoras. One day, Pythias in some way roused the anger of the tyrannical king Dionysius I, who put him in prison and condemned him to die in a few days.

Accepting his sentence, Pythias asked to be allowed to return home one last time to settle his affairs and bid his family farewell. Not wanting to be taken for a fool, the king refused, believing that, once released, Pythias would flee and never return. Damon, anxious to gratify his friend's last wish, went into the presence of the tyrant, offering himself as a hostage in Pythias' absence. When the king insisted that should Pythias not return by an appointed time, Damon would be executed in his stead, Damon agreed. So Pythias was released.

Pythias hastened home, where he bid farewell to his family, and then set out to return to Syracuse. However, on the way back, his ship was attacked by pirates and he was thrown overboard. Pythias swam to shore, but he did not have any money or a horse or any way of getting back to Damon. Nerved by the fear that his friend would die in his stead, he started to run as fast as he could towards the king's palace. The hot rays of the sun and the burning sands greatly increased his fatigue and faintness, and almost made him die of thirst. Still he sped onward as fast as his trembling limbs could carry him, for he knew that his friend would die if he were not in Syracuse by sunset.

In the meantime Dionysius was taunting Damon, and constantly telling him, "See! Pythias has abandoned you. I told you he'd never come back." He also insisted that Pythias was only too glad to escape death, and would be very careful not to return in time. Damon, who knew the goodness and affection of his friend, received these remarks with the scorn they deserved, and repeated again and again that he knew Pythias would never break his word, but would be back in time, unless hindered in some unforeseen way.

The last hour came. The guards led Damon to the place of crucifixion, where he again asserted his faith in his friend, adding, however, that he sincerely hoped Pythias would come too late, so that he might die in his stead. Just as the guards were about to nail Damon to the cross, Pythias dashed up, pale, bloodstained, and disheveled, and flung his arms around his friend's neck with a sob of relief. For the first time, Damon turned pale, and began to shed tears of bitter regret.

In a few hurried, panting words, Pythias explained the cause of his delay, and, loosing his friend's bonds with his own hands, bade the guards bind him instead. Dionysius, who had come to see the execution, was so touched by this true friendship, that for once he forgot his cruelty, and let both young men go free, saying that he would not have believed such devotion possible had he not seen it with his own eyes.

This friendship, which wrung tears from the grim executioners, and touched the tyrant's heart, has become proverbial. When men are devoted friends, they are often compared to Damon and Pythias, whose story has been a favorite with poets and playwrights. For example, in the works of William Shakespeare, Hamlet addresses his close friend Horatio as "O Damon dear".

正如达摩克利斯之剑的故事，达蒙和皮西厄斯的故事也是古罗马军事家、演说家、哲学家西塞罗最早讲述的。传说两人自儿时起便是要好的朋友，他们在西西里的重要城市锡拉库萨一起长大，并且都成了哲学家毕达哥拉斯的学生。有一天，皮西厄斯因为某种原因得罪了暴君狄奥尼西奥斯一世，最后被关进大牢，几天后处死。

皮西厄斯接受了判决，但他请求临死之前回家一趟，安排一下身后事，并向家人告别。国王不是傻瓜，自然不会答应这样的请求。达蒙听说后，觉得有必要帮助好友完成这最后的心愿。于是他来到国王面前，请求在皮西厄斯回来前把自己当作人质。国王同意了，但是他明确表示，一旦皮西厄斯不能按时回来，达蒙就将代替他受刑。达蒙同意了，于是皮西厄斯被释放。

皮西厄斯匆匆赶回家，和家人一一告别后，又快马加鞭地赶回锡拉库萨。然而返程时，他的船遭遇了海盗，他被海盗们扔进了大海。虽然皮西厄斯努力地游上了岸，但他身无分文，也没有任何交通工具。想到朋友正命悬一线，他开始向着王宫的方向飞奔而去。炙热的阳光和滚烫的沙地令他汗流浃背、精疲力竭，他几乎快要渴死了。但是他不敢停，也不能停，他知道自己必须在天黑之前赶到锡拉库萨，否则他的朋友就会为他丧命。

与此同时，狄奥尼西奥斯正在挖苦达蒙，不断地说着："你瞧！皮西厄斯已经把你抛弃了。我告诉过你他不会回来的。"他坚持认为皮西厄斯巴不得逃离死亡，根本不可能按时回来的。对于这番话，达蒙只是一笑置之，他丝毫不怀疑好友的为人和品德，他一遍又一遍地强调说皮西厄斯绝不会食言，他一定会按时回来的，除非发生了什么意外。

最后一刻到来了，卫兵们将达蒙押上了绞首架，此时的达蒙依然坚信他不会看错自己的好友。但他也希望皮西厄斯能晚一点到，这样他就能代替皮西斯死去。就在行刑的士兵把绞索套上达蒙的脖子之际，皮西厄斯冲了进来，他脸色苍白，浑身血迹斑斑，头发蓬乱、衣衫褴褛，他一把搂住达蒙的脖子，长舒了一口气。而此时的达蒙却突然面色晦暗，第一次落下了伤心遗憾的泪水。

皮西厄斯一边替达蒙解开套在他脖子上的绞索，一边上气不接下气地解释自己迟到的原因，他请求士兵把绞索套到自己脖子上。所有这一切，在一旁监督行刑的狄奥尼西奥斯都看在眼里，平生第一次，他那颗冷酷的心也被深深打动了。如果不是亲眼所见，他根本不可能相信这世上还有如此无私真挚的友情。他决定网开一面，将两个人都无罪释放了。

这份令严肃的行刑人员和专制的暴君都为之动容的友情，渐渐变成了一种众所部分知的表达方式。人们往往用达蒙和皮西厄斯来代表彼此全心全意地无私奉献的生死之交，这个故事也成了诗人和戏剧家们惯用的情节。例如，在莎士比亚的作品当中，哈姆莱特就以这样的方式来称呼其好友霍拉旭："哦，我亲爱的达蒙。"

Extra 拓展测试

Both Damon and Pythias were followers of Pythagoras, the Greek philosopher and mathematician known for a theorem in geometry. Do you know the Chinese name of this theorem?

达蒙和皮西厄斯都是毕达哥拉斯的追随者，这位古希腊哲学家和数学家因一项几何学定理著名。你知道这项定理的中文是什么吗？

（答案：毕达哥拉斯定理/勾股定理）

PART Ⅵ Myth and Customs

第六部分
神话与习俗

扫一扫,听本部分音频

CHAPTER 1 The Wine God Dionysus
第一章 酒神狄俄尼索斯

Word Knowledge 词汇知识

Dionysia(酒神节)

The Dionysia was a joyous spring festival held in honor of Dionysus, in the month of March, and lasted several days. During the festival, everything wore its holiday garb, everyone was costumed and wine was freely indulged in. The central events of the festival were the theatrical performances of dramatic tragedies and comedies. In fact, the Dionysia consisted of two related festivals: the Rural Dionysia and the City Dionysia. The modern Carnival in Greece is believed to have been evolved from this festival.

When introduced into Rome, the Dionysia festival of Athens was given the name Bacchanalia, which has now become a common noun in English, meaning any uninhibited or drunken revelry, such as in the following sentence: *What followed wasn't your average office retirement party, but a weeklong bacchanalia on a 65-foot schooner near St. Bart's.*

酒神节是为狄俄尼索斯而举行的春日庆典,一般在三月份举办,持续数天。节日期间,无论是人还是物都会披上节日的盛装,可以尽情享用美酒。而节日的核心内容是剧院里的悲剧或喜剧演出。事实上,酒神节分为两种:乡村酒神节和城市酒神节。如今,希腊每年举行的狂欢节据信便源自酒神节。

雅典的酒神节传到罗马后,改名为“大酒宴(Bacchanalia)”。而bacchanalia一词如今已经成了普通名词,可以表示任何形式的纵情狂欢，例如："随之而来的不是像平常人那样的退休派对，而是在圣巴特附近一艘五十英尺的纵帆船上长达一周的狂欢。"

Triumphal Progression(胜利游行)

Dionysus, as the wine god, had many followers, who gathered around him and traveled together with him. Wherever they went, people saw Dionysus seating in a chariot drawn by panthers, and leading a large army composed of men, women, fauns, and satyrs, all bearing in their hands the Thyrsus, and clashing together cymbals and other musical instruments. The progression was indeed like a celebration or parade after a military conquest. Hence Dionysus was considered the founder of the triumphal progression, or variably, triumphal progress/procession. Here are two examples: 1) *The triumphal progress of the president continued throughout the evening.* 2) *His only injury had occurred, ironically enough, while he was leading the triumphal procession into the open city of Rome.*

作为酒神的狄俄尼索斯有许多追随者，他们聚集在他身边，随他去各地旅行。所到之处，人们看到的是狄俄尼索斯端坐在由黑豹拉着的双轮马车里，后面跟着由男人、女人和半羊人所组成的长长队伍，每个人手上都拿着酒神杖，敲着钹，或演奏着其他乐器。这支队伍的确像是得胜凯旋的庆祝队伍，因此，狄俄尼索斯被认为是胜利游行的创始人。这里举两个例子：1)"总统的胜利游行一直延续到深夜。"2)"说来好笑，他唯一的伤发生在他率领凯旋队伍开进罗马城的途中。"

Liber(利柏耳)

Liber, or Liber Pater, was an ancient Roman god of wine, fertility and freedom. Therefore, he was identified with the Greek Dionysus, and worshipped under the name of Bacchus. The festival of Liber, called the Liberalia, was celebrated on the 17th of March, which was generally associated with free speech and the rights attached to coming of age.

The word "Liber", in Latin, means "the free one". Liber Pater means the free father. So it is not difficult to see the etymological origins of such English words as *liberty*, *liberation*, *liberal*, *liberalize*, *liberalism*, *litertarian*, *libertine* etc.

利柏耳,或利柏耳·佩特,是古罗马的酒神、丰产之神和自由之神。因此,后来人们把他和希腊神话中的狄俄尼索斯等同起来,并以巴克斯来称呼他。利柏耳的节日被称为"利柏耳利拉",是每年的3月17日,其主题通常为自由言论以及成年人的权利。

在拉丁语中,"Liber(利柏耳)"一词的意思是"自由的那一个","Liber Pater(利柏耳·佩特)"的意思就是"自由之父"。因此,我们不难看出这个词与下列英语单词的词源关系:liberty(自由)、liberation(解放)、liberal(开明的)、liberalize(自由化)、liberalism(自由主义)、libertarian(自由论者)、libertine(放荡不羁的人)等。

The Myths 神话故事

Dionysus, whose Roman name was Bacchus, was the ancient Greek god of wine, merriment, and theatre. Son of Zeus and his mortal lover Semele, Dionysus was snatched by Zeus from the devouring flames in which his mother perished at the sight of the almighty god in all his divine glory. He was reared in Zeus' thigh for several months before being born. Hence he was known as "the twice-born". The motherless child was first entrusted to the charge of

Hermes, who then transferred him to the fostering care of the nymphs of Mount Nysa. An aged satyr named Silenus, the son of Pan, became his educator and chief companion.

Dionysus passed an innocent and uneventful childhood, roaming through the woods and forests, surrounded by nymphs, satyrs, and shepherds. During one of these rambles, he found a fruit growing wild, of a most refreshing and cooling nature. This was the vine, from which he subsequently learnt to extract a juice which formed a most exhilarating beverage. He then set out to make a triumphal progress, accompanied by thousands of enthusiastic followers, through Syria, Egypt, Arabia, even as far as India, to teach people the cultivation of the vine.

One myth tells of Dionysus being abducted by pirates who were unaware of his identity. The wine god transformed the ship's mast into a huge vine, and a heavenly choir filled the air with music. Turning himself into a lion and assisted by a bear, Dionysus dispatched the pirate captain. In terror, the remaining crew members leapt overboard and were changed into dolphins. Only the helmsman survived the encounter as he had counselled his crewmates against abducting the stranger in the first place.

In another myth, Hera was trapped by her son Hephaestus in an ingenious throne. It was Dionysus who persuaded (probably with wine) the god of metallurgy to return to Mount Olympus and release her. Hera, therefore, in her gratitude ensured that Dionysus, actually a demigod, became a full Olympian god with permission to reside on Mount Olympus for all time.

Homer described Dionysus as the "joy of men" and Hesiod likewise depicted him as "much-cheering". Both made sense because Dionysus was credited with giving man the gift of wine. The Greeks usually drank wine diluted with water, mixed in a large krater vessel. Wine was drunk at banquets, festivals, and private parties, in particular, at a symposium, a kind of informal, male-only drinking session where guests reclined on a couch and engaged in conversation on topics ranging from gossip to philosophy.

Dionysus was regarded as the patron of the drama. At the state festival of the Dionysia, dramatic entertainments took place in his honour, for which all the renowned Greek dramatists of antiquity composed their immortal tragedies and comedies. It is believed that theatre sprang from a Dionysian frenzy as, like Dionysus' worshippers, actors strive to leave behind their own persona and become one with the character they are playing. Indeed, priests of Dionysus were given seats of honour in Greek theatres.

狄俄尼索斯的罗马名字叫巴克斯，是古希腊的酒神、欢乐之神和戏剧之神。作为宙斯和凡人女子塞墨勒的儿子，他是被宙斯从火堆里抢救出来的，因为宙斯在塞墨勒面前显露真容，令凡人姑娘瞬间化为灰烬。于是，在他出生之前，他又被放在宙斯的大腿里孕育了几个月，他的出生也成了“二次出生”。这位没有母亲的孩子最初被托付给赫耳墨斯，后来又被赫耳墨斯转移到倪萨山，交由那里的仙女们照顾。潘神的儿子、一位年长的半羊人塞列努斯成了他的老师和伙伴。

狄俄尼索斯的童年时光单纯而快乐、平静而闲散，每天，他穿梭在林木之间，与仙女、半羊人和牧羊人为伴。一次偶然的机会，他发现了一种野生植物，具有提神醒脑的作用，这就是葡萄藤。接下来，他学会了从葡萄藤中提取汁液，制作出了一种令人兴奋的饮品。于是，他开始四处云游，教授人们酿酒之术，他的身边常常跟着成百上千的追随者，仿佛胜利游行一般，他们的足迹到达了叙利亚、埃及、阿拉伯，甚至遥远的印度。

传说狄俄尼索斯曾被一群有眼无珠的海盗们绑架。他将船上的桅杆变成了巨大的葡萄藤，把自己变成了一头狮子，旁边还有一只熊作为助手，空气中则飘荡着唱诗班的仙乐之声。酒神只取了海盗船长的性命，而其余船员早已吓得纷纷弃船逃命，跳入水中后变成了一只只海豚。唯一幸存的下来的是舵手，因为他从一开始就反对其他船员的绑架计划。

当天后赫拉被儿子赫菲斯托斯所制作的神奇宝座困住的时候，据说也是狄俄尼索斯劝说(很可能带着酒去的)这位锻冶之神回到奥林匹斯山,从而解救了天后。此后,赫拉出于感激,将原本只是半神的狄俄尼索斯变成了真正的奥林匹斯之神,允许他永远住在奥林匹斯山上。

荷马称狄俄尼索斯为“男人的快乐源泉”,同样,赫西奥德也说他整天“令人非常快乐”。这些话不无道理,因为正是狄俄尼索斯带给了人们美酒。希腊人喝酒通常都会兑水,在一个大杯子里搅拌一下。他们在宴会上喝酒,在节日里喝酒,在私人聚会上喝酒,特别是在酒会上喝酒。这是一种只有男人参加的非正式聚会,客人们斜倚在沙发上,谈论着从流言到哲学的各类话题。

狄俄尼索斯也是戏剧的保护神。在酒神节的庆典上,各类戏剧节目为他献演。来自希腊各地著名的戏剧家们将他们所创作的古典悲剧或喜剧搬上舞台。人们相信,剧场的出现与酒神狂热有关,那些演员就好比狄俄尼索斯的崇拜者们,他们努力抛开自我,成为他们所要扮演的角色。事实上,在希腊各大剧场里,都有专门留给酒神祭司的座位。

Extra 拓展测试

1. Which of the following do you think is likely to be the Thyrsus?
   你认为下面哪一幅画很可能就是酒神杖?

A

B

2. The Bacchantes, the attendants or followers of the wine god Bacchus, or Dionysus, were noted for their noise and disorder. A most unruly, rowdy crowd, they drank, danced, and sang in a reckless way. The female Bacchantes were notorious for their excessive immodesty and scandalous excitement. In their rabid frenzy and intoxication, they committed atrocious violence. They once tore the most gifted musician into pieces. Do you know the name of the poor musician?

巴克恩提斯(酒神祭司)是酒神巴克斯,即狄俄尼索斯的侍者或随从,以吵闹混乱而著称。他们毫无节制地饮酒、唱歌、跳舞,时常惹是生非。女性酒神祭司也是臭名昭著,她们在酒后极端癫狂的状态下,会完全失去理智,甚至变得残暴。她们曾经将一位天才音乐家撕成了碎片。你知道这位可怜的音乐家叫什么名字吗?

(1. 答案:B)

(2. 答案:俄耳甫斯)

CHAPTER 2 The Myth of Orpheus
第二章　俄耳甫斯的悲情故事

Word Knowledge 词汇知识

Music(音乐)

Music, or *mousike*, was an integral part of life in ancient Greek world. The term covered not only music but dance, lyrics, and epics. A wide range of instruments were used to perform music which was played on all manner of occasions such as religious ceremonies, festivals, symposia, weddings, funerals, and during athletic and military activities. Music was also an important element of Greek education and dramatic performances held in theatres such as plays, recitals, and competitions.

For the ancient Greeks, music was viewed as quite literally a gift from the gods. The invention of specific instruments was attributed to particular deities: Hermes the lyre, Pan the syrinx, and Athena the *aulos*. The mythical figures strongly associated with music include the Nine Muses, and the wine god Dionysus and his followers. Amphion and Thamyris were both famed for their skills playing the *kithara*, whilst Orpheus was celebrated as a magnificent singer and lyre player.

音乐(mousike)是古希腊人生活中不可或缺的部分。这个词不仅仅指音乐,还包括舞蹈、抒情诗和史诗。演奏音乐的乐器种类繁多,场合千差万别,既可以是宗教仪式、节日庆典和宴会酒会,也可以是婚丧嫁娶、体育竞技或军事行动。同时,音乐也是古希腊教育和戏剧演出的重要元素,常常出现在舞台剧、朗诵会和比赛中。

在古希腊人看来，音乐无疑是神的礼物。不同的神发明了不同的乐器：赫耳墨斯发明了里拉琴，潘神发明了排箫，雅典娜发明了竖笛。与音乐密切相关的神话人物还包括九位缪斯女神、酒神狄俄尼索斯和他的追随者们。昂斐勇和塔米里斯均以擅长演奏基萨拉琴而著称，俄耳甫斯则拥有动人的歌喉及高超的里拉琴演奏技巧。

Orphism(俄耳甫斯主义)

Orphism is a mystic religion of ancient Greece, originating in the 6th or 7th century B.C. It is said to be based on poems (now lost) attributed to Orpheus, emphasizing the necessity for individuals to rid themselves of the evil part of their nature by ritual and moral purification throughout a series of reincarnation. Orphism is sometimes referred to as Orphic Mysteries, which is in sharp contrast with Dionysian Mysteries, a term derived from Dionysus or the god of wine. In the below tragic story about Orpheus and Eurydice, Orpheus was eventually torn into pieces by some crazy women called Maenads who were then performing the wild rites of Dionysus. The Dionysian Mysteries advocate liberating the individuals and helping them return to a natural state by using intoxicants and other trance-inducing techniques, such as dancing or music, so that the inhibitions and social constraints could be removed. A Dionysiac frenzy now refers to a state or period of uncontrolled excitement or wild behavior after drinking.

俄耳甫斯主义是古希腊一种神秘的宗教，发端于公元前 6 至 7 世纪。据说该宗教是以俄耳甫斯所创作的诗歌(已失传)为基础建立起来的。这首诗强调个体有必要借助仪式来去除人性中邪恶的部分，并通过一系列的转世轮回使道德得以净化。俄耳甫斯主义有时也被称为俄耳甫斯宗教仪式，它和酒神仪式形成了鲜明的对比，后者源自酒神狄俄尼索斯。在本章关于俄耳甫斯和欧律狄刻的悲情故事中，俄耳甫斯最终被一群疯狂的女子(酒神的女祭司们)撕成了碎片，而这些女子据说当时正处在酒神仪式的过程中。酒神仪式倡导的是解放自我，利用酒精或音乐舞蹈之类有麻醉或致幻作用的手段，来帮助个体摆脱社会的禁锢和束缚。酒神的狂热如今指人在酒后表现出的无法自控的狂躁状态。

The Furies(复仇三女神)

The Furies, or the Erinyes, were three female divinities of vengeance in Greek mythology. They were employed by Hades and Persephone in the underworld to punish and torment those who had committed crimes during their earthly career, and had not been reconciled to the gods before descending to Hades. Now "fury" has become a common noun in English to mean wild or violent anger, and its adjective "furious" is also frequently seen in daily communication.

复仇三女神，或称厄里倪厄斯，是希腊神话中三位代表复仇的女神。她们受雇于冥王和冥后，其工作就是惩罚和折磨那些前世作恶，而死后又没有得到众神宽恕的灵魂。如今 fury 一词在英语中已经成了普通名词，意思是"狂怒"或"暴怒"，而它的形容词形式 furious 也经常出现在人们的日常交流中。

The Myths 神话故事

Orpheus, the son of Apollo and the Muse Calliope, was known as the greatest of all poets and musicians. Having inherited from his father an extraordinary genius for music, he was also a teacher of the religious doctrines known as the Orphic Mysteries. Orpheus married a lovely nymph named Eurydice, the daughter of the sea god Nereus. Their married life was full of joy and happiness, but short-lived.

One day, when Eurydice tried to elude the pursuit of Aristaeus, the half-brother of Orpheus who also loved the beautiful nymph, she stumbled and was bitten in the foot by a poisonous snake hidden in the grass. By the time Orpheus reached her side, she was dead. Following Eurydice's funeral, Orpheus was overcome with a grief the human world could not contain. His longing to rescue her was so strong that he determined to journey to the lower world to entreat Hades to restore his beloved wife.

Armed with only his golden lyre, the gift of Apollo, he descended into the gloomy depths of Hades. When Orpheus reached the gates of the underworld, he began to strum his lyre. The music was so heavenly that Cerberus, the three-headed dog who guards the dead, lay down as Orpheus passed. Charon, the ferry captain who charged dead souls to cross the River Styx, was so moved by the melody that he brought Orpheus across free of charge.

When Orpheus arrived at the palace of Hades and Persephone, the king and queen of the underworld, he began to sing to the sound of his lyre. He sang of his love for Eurydice, saying that she had been taken away too soon. In the moment after Orpheus finished, all the hell stood still. Sisyphus no longer rolled his rock up the hill. Tantalus forgot his perpetual thirst. Even the Furies, the demonic goddesses of vengeance, shed tears.

Hades and Persephone granted Orpheus's plea, but on condition that he should not turn around to see if Eurydice was following behind him until they reached the upper world. Orpheus gladly sang his gratitude, and the reunited couple began their journey back home. Followed by Eurydice, Orpheus climbed the steep and gloomy path which led to the realms of life and light.

All went well until Orpheus was just about to pass the extreme limits of Hades. Forgetting for the moment the hard condition, he turned back to convince himself that his beloved wife was really behind him. The fatal glance destroyed all his hopes of happiness, for, as he yearningly stretched out his arms to embrace her, Eurydice was caught back and vanished from his sight forever. Orpheus endeavored to return to the underworld, but was refused entry this time.

For seven days, Orpheus stayed near the entrance to the underworld without food and drink. Overwhelmed with grief at this second loss, Orpheus swore never to love another woman again. Although he went on to sing songs that would melt the hearts of nearby beasts and mighty trees, he was cold towards the local maidens who were so charmed by him. One day, at his refusing to join them, a group of wild women, in their mad jealousy and fury, attacked Orpheus and tore him to pieces.

In pity for his unhappy fate, the Muses collected his remains, which they buried at the foot of Mount Olympus. The nightingale mourned Orpheus, as did the rivers, who made music as they babbled. While the world wept for the loss of two great souls, Orpheus found peace and his other half in the underworld. There, to this day, he walks with Eurydice along the banks of the River Styx. Sometimes, they stroll side by side, sometimes, she is in front, and sometimes, he takes the lead, turning to look back at her as often as he likes.

俄耳甫斯被公认为最伟大的诗人和音乐家。作为阿波罗和缪斯女神卡利俄珀的儿子，他遗传了父亲极高的音乐天分。此外，他还是俄耳甫斯宗教仪式的导师。俄耳甫斯娶了老海神涅柔斯的女儿，可爱的水宁芙欧律狄刻。他们的婚姻美满幸福，却异常短暂。

阿瑞斯泰俄斯是俄耳甫斯同父异母的兄弟，他也深爱着欧律狄刻。一天，在躲避阿瑞斯泰俄斯的追求时，欧律狄刻绊了一跤，结果脚被草丛中的一只毒蛇咬了一口。等到俄耳甫斯赶到之际，她已经香消玉殒了。埋葬了妻子后，俄耳甫斯的悲伤难以言表，为了唤回爱妻的生命，他决心到地下世界去走一遭，唤回所爱。

他只拿了父亲送给他的那把金色里拉琴，便向着黑暗的深渊出发了。来到冥界的大门口，俄耳甫斯掏出里拉琴开始演奏。那犹如仙乐般的旋律是如此动听，以至于看守大门的三头狗刻耳柏洛斯眼看着俄耳甫斯进门，却一动也没动。而冥河上负责超度亡魂的船夫卡戎也在感动之余，免费将俄耳甫斯渡过了河。

俄耳甫斯来到了冥王哈迪斯和冥后珀尔塞福涅的宫殿前，这次他开始伴着里拉琴歌唱，歌声中饱含了他对欧律狄刻的爱和失去她后的悲伤。歌声结束之时，整个地狱一片寂静：西西甫斯不再推石上山，坦塔罗斯忘记了他永久的饥渴，甚至连复仇三女神都潸然落泪。

冥王和冥后答应了俄耳甫斯的请求，但是有一个条件，就是在他走出冥界之前，他不能回头去看欧律狄刻有没有跟上。俄耳甫斯开心地连连道谢，这对团聚的夫妻踏上了返回光明世界的道路，俄耳甫斯在前，欧律狄刻在后，他们沿着冥界黑暗陡峭的道路向上攀登。

一切似乎都很顺利，可就在俄耳甫斯即将跨出冥府的边界之际，他忘记了那条重要的约定，回过头去想要确认一下心爱的妻子是否在后面。这致命的一瞥将所有幸福的希望全部打破，就在他伸出手去迫切地想要拥抱她的时候，欧律狄刻瞬间从他眼前彻底消失，重新坠入无底的黑暗。俄耳甫斯试图再次进入冥界，但是却再也不被接纳。

整整七天七夜，俄耳甫斯徘徊在冥界的入口处，不吃不喝，再次失去妻子的巨大悲伤让他发誓以后绝不再爱任何其他女人。尽管他仍然弹琴唱歌，那歌声足以融化野兽乃至树木的心，可他对于周围追求他的异性却冷若冰霜。这天，一群遭到拒绝的疯狂女人们，在嫉妒和愤怒的驱使下，野蛮地袭击并撕碎了俄耳甫斯。

缪斯女神怜悯他的不幸遭遇，将他的残躯收集起来，埋葬在奥林匹斯山脚下。夜莺为他唱起挽歌，河水汩汩地流淌，似乎也在重复他所留下的美妙音乐。当全世界都在为两个伟大灵魂的逝去而哀叹之际，俄耳甫斯却终于在冥界找回了他的另一半。直到今天，他依然会和欧律狄刻在冥河边漫步。他们悠闲地走着，时而肩并肩、手拉手，时而一个在前、一个在后，偶尔他还会回过头去，看看她是否安然无恙。

Extra 拓展测试

1. Which of the following do you think is the lyre of Orpheus?
你认为下面哪一把是俄耳甫斯的里拉琴?

A

B

2. *Black Orpheus* is a 1959 romantic tragedy film made in Brazil, which won the 1960 Academy Award for Best Foreign Language Film. Barack Obama, the former American president, mentions in his memoir *Dreams for My Father* (1995) that it was his mother's favorite film. The film is particularly noted for its soundtrack. Do you know which type of music it is?

《黑色俄耳甫斯》是巴西的一部浪漫悲剧影片,制作于1959年,于1960年获得奥斯卡最佳外语片奖。美国前总统奥巴马在他的回忆录《我父亲的梦想》一书中曾提到,这是他母亲最喜欢的电影。这部电影的音乐特别有名,你知道它属于哪种音乐吗?

(1. 答案:A)
(2. 答案:爵士乐)

CHAPTER 3 The Danaids
第三章 达那俄斯的女儿们

Word Knowledge 词汇知识

Marriage in Ancient Greece(古希腊的婚姻)

In Greek mythology, virginity was often considered a virtue denoting purity and physical self-restraint and is an important characteristic. There were three virgin Olympian goddesses: Artemis, Athena, and Hestia. Artemis was known as having a lot of followers who swore off men. Athena's children were literally born from her thoughts. As a result of the meeting of minds, this kind of birth was considered the purest kind of love. Hestia swore to Zeus that she would never marry.

All women were expected to marry, for there was no provision and no role in Greek society for single mature females. Young women were expected to marry as a virgin, and marriage was usually organized by their father or *kyrios* (guardian), who might be an uncle or a male relative. As the couple were often married at puberty, the matching probably had little to do with love. Of course, love may have developed between the young bride and groom, but the best that might be hoped for was *philia*—a general friendship or love sentiment, whereas *eros*, the love of desire, was often sought elsewhere by the husband.

A man would choose his wife based on three things: the dowry, her presumed fertility, and her skills, such as weaving. When a young woman was allowed to marry, the suitors would compete against each other by song, dance, or games for her hand in marriage. The chosen one and the girl's father would then proceed in a process known as *engysis*, meaning "giving of a pledge into the hand", which is like the modern engagement. In Athens the *engysis* or betrothal was in fact indispensable to the complete validity of a marriage contract. Children born from a marriage without such contract would lose their heritable rights.

The wedding day, called the "*gamos*" in Greek, began with nuptial bath in the women's quarters. An honored child would bring water from a nearby river to the bride. This special ceremony was intended to purify the bride and enhance her ability to have children. After the bath, the bride would put on the wedding gown and a veil, a symbol of purity, which was not removed until she was given in marriage to the groom.

在希腊神话中，处女之身是纯洁和自律的表现，代表一种美德和重要的品格。在奥林匹斯诸神中，有三位女神拥有处女之身：阿尔忒弥斯、雅典娜和赫斯提。跟随阿尔忒弥斯的众多女性都发誓远离男人。雅典娜的孩子据说都诞生于她的思想，作为智慧碰撞的产物，他们是最纯洁的爱的结晶。赫斯提向宙斯发誓永不结婚。

在古希腊，年轻女性都必须结婚，因为单身的成年女性既没有收入来源，也不被社会所认可。女孩子在结婚前最好是处女之身，她们的婚姻通常由父亲或监护人，也就是叔伯或某位男性亲属来安排。由于结婚时年龄很小，夫妻间谈不上相爱。当然，爱情是可以培养的，但是小夫妻间一般最多只能获得一种友谊或好感（philia），而爱欲（eros）这种东西，丈夫往往会去别处寻觅。

男人选择妻子的理由一般有三个：嫁妆、生育能力和持家能力，比如女红。一旦某位少女即将出嫁，追求者会通过歌唱、舞蹈或比赛的方式来相互竞争，入选的小伙子随后会和女孩的父亲进入婚誓（engysis）的程序，类似于今天的订婚仪式。在雅典，婚誓或订婚仪式是使婚姻契约合法有效不可或缺的一部分，假如没有这样的过程，那么生下来的孩子就会丧失合法的继承权。

婚礼日在希腊语中被称为gamos，新娘先要沐浴更衣。一位遴选出的儿童会从附近的河里取水供新娘沐浴，这样做的目的是为了洁净身体，促进生育能力。沐浴之后，新娘穿上婚纱，披上象征纯洁的头纱，头纱必须在婚礼当天由新郎亲手揭去。

The Danaids(达那伊得斯)

The Danaids were the fifty daughters of Danaus, king of Argos. All but Hypermnestra murdered their bridegrooms on the wedding night, for which they were condemned eternally. In Hades the forty-nine Danaids were punished to prepare their bridal baths by pouring water forever into a barrel or bathtub full of holes. If something is now compared to the Danaids, it is likely to involve futile work. An example is as follows: *It was like the cask of Danaids into which the public had been pleased to pour its deposits*.

达那伊得斯是阿尔戈斯国王达那俄斯的五十个女儿，除了许珀耳涅斯特拉之外，她们都在新婚之夜谋杀了自己的新郎，为此而遭到永久的天谴。在冥界，四十九位达那伊得斯被罚准备沐浴用水，但是盛水的大桶或浴缸满是破洞，因此永远也没办法装满。如今，假如什么东西被比作"达那伊得斯"，那么其含义很可能是无效的工作，例如："它就像达那伊得斯的竹篮，公众开心地将存款投入其中，最终却可能一无所获。"

The Myths 神话故事

Do you remember Io, the beautiful daughter of the river god Inachus and one of the mortal lovers of Zeus, who had been transformed into a white cow and chased and tormented by Hera incessantly? It was only when she reached Egypt that she eventually found rest and freedom from the persecutions of her enemy. On the banks of the Nile she resumed her original human form and gave birth to a son named Epaphus, who afterwards became king of Egypt, and built the famous city of Memphis. In fact, the royal lines of Egypt and Phoenician, of Argos, Thebes, and Crete, all looked back to Epaphus as their ancestor.

Epaphaus had two great-grandsons: Danaus and Aegyptus. The former fathered fifty daughters, while the latter, fifty sons. Aegyptus expected his sons to marry their cousins, but Danaus refused. He then took himself and his daughters off to live in exile in Argos. To press their claim, Aegyptus and his sons then led an army following them to Greece. Despite the stout resistance of the Argolians, the Egyptians got the upper hand and laid a close siege to the capital, Argos. When the city was about to fall, the fifty maidens, all in their wedding robes, rode out and offered to marry the princes on condition that they withdraw forthwith. The princes, who loved their cousins very much, immediately lifted the siege and returned to their camps.

The mass wedding was to be held that night. Danaus instructed each of his daughters to take a sword and kill the groom on the very night before her virginity could be taken. The vile deed took place as planned—or almost as planned. When morning came, the Egyptians found, to their consternation, that forty-nine of the fifty princes had been stabbed to death in their nuptial chambers, but the fifty daughters and the eldest prince, Lynceus by name, were nowhere to be found. The shock and grief was sufficient to kill Aegyptus and the Egyptians beat a hasty retreat. The fifty maidens came back to the city of Argos to a hero's welcome.

As the Argive king was killed in battle, Danaus became king of Argolis. When he found the body of Lynceus missing, he asked his eldest daughter, Hypermnestra, about the prince's whereabout. Hypermnestra told the truth. Lynceus was an honest young man. Unlike his brothers, he did not wish to consummate the marriage with Hypermnestra before actually won her heart. Moved by his noble love, Hypermnestra disclosed to him the insidious plan of her father, and urged him to seek asylum in a sanctuary.

At this Danaus flew into a rage. He was about to condemn her to death when Aphrodite, the goddess of love, intervened on the maiden's behalf. In due course, Hypermnestra was married to Lynceus. When Danaus died without a male heir, Lynceus succeeded to the throne, and the descendants of their marriage became rulers of Argos, including the great hero Perseus.

The fate of the forty-nine sisters of Hypermnestra could only be defined as miserable. Since they could not avoid marriage forever, Danaus arranged a footrace for all their suitors, and the first across the line took his first choice of woman, the second chose second, and so on, until all forty-nine were accounted for. Nor could the Danaids avoid punishment for their terrible crime: in Hades they were condemned eternally to carry water in a vessel which, being leaky, would never fill.

还记得美丽的河神之女艾奥吗?作为宙斯的一位凡间情人,她被变成了一头白牛,但依然遭到赫拉的追捕和折磨?最终她逃到了埃及,在那里她总算摆脱了情敌的迫害,得以享受安定的生活。在尼罗河畔,她变回了人形,生下了一个儿子名叫厄帕福斯,就是后来的埃及国王,是他建造了著名的埃及古城孟斐斯。事实上,埃及、腓尼基,到阿尔戈斯、底比斯、克里特这些城邦国家的皇室血脉,均可以追溯到厄帕福斯这位祖先。

厄帕福斯有两个曾孙:达那俄斯和埃古普托斯,前者生了五十个女儿,后者生了五十个儿子。埃古普托斯希望自己的儿子能娶他们的堂妹为妻,但遭到了达那俄斯的拒绝。达那俄斯带着自己的五十个女儿离开家乡,流亡到阿尔戈斯生活。埃古普托斯不愿轻易放弃,他和自己的儿子们率领军队一路追到了希腊。尽管阿尔戈斯军队顽强抵抗,但埃古普托斯的埃及军队还是占了上风,他们将都城阿尔戈斯团团包围。眼看着城池即将陷落,五十位穿着婚纱的少女出现在阵前,她们表示愿意嫁给她们的堂兄,但条件是必须立刻撤军。王子们对于这场婚姻都很向往,于是立刻解散了包围圈,撤回到了自己的营地。

集体婚礼就安排在那天夜里。达那俄斯授意自己的女儿每人带一把匕首，在新婚之夜杀死她们的新郎。计划如期进行——或者说，几乎是如期进行的。当清晨来临，埃及人惊恐地发现五十位王子中有四十九位都惨死在洞房之中，而五十位新娘及长公子林瑟斯则不见了踪影。巨大的打击击垮了埃古普托斯，令其丧命，埃及军队仓皇撤退。五十位姑娘回到阿尔戈斯城，受到了英雄凯旋般的热烈欢迎。

由于阿尔戈斯国王丧命，达那俄斯成了新的国王。发现林瑟斯的尸体不见了之后，他叫来大女儿许珀耳涅斯特拉询问缘由，女儿便实话实说。她告诉父亲，林瑟斯是一位诚实的青年，和他的兄弟们不同，他没有强迫她，而是希望在赢得她的芳心之后再和她结合。这让许珀耳涅斯特拉非常感动，她不仅将父亲的阴险计划和盘托出，还催促他快点找一座神庙避一避。

女儿的这番话令达那俄斯勃然大怒，他决定要杀了这个不孝之女。危急时刻，女神阿芙洛蒂忒出现了，她不仅阻止了国王的愚蠢行为，还做主将许珀耳涅斯特拉嫁给了林瑟斯。达那俄斯死后，由于没有男性继承人，林瑟斯便继承了王位。他们两人的后代成了阿尔戈斯的统治者，其中就包括大英雄珀尔修斯。

许珀耳涅斯特那四十九位妹妹的命运只能用悲惨来形容，因为她们不可能一辈子不嫁人，所以达那俄斯便安排求亲者进行了一场脚力竞赛，获得冠军的可以优先选择一个女儿做新娘，亚军就第二个选，以此类推，直到四十九个女儿全部名花有主。而这四十九个姑娘死后全都进入地狱，为她们所犯下的罪行接受惩罚：那就是用一个满是破洞的容器盛满水——一项永远无法完成的任务。

Extra 拓展测试

1. Could you add a few lines to make the following vessel like that of the Danaids?

   你能加上几笔把下面这个水缸变成达那伊得斯的水缸吗？

2. *Crime and Punishment* is a famous novel written by a Russian author and published in 1866. Do you know the name of this Russian novelist?

《罪与罚》是一部由俄国作家创作的、发表于1866年的著名小说。你知道这位俄罗斯作家叫什么名字吗?

(2. 答案:陀思妥耶夫斯基)

CHAPTER 4 Atalanta's Race

第四章 阿塔兰忒的竞赛

Word Knowledge 词汇知识

The Calydonian Boar Hunt(狩猎卡吕冬野猪)

When Artemis was forgotten at a sacrifice by King Oeneus, she was so angry that she sent the Calydonian Boar, a wild boar that ravaged the land, men, and cattle and prevented crops from being sown. Meleager, the son of Oeneus and a hero in Argonautic expedition, felt it his lot to kill the beast. Manlike and hardy, Atalanta offered herself as a member of the band of heroes assembled under Meleager for the dangerous adventure. At first the men demurred to her request, but Meleager, who loved her at first sight, quickly silenced any opposition. The group went on the boar hunt.

The boar rushed right and left, and some warriors met their untimely death. However, the young woman was not to be daunted. Very soon she was able to inflict a severe spear wound on the boar, and Meleager had the honor to thrust his sword into its reeking sides, thus killing it for good. The hide of the boar, promised as the top prize, was duly awarded to Meleager, who then gave it to his beloved. Out of protest and jealousy, two of Meleager's uncles, tried to snatch the skin away from the girl, which enraged the prince who killed them in order to restore the prize to its rightful owner. Wild with grief, Althaea, Meleager's mother, threw a charmed log on the fire, and thus consumed her son's life as it burned.

在一次献祭活动中，国王俄纽斯遗忘了阿尔忒弥斯而令女神异常生气，她派出了卡吕冬野猪到他的国土上肆意破坏、糟蹋庄稼和牲畜，百姓苦不堪言。俄纽斯的儿子墨勒阿格尔曾是阿尔戈号远征的英雄之一，他意识到自己有责任为民除害，而刚强坚毅的阿塔兰忒则主动要求加入他的狩猎队伍。起初，队伍里的男人们都表示反对，但墨勒阿格尔对这位姑娘一见钟情，力排众议，很快，狩猎队伍正式出发。

野猪横冲直撞，不少猎手因躲避不及而被拱死。然而，这位年轻姑娘毫不畏惧，很快，她用一根长矛重重地扎入了野猪的身体，墨勒阿格尔紧随其后，用利剑刺中了野猪的要害部位，野兽终于一命呜呼。作为最高奖赏的野兽皮颁给了墨勒阿格尔，而他却转手送给了自己的心上人。他的两个舅舅对外甥的这种做法非常不满，试图从姑娘手中抢回兽皮，墨勒阿格尔一怒之下，杀死了他们，将兽皮物归原主。墨勒阿格尔的母亲阿尔泰娅悲伤之余，将一块施了魔咒的木头投入火中，随着木头的燃烧殆尽，墨勒阿格尔的生命也随之消亡。

Footrace(竞走)

The Greek word “atalantos” literally means “equal in weight”, which may well be related to the success of Atalanta in various contests with men, such as in hunting, footrace, and wrestling. The ancient Greeks enjoyed sporting events, particularly footracing. Wealthy admirers or spectators would often give large gifts to successful athletes. Though footraces were physically challenging, if successful, athletes could become very rich.

There were many lengths and types of footraces in ancient Greece. The standard distance that these races were measured in was the stade (where one stade is approximately 185 meters), which the mythical founder of Olympic Games could allegedly cover in one breath.

What is called a marathon today gets its name from the 280-mile (451 km) distance covered by the runner Pheidippides over the course of three to four days from Athens to Sparta and then back to Marathon in 490 BC. He was sent to gain the help of the Spartans against the attack of the Persian army in Marathon.

Another event in the ancient Olympic Games was the pentathlon, which was a combination of five events: discus, javelin, jumping, running and wrestling. This race reflected the ancient Greek belief that one's body should be strong as a whole and not just in one area. Aristotle describes a man's ultimate physical beauty as a body capable of enduring all challenges. This is why he viewed the athletes in the pentathlon as the most beautiful of them all.

在希腊语中 atalantos 的意思是"势均力敌",它很好地诠释了阿塔兰忒在与男人们的各种较量,如狩猎、竞走、摔跤中的完美表现。古希腊人热衷于体育运动,尤其是竞走,那些有钱的观众或爱好者常常愿意花重金奖赏比赛的胜利者。因此,虽然竞走是对体力的考验,但是成功者也有可能一夜暴富。

在古希腊,竞走的方式和距离有很多种,一般标准距离的测量单位是"斯塔德"(一个"斯塔德"约为 185 米)。据说这个距离对于传说中的奥运会创始人来说一口气就能走完。

我们今天所说的马拉松比赛始于公元前 490 年,一位名叫斐迪庇蒂斯的希腊士兵在三到四天时间里,先是从雅典跑到斯巴达,后又从斯巴达跑到马拉松,共计跑了 280 英里(451 千米),以恳请斯巴达人共同抵御波斯军队的进攻。

古代奥运会的另一个项目是"五项全能",包括铁饼、标枪、跳高、长跑和摔跤。在古希腊人看来,一个人身体的强壮不应是单一的某个方面,而应是全方位的,这项比赛恰恰是这种思想的反映。亚里士多德将人的极致之美描绘成一个能够承受各种挑战的身体,这也是为什么在他看来,参加"五项全能"的运动员是世界上最美的人。

The Myths 神话故事

An Arcadian king had an ardent desire to have a male heir. When, to his utter frustration, a daughter was born to him, he ordered the baby to be thrown out to die on top of a mountain. A she-bear which happened to be passing by found the little thing interesting and began to suckle it. Later, she was snatched away from the bear's den by hunters, who brought her up as one of their number. Her name was Atalanta. She was a fair and brave girl, but she had a heart every bit as hard as her father's.

But her stony heart was for once stirred to tenderness when she saw Meleager, the handsome son of King Oeneus. To avoid losing him, she joined the Argo as the only woman and played a major part in various adventures of Jason's crew. After the Calydonian boar hunt, Atalanta was rediscovered by her father, who wanted her to be married. As suitors swarmed into the house every day, she declared that she would only be won if someone could outrun her in a footrace. Her hand was to be the reward of the conqueror, but death the penalty of the vanquished.

Since she was the swiftest of foot, she thought that the condition would be enough to scare any suitor away. Nevertheless quite a few came and not willingly died. A spectator, Hippomenes by name, was at first quite skeptical about the wisdom of having to stake so much on the love of a lady, beautiful as she was. But as he watched the delicate form of the maiden rushing along, he was increasingly thrilled by her bewitching beauty. When the fourth youth paid the penalty of the vanquished, Hippomenes announced his intention to enter into the race.

Before he offered himself for the trial, however, the youth had called upon Aphrodite to help him. Having heard his prayers, the goddess gave him three golden apples of the Hesperides, and taught him the artful means of surpassing the cold-blooded maiden. Soon after the youth and Atalanta started to run, all the spectators fell certain that the youth was doomed, because Atalanta had darted far ahead. But very soon all were amazed to see a golden apple fly from Hippomenes' right hand. Atalanta hesitated for a second, but she stopped to pick it up, for curiosity and greed were too strong for her.

Though the youth had run ahead, she had no difficulty catching up. When the second apple was thrown out and Atalanta stopped again to pick it up, she caught up with the young man soon once more and dashed forward. Hippomenes, now panting for breath and about to give up in despair, exerted his last ounce of energy to fling the third apple as far away from the course as possible. When Atalanta went out of her way to snatch up the glittering apple for the third time, she lost out to her fellow runner.

In this way, Hippomenes won the footrace and came to marry Atalanta. They had a son Parthenopaeus, who later was one of the Seven who fought against Thebes. The marriage was a happy but short-lived one, for Hippomenes forgot to pay Aphrodite, his patroness, her dues. The infuriated goddess was not prepared to let the neglect go unpunished. When the young couple was one day passing the temple of Rhea, mother of the gods, Aphrodite aroused such unholy desire in Hippomenes that the youth defiled the holy place with his unlawful lust. Rhea turned them both instantly into lions and harnessed them to her chariot.

阿卡狄亚国王一心想要个儿子，因此，当他看到生下来的是个女儿，便下令将婴儿扔到山顶上，让她自生自灭。一只母熊恰巧经过，发现了这个小东西，便开始给她喂奶。后来，附近的猎人们从熊窝里夺回了孩子，并把她抚养长大。她的名字叫阿塔兰忒，她美丽而勇敢，然而她的心却像她的父亲一样冷酷。

不过，这颗冷酷的心也曾经泛起过温柔的涟漪，那是当她看到英俊的王子墨勒阿格尔的时候。因为害怕失去他，她作为唯一的女性加入了阿尔戈号远征的队伍，并在伊阿宋的数次冒险经历中起到了重要的作用。卡吕冬狩猎结束后，阿塔兰忒被召回了父亲身边，父亲希望她能快点嫁人。面对蜂拥而至的求婚者，阿塔兰忒宣布假如有谁能在竞走中赢过她，她就嫁给他，而如果输了的话，就必须以死谢罪。

作为脚力最佳的姑娘，她认为这样的条件足以吓退所有的求婚者，然而，总有那么大胆前来应战的人，结果自然是因此丢了小命。有一个名叫希波墨涅斯的小伙子，起初对此不屑一顾，认为就算再美，为一个女子丢了性命也未免太可笑了。然而，当他亲眼看到那个骄人的身姿从眼前一闪而过时，他的目光再也离不开她了。眼看着第四位求婚者也败下阵来，希波墨涅斯决定报名参赛。

不过在正式比赛之前，年轻人来到阿芙洛蒂忒面前寻求帮助。听到他的请求，女神给了他三个赫斯珀里蒂斯的金苹果，并秘授他战胜冷血少女之计。不久，比赛正式开始，所有观众都以为小伙子注定会以失败告终，因为阿塔兰忒简直太快了！突然，不可思议的事情发生了：希波墨涅斯右手一挥，一只金苹果飞了出来！阿塔兰忒迟疑了一下，从地上捡起了苹果，毕竟好奇和贪婪是人之常情。

尽管年轻人一度超过了她，但阿塔兰忒毫不费力便追了上来。这时，希波墨涅斯又扔出了第二只苹果，阿塔兰忒再次弯腰捡起来，随后又很快追上了他。此时，希波墨涅斯已经气喘吁吁了，绝望之际，他拼尽全力将第三只苹果扔向了远方，阿塔兰忒不得不离开赛道去捡那只金光闪闪的苹果，最终，她输给了希波墨涅斯。

希波墨涅斯凭借这样的方式赢得了比赛，并迎娶了阿塔兰忒，他们的儿子名叫帕耳忒诺派俄斯，是后来攻打底比斯的七雄之一。他们的婚姻幸福而短暂。传说因为希波墨涅斯忘记了回报帮助了他的女神，令阿芙洛蒂忒恼怒不已，她决定要教训一下这个忘恩负义的家伙。于是有一天，当夫妻俩途经第二代地母瑞亚的神庙时，阿芙洛蒂忒暗地里勾起了希波墨涅斯的欲望之火，两人在神庙中行了不洁之事，这种大逆不道的行为令瑞亚当场将他们都变成了狮子，此后只能套上枷锁替她拉车。

Extra 拓展测试

1. Which of the following was not included in the pentathlon in ancient Greece?
下面哪一个项目不属于古希腊的“五项全能”？

A

B

2. Bears are wild but unique animals, which are popular not only in Greek mythology but also in legends of many cultures around the world including those of Asian, North American and European myths. In 1902, the American President Theodore Roosevelt was on a hunting trip along the Mississippi, but showed mercy to an old bear he could have easily taken as a trophy. The story of this act spread quickly, and led to the birth of a soft toy in his honour. Can you guess the name of this toy?

熊是一种独特的野生动物，无论是在古希腊神话中，还是在亚洲、北美和欧洲的神话传奇中，它都是一种非常受欢迎的动物。1902 年，时任美国总统的西奥多・罗斯福沿着密西西比河打猎，途中因对一只老棕熊心生怜悯，而将到手的战利品放生。这则故事广为流传，后来人们为了纪念它，创造了一种毛绒玩具。你知道这种玩具熊的名字吗？

(1. 答案：B)

(2. 答案：泰迪熊，因为“泰迪”是西奥多的昵称。)

CHAPTER 5 Seven Against Thebes
第五章 七雄联攻底比斯

Word Knowledge 词汇知识

Burial Practices(殡葬传统)

Ancient Greeks believed in gods and the afterlife, so, for them, funerals were an important aspect of the transition from life to death. In order to help the body to enter its afterlife peacefully, they created elaborate burial rituals, which consisted of three parts: the *Prothesis* (laying out the body), the *Ekphora* (funeral procession), and the *Perideipnon* (interment). Although it was dire to perform a proper burial, not having one was insulting to the human pride and a potential sendoff to the dark side of the underworld.

As a general tradition, women were in charge of preparing the body, which was washed, anointed and adorned with a wreath. The mouth was sometimes sealed with a coin, "Charon's obol" or a payment for the ferryman of the dead to convey the soul from the world of the living to the world of the dead. Such burial rites helped people view death not only as something frightening but also beautiful. For the Greeks, immortality lay in continued remembrance of the dead by the living. Death was not the end, but the beginning.

古希腊人相信神，也相信有来生，因此葬礼是由生过渡到死的重要环节。为了帮助死者顺利地进入来世，他们创建了复杂的殡葬仪式，包括三个部分：净化仪式、出殡仪式和入葬仪式。虽然整个丧葬过程压抑肃穆，但是不举行葬礼是对死者尊严的亵渎，是有可能要下地狱的。

根据古希腊的传统，为死者净化身体的工作通常由女人们来完成，包括清洗、敷油和用花圈装饰。他们时常会在死者的嘴里放上一枚硬币，称作“卡戎的银币”，是用来付给冥界船夫的买路钱，超度亡魂从阳世转入阴间。此类丧葬仪式有助于人们更好地看待死亡，在恐惧之外也能感受到一丝美好。对于希腊人来说，永生来自活着的人对于亡者不断的怀念，死亡并不是终点，而是开端。

Necklace of Harmonia(哈耳摩尼亚的项链)

The necklace of Harmonia was a magical object created by Hephaestus, the god of blacksmith, as a curse on the offspring of his wife Aphrodite and her extramarital lover Ares. The exquisite necklace was first given as a wedding gift to Harmonia, daughter of Aphrodite and Ares, when she was married to Cadmus, the first king of Thebes. According to legend, the necklace would make any woman wearing it remain eternally young and beautiful. However, it would bring ill fortune to all of its wearers and owners.

This was how things were, for Harmonia and Cadmus were later both transformed into serpents, and their daughter Semele was destroyed when she foolishly demanded Zeus to reveal his true identity. Oedipus, as well as his descendants and relations, all suffered various personal tragedies due to this family heirloom. It was said that after the expedition against Thebes, the grandsons of Polynices eventually dedicated the necklace to the Temple of Athena at Delphi to prevent further disaster amongst human wearers.

哈耳摩尼亚的项链是由锻冶之神赫菲斯托斯打造的一件神奇首饰，作为他对妻子阿芙洛蒂忒及其婚外恋情人阿瑞斯后代的诅咒。哈耳摩尼亚是阿芙洛蒂忒和阿瑞斯的女儿，因此在她嫁给底比斯的第一位国王卡德摩斯时，这条精致的项链便成了她的结婚礼物。传说戴上这条项链的女人能够永葆青春和美貌，但同时也会给拥有它的人带来厄运。

事实的确如此。因为哈耳摩尼亚和卡德摩斯后来被变成了两条巨蟒，而他们的女儿塞墨勒则在愚蠢地要求宙斯显露真身后活活被烧死。俄狄浦斯以及他的后代亲属皆因这一祖传宝物而厄运不断。据说在七雄攻打底比斯之后，波吕尼克斯的孙子最终将这条项链献给了特尔斐的雅典娜神庙，以避免它继续祸害人类。

Antigone(安提戈涅)

Antigone was the daughter of Oedipus and Jocasta, and the subject of a tragedy by Sophocles, one of the ancient Greek dramatists. She was sentenced to death for defying her uncle Creon, king of Thebes, by giving the dead body of her brother Polynices the last rites of burial herself. The name Antigone in Greek literally means "worthy of one's parents". Here the "parents" should be understood as gods rather than her own parents because what she did, though against the king's order, was in conformity to the principles of the gods.

The prefix "*anti-*" is therefore used to form compounds denoting something either opposed to a particular system or practice, such as in *anti-apartheid*, *anti-abortion*, *anti-American*, or intended to prevent something from happening, such as in *anti-poverty*, *anti-freeze*, *anti-aircraft* etc.

安提戈涅是俄狄浦斯和伊俄卡斯特的女儿，也是古希腊戏剧家索福克勒斯所创作的悲剧人物之一。她因擅自为哥哥波吕尼克斯的尸体行葬礼仪式而冒犯了底比斯国王，自己的舅舅克瑞翁，最终被判了死刑。在希腊语中，安提戈涅这个名字的字面意思是“对得起父母的人”，这里的“父母”并非生身父母，而应当是神，因为她所做的一切虽然违背了国王的命令，却符合神的旨意。

因此，anti-这个前缀用来构成复合词，意思既可以是“反对某种制度或活动”，诸如 anti-apartheid(反种族隔离)、anti-abortion(反堕胎)、anti-American(反美)等，也可以是“试图防止某事发生”，如 anti-poverty(脱贫)、anti-freeze(防冻剂)、anti-aircraft(防空)等。

The Myths 神话故事

Eteocles and Polynices were sons of Oedipus, the king of Thebes who unwittingly killed his father and married his mother. When they came of age, both brothers wanted the throne, so they adopted a compromise that was bound to fail. Each of them would rule for a year, while the other made himself scarce. Eteocles ruled first, with Polynices spending the year in Argos, at the court of king Adrastus. As insurance, he took with him the family heirloom—the fabulous necklace made for Harmonia by Hephaestus.

Nevertheless, at the end of the year, Eteocles refused to give up the throne. Power had gone to his head. During his year of exile Polynices had married one of Adrastus' daughters, so the Argive king now promised to help restore him to his throne. Adrastus assembled an army that was led by seven champions: himself, Polynices, Tydeus, Capaneus, Hippomedon, Parthenopaeus, and the soothsayer Amphiaraus.

The Seven descended on Thebes, the seven-mouthed city well defended by seven warriors, who had volunteered to hold the gates against the enemy. The Seven met the seven Theban champions in single combat to decide the war, one at each of the city's gates. It was an outright victory for the Thebans. Of the Seven, only Adrastus and Amphiaraus survived the failed siege of Thebes. They fled the battlefield. Adrastus made it safely back to Argos, but the earth gaped before Amphiaraus as he was driving his chariot away.

As for the two brothers, Eteocles and Polynices, they traded blows and wounds in a fight that was so close and fierce that in the end they both died. Their uncle Creon, once again the emergency ruler of Thebes, gave orders that Polynices, being a traitor, was not to be honoured with burial. Antigone, the daughter of Oedipus, could not abide this sin against her dead brother. Regardless of warnings from her sister Ismene, she defiantly gave Polynices at least the symbolic burial of three handfuls of dust thrown on his corpse. She preferred the unwritten law of the gods to Creon's edict, and was prepared even to suffer death for it.

Creon was so angry that he had Antigone imprisoned in a cave and left her there to die. His son Haemon, who was in deep love with Antigone, broke in to rescue her, but only to find that she had hanged herself with her girdle. In despair, Haemon slew himself on the spot with his own sword. And Queen Eurydice did the same when she heard of the death of her son. Creon was well repaid for ignoring the gods' wishes.

厄忒俄克勒斯和波吕尼克斯都是俄狄浦斯的儿子,就是那个无意中杀了自己的父亲,娶了自己母亲的底比斯国王。兄弟俩长大成人后,都想继承王位,互不相让,于是选择了一个折中,但注定要失败的办法:每人一年轮流称王。厄忒俄克勒斯先坐上了王位,波吕尼克斯为了避嫌,转而来到阿尔戈斯,成了国王阿德拉斯托斯的手下。作为信物,他随身带着家传的宝物——由赫菲斯托斯专门为哈耳摩尼亚打造的神奇项链。

然而,一年期满,厄忒俄克勒斯却拒绝让出王位,权力欲望已经充斥了他的大脑。而同一年中,流放中的波吕尼克斯娶了阿德拉斯托斯的女儿,因此得知此事后,阿尔戈斯国王承诺帮助女婿夺回王位。阿德拉斯托斯召集了一支精锐部队,由包括他自己在内的七名强悍勇士组成,另外六名是:波吕尼克斯、提丢斯、卡帕纽斯、希波墨冬、帕耳忒诺派俄斯和占卜师安菲阿拉俄斯。

七雄突袭了底比斯。这座城池有七个城门,每个城门分别由一位武士自愿把守。于是,一对一的较量成为决定战争胜利的关键。结果,底比斯人完胜。七雄之中,只有阿德拉斯托斯和安菲阿拉俄斯在围攻底比斯的战斗中得以幸存,两人逃离战场后,前者成功地回到了阿尔戈斯,而后者则在驾驶战车狂奔的半路上,突然遭遇地面塌陷,连人带车一起消失不见了。

至于厄忒俄克勒斯和波吕尼克斯两兄弟，由于在搏斗中势均力敌，两败俱伤，双双毙命。他们的舅舅克瑞翁在非常时期再次成为底比斯国王，他下令称波吕尼克斯是忤逆者，将不得下葬。俄狄浦斯的女儿安提戈涅认为如此对待死去的兄长是对神旨的公然藐视，她不顾姐姐伊斯墨涅的警告，来到战场上为曝尸荒野的哥哥行殡葬之礼。尽管只是象征性地撒了三把土到尸体上，她认为这是神所制定的不成文法规，所以即便这与克瑞翁的命令背道而驰，她也要这么做。

克瑞翁大为震怒，下令将安提戈涅关进一个洞穴里饿死她。他的儿子希门深深爱着安提戈涅，闯进洞穴试图营救她，却发现自己的心上人业已香消玉殒，她用身上的腰带结束了自己年轻的生命。悲痛欲绝的希门不愿独活在世上，他举起手中的宝剑自刎而死。王宫里，得知儿子的死讯，欧律狄刻王后也追随儿子而去。克瑞翁品尝到了因违背神旨而自酿的苦果。

Extra 拓展测试

1. The necklace of Harmonia was usually described as a sparkling chain made of gold and ornamented with various jewels, in the shape of two serpents whose open mouths formed a clasp. Could you add a few lines to make the following picture the necklace of Harmonia?

   哈耳摩尼亚的项链通常被描绘成一条闪闪发光的金项链，上面装饰着各类珠宝，构成两条蛇的形状，蛇口相交构成一个搭扣。你能将下图加上几笔，让它变成一条哈耳摩尼亚项链吗？

2. *The Necklace* is a famous short story and morality tale written in 1884 and widely read in classrooms throughout the world. Do you know who wrote this short story?

《项链》是一篇著名的短篇小说和道德故事，创作于 1884 年，曾在全世界的课堂上被广泛阅读。你知道这部短篇小说的作者是谁吗？

（2. 答案：法国作家莫泊桑）

FURTHER READING　Sisyphus
延伸阅读　西西弗斯

Sisyphus was known in Greek mythology as a complicated and crafty figure who was doomed to forever rolling a huge boulder up a steep hill in the Underworld. Each time when he was near the top of the hill, the boulder would fall miraculously back of its own weight, forcing Sisyphus to repeat the futile labor endlessly. This eternal task was imposed on him as a punishment for his misdeeds in life, particularly his continual cheating and scorn of the gods.

Being the son of the windgod Aeolus, Sisyphus was the founder and the first king of Ephyria, which was said to be the original name of Corinth. He first came to the attention of the gods as being a cruel and ruthless tyrant. Instead of showing hospitality and generosity on his guests, he occasionally broke the *xenia* by killing them, and thus making Zeus, the king of gods who was in charge of maintaining *xenia*, very displeased.

However, Sisyphus appeared to be a good king who cared about his people and the land. When Aesopus, a river god and son of Poseidon, complained to him about the sudden disappearance of his daughter Aegina, Sisyphus, who knew the girl had been abducted by Zeus, promised to tell him about it on the condition that an eternal spring for his city was created. To the celestial thunderbolts he preferred the benediction of water.

Incensed by such bold revelation of the divine secrets, Zeus ordered Thanatos, the god of death, to bring Sisyphus to Hades. When he was confronted by Thanatos, Sisyphus pretended to have great interest in the chain Thanatos held in hand and asked him how it worked. Thanatos, unaware of the artifice, was then tricked into demonstrating the use of it by trapping himself in his own chain. So it turned out that the god of death was kept locked up in a closet at Sisyphus' house for many a day.

Now with Death being a prisoner of Sisyphus, no one on earth would die. Even a soldier being chopped to bits in battle could still show up later at a camp for dinner. In the end, Ares, the god of war, found it so unbearable that he had to intervene. So Death was liberated. Then he would go on to complete his mission by fetching Sisyphus. But once again the wily mortal king had another trick up his sleeve.

Knowing that he would not be able to keep Thanatos for long, Sisyphus instructed his wife, Merope, to leave his corpse unburied and forgo the necessary funerary rites. Once in the land of the dead, Sisyphus approached Persephone, the queen of the dead, and complained to her about what his wife had done to his body. He requested to be sent back to the realm of the living so that he could punish his wife. The request was granted.

Having returned to the mortal world, Sisyphus no longer wanted to go back to the infernal darkness. Recalls, signs of anger, warnings were of no avail. Many years more he lived facing the curve of the gulf, the sparkling sea, and the smiles of the earth. A decree of the gods was necessary. Hermes came and seized the impudent man by the collar and, snatching him from his joys, led him forcibly back to the underworld, where his rock was ready for him.

The gods had the last laugh indeed, yet, to some extent, Sisyphus was a hero, an absurd hero though. His scorn of the gods, his hatred of death, and his passion for life won him that unspeakable penalty in which the whole being was exerted toward accomplishing nothing. The torture was the price that must be paid for the passion of this earth. But the myth was tragic only at rare moments because there is no fate that cannot be surmounted by scorn.

在希腊神话中,西西弗斯以性格复杂、诡计多端而著称。他命里注定要将一块巨石推上陡峭的山坡,而每一次他快要到达山顶的时候,那块巨石就会神奇地自动滚落,迫使西西弗斯从头再来。这项永无止境的工作是众神给他的惩罚,为了他在阳世所做的坏事,尤其是对众神的反复欺骗及嘲弄。

西西弗斯是风神埃俄罗斯的儿子,也是埃佛勒的创立者和首位国王,据说埃佛勒就是科林斯原来的名字。首先引起众神注意的是西西弗斯的残酷和专制。他不愿遵循待客之道,在客人面前,不仅小气吝啬,甚至有时还会杀了他们。而众神之王宙斯恰恰是主司待客礼仪的,这种对神礼的违背和藐视无疑令他非常不满。

然而,作为国王的西西弗斯似乎还是不错的,既体恤百姓,又爱护城池。这天,波塞冬的儿子,河神伊索普斯向他抱怨自己的女儿埃伊娜突然消失不见了。西西弗斯知道姑娘是被宙斯掳走了,于是他向伊索普斯保证,只要河神给他的城池造出一口生命之泉,他便将事情的真相和盘托出。相比天神的雷雨,西西弗斯更喜欢河水的滋润。

这种将神的秘密公之于众的大胆行为彻底激怒了宙斯,于是他下令让死神萨纳托斯将西西弗斯打入地狱。当萨纳托斯出现在西西弗斯面前时,后者假装对他手里的铁链很感兴趣,询问他这个东西怎么用。萨纳托斯不知是计,就演示给他看,最终被自己的铁链锁住而动弹不得。结果死神被关在西西弗斯家的壁橱里,一待就是好多天。

既然死神成了西西弗斯的囚徒,那么尘世的人们都不会死,甚至连战争中被大卸八块的士兵,随后依然会出现在野外的餐桌旁。终于,战神阿瑞斯再也看不下去了。他从中干涉,将死神放了出来。获得自由的死神紧接着便将西西弗斯抓获归案。想不到的是,这个狡猾的人类国王还留着一手。

西西弗斯料到了自己没办法长时间控制死神,他嘱咐妻子美罗珀在自己死后不要把尸体下葬,也不要举行任何葬礼仪式。待他真正进入冥界后,他便立刻跑到冥后珀尔赛福涅面前诉苦,指责妻子行为不端,让自己曝尸荒野,并请求允许他回到阳界去教训一下自己的妻子。冥后答应了。

重返人间的西西弗斯哪里还愿意再回到那阴森的地狱里去,他对于所有的呼唤、愤怒和警告充耳不闻。就这样,他又享受了很多年日升月落的幸福时光。神的法令岂容如此藐视。最终赫耳墨斯出现了,他一把拎起这个家伙的领子，将这个胆大妄为的人强行带离阳世，再次投入哈迪斯的领地，在那里，一块巨石正等待着他。

虽然众神的确笑到了最后，但从某种程度上来说，西西弗斯算得上一个英雄，一个略显滑稽的英雄。他对神的藐视、对死的仇恨和对生的渴望，最终换来了一场徒劳无功、永无止境的惩罚。这种折磨是他必须付出的代价。然而，我们很难说这则故事是出悲剧，因为没有一种命运是嘲讽和藐视所不能战胜的。

Extra 拓展测试

Derived from the myth of Sisyphus, Sisyphean is now used as a common adjective, as in the following sentence: *One evening I found him in his chamber engaged upon his Sisyphean labour of "tidying up".* Can you try to translate it into proper Chinese?

Sisyphean 这个词源自西西弗斯的神话故事，但它如今已经被当作普通的形容词来使用了，例如下面这句话："One evening I found him in his chamber engaged upon his Sisyphean labour of 'tidying up'."你能试着把它翻译成中文吗？

（答案：一天晚上，我发现他在屋里徒劳地收拾整理。）

PART Ⅶ Myth and Fantasy

第七部分

神话与奇幻

扫一扫，听本部分音频

CHAPTER 1 Eros and Psyche
第一章 厄洛斯和普赛克

Word Knowledge 词汇知识

Eros(厄洛斯)

Eros was the Greek god of carnal love. In Latin, his name was Amor (love) or Cupid (desire). Eros was the constant companion, or, in some versions, son of Aphrodite, the goddess of love and fertility. While lighting the flame of love in the hearts of gods and men, armed with either a bow and arrows or a flaming torch, he himself lost his heart to the breathtaking beautiful Psyche.

In art, Eros is often portrayed as a winged and chubby boy with a bow and arrow. Such a figure is also known as a "putto". Putti (plural form of putto) are frequently depicted together, and in such cases they are not always involved with love. A blindfolded Eros usually stands for lust. Alternately, when he slumbers, it means suppressed sensuality. Two putti fighting each other could represent Eros and his opposite, Anteros, the requited love. Eros with a torch held downward is a symbol of death.

厄洛斯是希腊神话中代表肉体之爱的神。在拉丁语中,他的名字叫阿莫尔(爱)或丘比特(欲望)。厄洛斯是陪伴阿芙洛蒂忒的助手,在有些神话版本中,也被认为是这位主司爱情和生育的女神的儿子。他手持弓箭或燃烧的火炬,在人与神中间点燃爱的火种,而他自己的心则为美丽绝伦的普赛克所倾倒。

在艺术作品中,厄洛斯常被塑造成一个拿着弓箭、长着翅膀的胖嘟嘟的小男孩，这种形象也被称为“布托(putto)”。布提(putti，布托的复数)经常成对出现，但是这样的布托并非总和“爱”有关。蒙着眼睛的厄洛斯往往代表着“色欲”，而睡眠中的他则意味着“禁欲”；两个打架的布提可以理解为厄洛斯和他的弟弟安忒洛斯(回报的爱)；手举向下火把的厄洛斯则是死亡的象征。

Anteros(安忒洛斯)

There is a myth about Anteros, the younger brother of Eros. Aphrodite worried about Eros being small in stature, so she took the advice of Themis by giving Eros a brother as his playmate. Curiously, Eros began to grow and thrive in company with Anteros. The word Anteros in Greek means requited love, or love returned. The rationale behind the myth is that love must be answered if it is to prosper.

有一则关于厄洛斯的弟弟，安忒洛斯的神话，说阿芙洛蒂忒因为担心厄洛斯长不大，便听从西弥斯的建议，给他一个弟弟作为玩伴。有意思的是，在安忒洛斯的陪伴下，厄洛斯果真开始快速地长大。在希腊语中，安忒洛斯的意思是“爱的回报”或“回报的爱”。这则故事告诉我们：爱要成长，必须得到回应。

Psyche(普赛克)

Psyche was a mortal girl with stunning beauty which made people worship her instead of the goddess Aphrodite. Due to jealousy of her, Aphrodite plotted to ruin Psyche. Although the story has a happy ending, the union between Eros and Psyche has not at all been easy. The myth signifies that Psyche, which is the Greek word for the soul, must be purified by the chastening sorrows and sufferings of its earthly career before it can be reunited with Eros, the symbol of love, and its original divine essence.

Apart from the meaning of soul or mind, the word psyche in modern English may also be interpreted as self. There are such words as *psychology*, *psychiatry*, *psychoanalysis* etc.

普赛克是一个拥有惊人美貌的凡人女子,由于人们崇拜她而忽视了阿芙洛蒂忒,令女神心生嫉妒,于是设计陷害普赛克。虽然故事的结局是完美的,但是厄洛斯和普赛克结合的过程却并不容易。这则神话传递出如下信息:在希腊语中代表灵魂的普赛克在与爱情化身的厄洛斯结合之前,必须经历人世间痛苦磨难的洗涤,才能找回自身原始的神圣品质。

除了可以表示灵魂或心理外,psyche 这个词在当代英语中还有"自我"的含义,可以构成诸如 psychology(心理学)、psychiatry(精神病学)、psychoanalysis(心理分析)这样的词。

The Myths 神话故事

As a genre of children literature, fairy tales are generally defined as stories about fairies or other magical creatures, while myths are stories of deities handed down through history. Therefore, many popular fairy tales had in fact been inspired by ancient mythology. The myth from which fairy tale writers have drawn most inspiration must be the love story between Eros and Psyche.

In this myth, Eros, the lovegod and son of Aphrodite, was not a naked infant as what is often portrayed in modern artistic works, but a handsome young man who had sparkling wings to fly. One day, Aphrodite asked her son to shoot his gold-tipped arrow into a girl named Psyche to make her fall in love with a monster, for the goddess was jealous of the radiant beauty of the mortal girl. However, even Eros himself was bewitched when he caught sight of the girl and decided to take her as his own lover.

With the help of Zephyrus, god of the west wind, Eros kept Psyche in a grand palace. Every night, he would come and meet his dear lover in darkness, but he wouldn't allow her to see him and warned her not to do that. Psyche felt curious and lonely. To relieve her homesickness, Eros agreed to let her two sisters come and visit her. Upon seeing the magnificent palace with plenty of riches, her two sisters became maliciously jealous. They coaxed Psyche into believing that her lover must be an ugly and frightful monster.

Driven by strong inquisitiveness and fear, Psyche rose in the dead of night, taking a lamp in one hand and a dagger in the other and tiptoed to the bed of her lover. The beauteous form of the love god greeted her view. As she was trying to take a close look at him, a drop of burning oil fell on his shoulder, which alarmed and woke him. Sorrowfully reproaching her for her treacherous design, Eros spread out his wings and flew away. Then the palace vanished with him.

In desperate yearning for her lost love, Psyche wandered all over the world in search of Eros. At length she appealed to Aphrodite to take compassion on her, but the goddess of beauty imposed upon her the hardest tasks, such as sorting out the various seeds and grains she had mixed together, fetching a lock of golden fleece from the sheep grazing on a steep mountain side, or filling a crystal urn from the icy source of Cocytus. Although appeared impossible, Psyche accomplished each task with the assistance of some invisible beneficent beings.

At last Aphrodite commanded Psyche to descend into the underworld, and obtain from Persephone a box containing all the charms of beauty. Again Psyche got help and instructions from a mysterious voice and eventually found the box. Despite the fact that she had followed all the injunctions from that voice, she neglected the last warning of not opening the box. Unable to resist the curiosity that devoured her, Psyche raised the lid of the box with eager expectation. Out from the casket issued a dense black vapour, which threw her immediately into a death-like sleep.

Fortunately, Eros awoke her out of the swoon with the point of one of his golden arrows. Then he went to Zeus for help. The father of gods and men eventually persuaded Aphrodite to reconcile with the girl whose status had been elevated to that of the immortals. A grand feast was spread to celebrate the eternal union of the pair. Psyche was happy in the embrace of her love again.

作为儿童文学的一种形式，童话一般是指关于仙女或其他神奇生物的故事，而神话则是历史上流传下来的关于神的故事。因此，许多家喻户晓的童话故事其实是受古代神话故事的启发而创作出来的，其中对童话创作影响最大的一则神话无疑是厄洛斯和普赛克的爱情故事。

在这则神话故事中，爱神厄洛斯并不是现代艺术作品中常见的裸体婴儿形象，而是一位有着闪光翅膀的英俊少年。一天，他的母亲阿芙洛蒂忒出于嫉妒，让他用金头的箭去射一位名叫普赛克的凡间女孩，使她爱上一头野兽，没想到，厄洛斯自己却被女孩惊人的美貌所吸引，决定将她占为己有。

在西风之神仄斐若斯的帮助下，厄洛斯将普赛克带到了一座华丽的宫殿里。每天夜晚，他都会在黑暗中与她相会。但是，他警告女孩不要试图看他的长相，普赛克感到既好奇又孤单，为了缓解她的相思之苦，厄洛斯允许她的两个姐姐前来看望她。当她的两个姐姐看到如此金碧辉煌的宫殿后，她们心生妒忌，于是极力贬低普赛克的爱人，让她相信那个人一定是一个恐怖的丑八怪。

夜深人寂，在强烈的好奇和恐惧驱使下，普赛克一手举着油灯，一手拿着匕首，蹑手蹑脚地来到厄洛斯的床前，映入眼帘的是一张无与伦比的美丽面孔。正当她想仔细端详一下时，一滴油落在了厄洛斯的肩上。惊醒后的爱神非常难过，他责备普赛克违背了诺言，随后便张开翅膀飞走了，整座宫殿也随之消失不见。

普赛克四处奔赴，想要找回自己的爱人，最后她来到阿芙洛蒂忒面前，请求她的帮助。然而，美丽的女神却将一连串最艰难的差事指派给她，例如将混在一起的种子和谷粒分开，到悬崖边吃草的羊身上去取一把金色的羊毛，将冰冷的科赛特斯河上的水晶缸填满等。尽管每一项任务看上去都难以完成，但是在某些看不见的好心人的帮助下，普赛克却神奇地把它们一一完成了。

最后，阿芙洛蒂忒要求普赛克前往冥界，从冥后珀尔塞福涅那里取回一只装着所有美丽的盒子。一个神秘的声音再次帮助并引导了普赛克，使她成功地找到了盒子。尽管她听从了来自那个声音的所有指令，但她却忽略了最后一个警告：不要打开盒子。无法抗拒的好奇心让普赛克急切地打开了盒子的盖子，从盒子里飘出一阵浓密的黑雾，普赛克立刻陷入了死一般的沉睡。

幸运的是，厄洛斯用他的金箭头将沉睡中的普赛克唤醒，随后向宙斯寻求帮助。人神之父赋予了女孩不朽之身，并最终说服阿芙洛蒂忒与之和好。为了庆祝有情人终成眷属，奥林匹斯山上举行了盛大的婚宴，普赛克为重新回到爱人怀抱而兴奋不已。

Extra 拓展测试

1. Which of the following putti represents death?
   下面哪个布提代表了死亡？

A

B

2. Which popular fairy tale does this myth remind you of?
这则神话故事让你想到了哪个著名的童话故事呢?

(1. 答案:B)
(2. 答案:《美女与野兽》《灰姑娘》《睡美人》)

CHAPTER 2 Those Strange Creatures

第二章　奇怪的生物

Word Knowledge 词汇知识

Unicorn(独角兽)

If you have ever watched some fantastic films, such as *The Lord of the Rings*, *The Chronicles of Narnia*, and the *Harry Potter* series, you must have noticed some strange creatures in the stories. In fact, the creatures contained in these works are largely derived from or greatly inspired by Greek mythology: centaur, minotaur, satyrs, nymph, Pegasus, Cerberus, dragon, mermaid ... to name a few.

While many mythic creatures are man-eating monsters or evil spirits, others, like unicorns, are powerful and peaceful. Over two thousand years ago, Greek travelers told tales of unicorns living in far-off lands. They caused no harm to humans, but such a favor was returned only by human hunting unicorns and luring them into traps. The reason for that was the magical properties of the unique horn, which was believed to range from detecting and neutralizing poisons and curing fevers to prolonging youth and acting as an aphrodisiac.

The word "unicorn" consists of two parts: the prefix *uni-*, meaning "one", and the root *corn*, "horn". As a productive prefix, *uni-* is used to form such English words as *universe*, *uniform*, *university*, *unicycle*, *unify* etc. Its Greek equivalent was *mono-*, which appears in words like *monologue*, *monotonous*, *monorail*, *monolingual*, *monopoly*, *monogamy* etc.

假如你看过《指环王》《纳尼亚传奇》《哈利波特》这类奇幻电影的话，你一定对故事中那些奇怪的生物留有印象。事实上，这些故事中的怪物大多源自希腊神话，或者多多少少受到希腊神话的启发，比如：半人马、牛头怪、半羊人、仙女、飞马珀加索斯、三头狗刻耳柏洛斯、喷火龙、美人鱼等。

虽然许多神话中的生物都是吃人的怪物或邪恶的精灵，但也不乏像独角兽这类强大却温和的物种。在两千多年前的古希腊就有关于独角兽的记载，它们居住在遥远的地方，对人类毫无恶意，然而，这份友好换来的却是人类四处设置的陷阱、对它们的大肆捕杀。原因就在于它们那神奇的独角，古人相信独角兽的角能够检测并中和毒剂、治疗发烧、延缓衰老、刺激性欲。

单词 unicorn（独角兽）包含两部分：前缀 uni-的意思是“一”，词根 corn 的意思是“角”。uni-是一个很常见的词缀，可以构成诸如 universe（宇宙）、uniform（制服）、university（大学）、unicycle（独轮车）、unify（统一）这些词。而与之对应的希腊词缀 mono-则构成了 monologue（独白）、monotonous（单调的）、monorail（单轨列车）、monolingual（单一语言的）、monopoly（独裁）、monogamy（一夫一妻制）等。

Pan(潘神)

The word “panic” is defined as sudden and uncontrollable fear or anxiety, which is derived from Pan, the Greek god of flocks and herds. As Pan possessed a frightful and most discordant voice, his sudden appearance was supposed to cause terror similar to that of a frightened and stampeding herd. It is said that Pan assisted Athenian victory over the Persians at Marathon by making the Persians panic and flee.

The name of Pan literally means “all”, from which derived such words as *panorama*, *panacea*, *panoply*, *pan-Pacific*, *pantheism*, *pandemonium*, *pancosmism*, *pandemic*, etc.

单词 panic 表示突然、不由自主的害怕和恐慌，该词汇源自希腊放牧之神潘。因为他的嗓音刺耳吓人，他一出现就会引起恐慌，使得羊群受惊四处奔逃。据说在马拉松战役中，潘令波斯人恐慌奔逃，从而帮助雅典人赢得了胜利。

潘的名字原意是"所有"，由它构成的词汇包括 panorama（全景）、panacea（万灵药）、panoply（全副盔甲）、pan-Pacific（泛太平洋）、pantheism（泛神论）、pandemonium（大混乱）、pancosmism（泛宇宙论）、pandemic（大范围流行）等。

Ixion's Wheel(伊克西翁之轮)

Ixion, the king of Thessaly, was said to be the father of the centaurs. As suggested by his name, Ixion was a hot-tempered man, who first killed his father-in-law, and then attempted to seduce Hera. Zeus transformed a cloud into his wife, which the impious king made love to and impregnated. To punish him, the infuriated Zeus cast Ixion down to the underworld and had him bound to a fiery wheel, which rolled unceasingly for all eternity.

Ixion's wheel, a symbol of eternal punishment, can now be used to connote a torture or a painful method of execution as in the following example: *He was so brave to face the Ixion's wheel that he refused to tell anything to the enemy.*

据说塞萨利国王伊克西翁是所有半人马的祖先。正如他的名字所暗示的那样，伊克西翁是一个脾气暴躁的人，他先是杀了自己的岳父，后来又对赫拉图谋不轨。宙斯将一朵云变成妻子的模样来试探伊克西翁，结果伊克西翁不仅奸污了"她"，还使"她"怀了孕。宙斯勃然大怒，为了惩罚伊克西翁，将他投入地狱，并下令将他绑在一个不停滚动的火轮之上，永无脱身之日。

伊克西翁之轮作为永久惩罚的象征，如今可以用来形容折磨或酷刑，例如："面对酷刑他表现得异常勇敢，拒绝向敌人透露半个字。"

The Myths 神话故事

Centaurs are ancient Greek chimeras, half man and half horse. They are defined by a blend human and horse characteristics, which might take a number of different shapes. Generally speaking, their ears are pointed, their hair, unruly, and their skin, browned by the sun. Early on, the centaurs lived a savage and artless lifestyle, but a handful of centaurs rose above their beast-like brothers to become allies of Greek heroes and gods.

Chiron was by far the most notable centaur. According to an archaic myth, Chiron was sired by the Titan Cronus when he had taken the form of a horse and impregnated the nymph Philyra. Unfortunately, his parents were horrified when they saw his chimeric form, and abandoned him at birth. It was Apollo and Artemis who took pity on the orphan and raised him, teaching him their knowledge and skills as well as the rules of civilization. A great healer, astrologer, and a respected oracle, Chiron was said to be the first among centaurs and was highly revered as a teacher and a tutor. Among his pupils were many of the Greek finest heroes, such as Theseus, Achilles, Jason, Perseus, and sometimes Heracles.

After training dozens of heroes, the noble and immortal Chiron met a painful death. Heracles, one of his beloved students, had brought a new weapon for Chiron to examine: a spear poisoned by the blood of Medusa. The spear accidentally struck Chiron in the hoof and he was immediately wracked with pain from the poison. As an immortal, he couldn't die, even though he was in terrible pain, so he had to come up with a creative way to exit the world. He offered his life to Zeus, but, in exchange, he asked the king of the gods to allow Heracles to free Prometheus. The sacrifice was accepted, and Chiron passed into the stars as the constellation of Centaurus or Sagittarius.

The satyrs were a race of woodland spirits. In Greek art they were represented as a man with a horse's ear and tail, but in Roman representations as a man with a goat's ears, tail, legs and horns. Being the companions of Dionysus, the god of wine, they were the original party animals. Their chief was Silenus, who was the tutor of Dionysus. Due to their love of wine, they are often depicted as holding wine cups, and their image tend to appear on the decoration of wine cups.

Pan, the god of fertility, and the patron of shepherds and huntsmen, had the appearance of a satyr. Like Chiron, Pan was also abandoned by his mother, a wood nymph, right after birth, but Hermes, his father, took him to Olympus, where he became popular among the immortals. He was named Pan (all) because he had delighted them all.

Pan was a great lover of music. The myth about the origin of Pan's pipe was related to a beautiful nymph called Syrinx. Appalled at his terrible appearance, the nymph fled from her unwelcome suitor. Pan pursued her to the bank of the river Ladon. Just as Pan was about to seize her, Syrinx, feeling escape impossible, called on the gods for assistance, who, in answer to her prayer, transformed her into a reed. In memory of his lost love, Pan, by cutting seven of the reeds of unequal length and joining them together, produced the famous pipe, called the syrinx.

半人马是古希腊人虚构出来的一种半人半马的生物,他们兼具人和马的特质,这些物质表现在不同的方面。一般来说,他们有尖尖的耳朵、毛发蓬乱、皮肤黝黑。早期的半人马都过着野蛮而粗糙的生活,后来,他们中的一小部分开始脱离野兽似的同伴,成为希腊诸神和英雄们的盟友。

喀戎可以说是迄今为止最著名的半人马了。根据古神话记载，喀戎的父亲是提坦巨人克罗诺斯，他化身为马让仙女斐莱拉怀上了身孕，生下了喀戎。不幸的是，刚一出生，他的父母就因为他奇怪的样子而抛弃了他。是阿波罗和阿尔忒弥斯可怜这个孤儿，领养了他，并教给他知识、技能以及文明礼仪。据说在所有的半人马中，喀戎是第一位治疗师、占星师和德高望重的神谕司，同时，他也是一位颇受推崇的老师和私教，培养出了众多希腊最杰出的英雄，例如忒修斯、阿喀琉斯、伊阿宋、珀耳修斯等，有时还包括海格立斯。

在培养出了十多位希腊英雄之后，喀戎这位高贵且原本拥有不死之身的仁师却痛苦地离世了。一天，喀戎的爱徒海格立斯带给他一件新武器让他检验：一把沾了美杜莎血的长矛。一不留神，长矛刺中了喀戎的马蹄，矛尖的毒液瞬间令喀戎痛苦不堪，然而，即便苦不堪言，他依然不会死去，因此，他决定以一种特殊的方式告别这个世界。他来到宙斯面前，提出将自己的生命与普罗米修斯的生命进行交换，请求允许海格立斯去解救普罗米修斯。宙斯成全了他，牺牲后的喀戎升上天空，变成了我们熟知的人马座或射手座。

半羊人是一种生活在林地的精灵。在希腊的艺术作品中，他们的形象是拥有马耳和马尾的人，而古罗马人则把他们描绘成拥有羊耳、羊尾、羊蹄和羊角的人。他们是酒神狄俄尼索斯的同伴，是最早的派对动物。他们的族长塞列努斯是酒神的老师，由于对杯中物的喜爱，他们高举酒杯的形象时常作为装饰出现在各类酒具器皿上。

拥有半羊人之身的潘既是生育之神，也是牧羊人和狩猎者的保护神。和喀戎一样，潘也是一出生就遭到母亲林木仙女的遗弃，好在其父赫耳墨斯把他带到了奥林匹斯山，在那里他成了众神的宠儿，大家叫他“潘(所有)”，因为他能给所有人带来欢乐。

潘酷爱音乐。关于潘神的排箫，有这样一则神话故事，讲的是潘爱上了一位名叫绪任克斯的美丽仙女，但他的丑陋相貌吓跑了对方。潘不死心，一路追到拉冬河畔，眼看潘就要抓住自己了，绝望中的仙女大声求助，诸神听到她的呼唤，便把她变成了一排芦苇。为了纪念这段逝去的爱情，潘将那些芦苇削得长短不一后重新排列组合，制作成了著名的绪任克斯排箫。

Extra 拓展测试

1. Which of the following do you identify as Pan's pipe?
   你觉得以下哪一幅图是潘神的排箫?

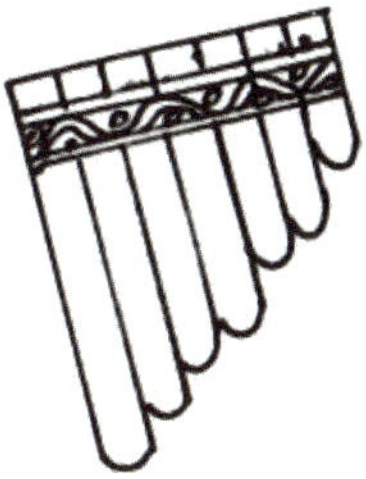

A

B

2. The word "centaur" is sometimes transliterated into Chinese *shentuo*, which literally means a magical camel, but the image of *shentuo* in Chinese culture is a world different from that of a centaur in Greek mythology. There is a legendary story about *shentuo* helping a Mongolian warrior-ruler climb an unsurmountable mountain in ancient China. Can you guess the name of this Mongolian conqueror?

   单词centaur(半人马)有时会被音译成汉语的"神驼",字面意思就是"神奇的骆驼",然而,中国文化中的"神驼",其形象与希腊神话中的半人马相去甚远。在古代中国,有一个传奇故事讲的是一位蒙古领袖得到神驼的帮助,从而翻过了一座无法逾越的高山,你能猜出这位蒙古征服者是谁吗?

(1. 答案:A)

(2. 答案:成吉思汗)

CHAPTER 3 The Labyrinth

第三章 迷宫的故事

Word Knowledge 词汇知识

Labyrinth(迷宫)

Labyrinth is a complex structure and an ancient archetype dating back 4,000 years or more. All the labyrinth stories owe their credit to the labyrinth on Crete in which the Minotaur was kept. This labyrinth was invented by Daedalus, a skillful craftsman and architect. Some Greeks would relate him to Hephaestus, the god of blacksmith. The Greek philosopher Socrates claimed to be a descendant of Daedalus in at least three of Plato's books.

Myth has it that to prevent Daedalus' knowledge of labyrinth from spreading to the public, Minos imprisoned him and his son Icarus. The ingenious Daedalus then designed a pair of fabricate wings for both his son and himself. As the feathers were secured with strings at their midpoints and wax at their bases, Daedalus warned his son neither to fly too high nor too low when they were prepared to escape. Unfortunately, Icarus, once in the sky, forgot his words and began to soar higher and higher. As a result, the blazing sun softened the wax that held the feathers. The poor youth fell quickly into the sea and was drowned.

Although labyrinth and maze are often used interchangeably, the two words are not exactly the same. A maze is a complex branching puzzle that includes choices of path and direction, whereas a labyrinth is unicursal, which means that it has only a single non-branching path leading to the center. Therefore, mazes are often used in scientific experiments to test people's spatial awareness or intelligence, while the word "labyrinth" seems to entail more spiritual significance. Both words are figuratively used to mean something complex or confusing, such as: 1) *I remember the first time I took a subway in New York, it was just like a labyrinth to me.* 2) *They were trapped in a menacing maze of corridors.*

迷宫是一种复杂的结构,最早的迷宫已经有四千年以上的历史了。所有关于迷宫的故事或多或少都受到了克里特迷宫的影响,这座藏着牛头人身怪物弥诺陶洛斯的迷宫是由技艺高超的工匠代达罗斯发明的。有些希腊人认为他是锻冶之神赫菲斯托斯的后人,古希腊哲学家苏格拉底自称是代达罗斯的后代,柏拉图在至少三本书里都记载过此事。

传说为了防止代达罗斯建造迷宫的技艺流传于世,克里特国王弥诺斯下令将代达罗斯和他的儿子伊卡罗斯囚禁起来。于是,聪明的代达罗斯便动手设计了两对机械翅膀,由于翅膀上的羽毛是用绳子和蜡固定的,在起飞之前,代达罗斯叮嘱儿子不要飞得太高,也不要飞得太低。不幸的是,伊卡罗斯飞上天后,就忘记了父亲的警告,越飞越高。结果,炽热的阳光晒化了连接翅膀的封蜡,可怜的少年迅速坠落、葬身大海。

尽管 labyrinth 和 maze 常常被互换使用,但两者的意思是有区别的。单词 maze 所指的迷宫可以包含不同的路线和方向,而 labyrinth 却是单行线,也就是说只包含一条通向中心的道路。因此,maze 类的迷宫多用于科学实验,能够验证人们的空间感和智商,而 labyrinth 似乎具有更多的精神意义。引申开来,两个词都可以表示复杂混乱的东西,例如:1)"我记得第一次在纽约坐地铁时,那里就像一个迷宫(labyrinth)。"2)"他们被困在一群回廊构成的迷宫(maze)中出不去了。"

Minotaur(弥诺陶洛斯)

The name Minotaur means "Minos' Bull" in ancient Greek. Minos, son of Zeus and Europa, was a legendary king of Crete who became one the judges of the Underworld after death. According to the myth,

Poseidon once sent him a snow-white bull for sacrifice. Instead of sacrificing it, however, Minos kept it alive, which infuriated the god. As a punishment, Poseidon made Pasiphae, wife of Minos, fall in love with the white bull, and later give birth to Minotaur, a monster with the body of a man and the head of a bull. To hide his family shame, Minos then gave the order for Daedalus to construct the labyrinth in which Minotaur would be shut up.

Bulls are honored as sacred in both eastern and western cultures. In Hinduism, for example, Shiva's Steed is Nandi, the Bull. Taurus, the constellation and the second sign of the Zodiac, is said to represent a bull that was tamed by Jason.

在古希腊语中,弥诺陶洛斯的意思就是"弥诺斯的公牛"。弥诺斯是宙斯和欧罗巴的儿子,这位克里特岛的传奇国王死后成了冥府的三大判官之一。传说波塞冬曾送给他一头雪白的公牛作为祭品,然而,他非但没有献祭,还把那头牛养了起来,这让波塞冬大为光火。为了惩罚弥诺斯,他使王后帕西淮爱上了白牛,并随后产下了牛头人身的怪物弥诺陶洛斯。为了避免家丑外扬,弥诺斯命令代达罗斯修建迷宫来关押这个怪物。

无论是在东方还是西方文化中,公牛都是尊贵神圣的象征。例如,印度教中的湿婆神,其坐骑南迪就是一头公牛。而黄道十二宫的第二宫金牛座,据说是由伊阿宋驯服的一头公牛变的。

Theseus Paradox(忒修斯悖论)

Theseus paradox, also known as the ship of Theseus, is a thought experiment that raises the question of whether an object that has had all its components replaced remains fundamentally the same object. Suppose that the famous ship sailed by the hero Theseus in a great battle has been kept in a harbor as a museum piece. As the years go by, some of the wooden parts begin to rot and are replaced by new ones. After a century or so, all of the parts have been replaced. Is the "restored" ship still the same object as the original? The paradox appears in some applied fields of philosophy. For example, texts and computer programs may be edited gradually but so heavily that none of the original remains, posing the legal question of whether the owners of the original have any claim on the result.

忒修斯悖论,或忒修斯之船,是一种思维实验,它提出了这样一个问题:当一个物体所有的零部件都被替换掉了之后,它还是原来的那个物体吗?假设英雄忒修斯曾坐过的那艘著名的战船在某个港口展出。若干年后,船上的木头开始腐烂,需要更换。百年之后,船上所有的零部件都已经换过新的了,那么这艘"修复"后的战船还是原来的那艘吗?这样的悖论出现在一些哲学应用领域,譬如:文本和计算机程序可以逐步被编辑修改,而有朝一日,当所有的内容都已经被改过之后,那些原有文本和程序的发明者对修改过的版本依然拥有著作权吗?

The Myths 神话故事

Theseus, son of Aegeus of Athens, was brought up by his mother in a small town called Troezen. On his sixteenth birthday, his mother led him to a huge rock and challenged him to remove it. Being strong and intelligent, Theseus lifted the boulder and found under it a sword and a pair of sandals left by his father as a token of his royal parentage. Theseus then embarked on a journey back to Athens to claim his birth right.

After Theseus united with his father, he discovered that Athens was under constant threat from the neighboring kingdom of Crete, whose powerful King Minos imposed a terrible tribute on Aegeus. Each year seven men and seven women in Athens would be selected and sent to Crete where their fate was doomed, for at the palace of King Minos was a huge stone labyrinth, in the center of which was a ferocious beast called the Minotaur, a half man and half bull monster which fed on only human flesh. Both the complex labyrinth and the blood-thirsty monster made it impossible for anyone entering to survive.

Theseus, who vowed to save the kingdom and release his people from the fate of the dreadful labyrinth, went in the place of one of the seven men. Before he departed, Theseus told his father to beware of the color of the sails, which would be turned from black to white had he succeeded. When Theseus arrived in Crete, Ariadne, the daughter of King Minos, fell in love with the brave and handsome young man at the first sight and determined to help Theseus in whatever way she could.

Princess Ariadne first paid a visit to Daedalus, the famous architect and inventor who designed the labyrinth. Ariadne implored him for the key to the maze, which he granted her. Then she sneaked into the dungeon where Theseus was being held, sharing with him the secrets about the labyrinth and gave him a pool of shining thread, which could be unwound and rewound. The love-struck also made an appointment to meet at the door of the labyrinth.

The next morning, Theseus was put into the labyrinth under the watchful eyes of King Minos, who was certain that the youth would be the breakfast of the Minotaur. He was wrong. Theseus rolled out the thread ball, as instructed by the princess, as soon as he stepped into the labyrinth and was led soon to the monster, which was still fast asleep. Being well trained in the arts of fighting and wrestling, Theseus took the creature by surprise and killed it on the spot. He then followed the thread back to the door of the labyrinth, where his beautiful lover was waiting as promised.

The story, however, did not have a happy ending because King Aegeus knew nothing of Theseus' success with the Minotaur. Every day he went to the cliffs to look

for the return of his son's ship, desperately hoping that the sails would be white. Tragically, in all the excitement with the Minotaur, Theseus forgot to change the color of the sails. Seeing the sails were black, Aegeus was sure that Theseus was dead. Overcome with grief, the heartbroken king threw himself down in the water below.

忒修斯是雅典国王埃勾斯的儿子,他从小生活在一座名为特罗曾的小镇,由母亲抚养长大。在他十六岁生日那天,母亲把他领到一块巨石面前,让他尝试搬起巨石。强壮而聪明的忒修斯抬起巨石,发现了藏在下面的宝剑和草鞋,这是父亲留给他的王族象征。于是,忒修斯踏上了去雅典寻找父亲的旅程。

和父亲团聚之后,忒修斯发现雅典正不断地受到邻国克里特的威胁,那里的国王弥诺斯要求埃勾斯国王每年都要上交贡品:七个童男和七个童女。这些不幸的孩子抵达克里特岛后,会被投进王宫深处的一座石头迷宫,在迷宫的中心住着一头半人半牛的吃人怪物,名叫弥诺陶洛斯。复杂的迷宫和嗜血的妖怪足以使得进入迷宫的所有人都无法生还。

忒修斯发誓要拯救王国,打破可怕的迷宫魔咒,于是,他主动要求成为七名童男之一,去克里特岛走一遭。临别之际,他告诉父亲,假如他看到归来的船帆从黑色变成了白色,那就代表他已经取得了胜利。当年轻英俊的忒修斯抵达克里特岛后,国王弥诺斯的女儿阿里阿德涅对他一见钟情,下决心要尽可能地帮助他。

阿里阿德斯公主首先去拜访了迷宫的设计者——著名的工匠和发明家代达罗斯,恳请代达罗斯告诉她走出迷宫的方法。接着,她悄悄潜入关着忒修斯的地牢,把她听到的所有信息转述给忒修斯,并交给他一团既可以展开又可以收起的金线,这对坠入爱河的年轻人还相约第二天在迷宫门口碰头。

翌日清晨,国王弥诺斯眼看着忒修斯被推进了迷宫,确信他不久就会成为弥诺陶洛斯的早餐。他错了!忒修斯按照公主的建议,一踏进迷宫,立刻展开了金线团,并跟着它很快地找到了牛头怪物。发现怪物还在酣睡,忒修斯施展出高超的格斗技巧,快速出击,当场杀死了它。随后,他在线团的指引下很快地走出了迷宫,与等在门口的心上人成功会合。

可惜的是，故事的结局并非喜剧，因为国王埃勾斯对于儿子的英雄行为一无所知。每天，他都会到悬崖边眺望，期待看到远方的船只飘着白帆。不幸的是，忒修斯此时正陶醉于胜利的喜悦中，完全忘记了要改变船帆的颜色。当埃勾斯发现远处的船帆依然是黑色时，他以为儿子肯定死了，于是悲痛欲绝的父亲从悬崖上纵身跃入了大海。

Extra 拓展测试

1. Which of the following do you think is the Minotaur?
你觉得以下哪一幅图会是弥诺陶洛斯？

A

B

2. In honor of the grief-stricken king, the part of the ocean where Aegeus fell into is known as the Aegean Sea to this day. Do you know its Chinese name?

为了纪念绝望自杀的国王埃勾斯，那片他纵身跃入的海域如今便以他的名字命名。你知道它的中文名字吗？

（1. 答案：A）
（2. 答案：爱琴海）

CHAPTER 4 Perseus
第四章 英雄珀尔修斯

Word Knowledge 词汇知识

Cap of Invisibility(隐身帽)

As a demigod favoured by the gods, Perseus received several temporary gifts that would help him slay Medusa, among which the most powerful and miraculous must be the cap of invisibility. According to Greek myth, this cap of invisibility, also known as Helm of Darkness, belonged to Hades, god of the Underworld, who lent it to Hermes who then handed it over to Perseus. With this magical cover, the hero not only killed Medusa but also the sea monster Cetus, to which Princess Andromeda had been sacrificed.

The cap of invisibility has inspired and influenced many writers, who entailed similar device and fictional theme in their own works. For example, in the *Harry Potter* series of novels by J. K. Rowling, there is a cloak of invisibility, with which Harry sneaked into forbidden areas of his school and remained unseen. It is later revealed that the cloak was once owned by Death himself, making it one of the Deathly Hallows.

作为受到神的庇护的英雄人物,珀尔修斯得到了几件神奇的礼物,帮助他最终杀死了美杜莎,而这些礼物中最为传奇和强大的无疑是隐身帽。根据希腊神话,这顶帽子属于冥王哈迪斯,因此也称为"暗夜头盔"。冥王将他借给了赫耳墨斯,后者再转借给了珀尔修斯。有了这一神奇的掩护,英雄珀尔修斯不仅杀死了美杜莎,还杀死了海怪刻托斯,从而解救了公主安德洛墨达。

隐身帽启发并影响了后来众多的作家，他们纷纷将这一虚构的主题和类似的物品引入自己的作品当中。例如，在罗琳的《哈利波特》系列小说中，就有一件隐身衣，哈利穿着他潜入了学校的禁地而没人发现。后来，书中揭晓了隐身衣的起源：这件物品原本属于死神，是死亡圣器之一。

Aegis(羊皮盾)

The aegis had been interpreted as an animal skin or a shield, sometimes bearing the head of a Gorgon. With its roots in Greek mythology, the word aegis is identified with protection by a strong force. The modern concept of doing something "under someone's aegis" means doing something under the protection of a powerful, knowledgeable, or benevolent source. Here is an example: *There are many societies run under the aegis of the Students' Union*.

羊皮盾通常指一块兽皮或盾牌，有时上面会有戈耳戈的头像。单词aegis源自希腊神话，用来表示"强有力的保护"。现代英语中有doing something under someone's aegis这样的表达，意思就是"得到有知识、有仁心者的强大庇护"，例如："有许多社团都是在学生会的支持下运转的。"

Graeae(格里伊)

The Graeae, also three in number, were the sisters and servants of the Gorgons. Being hags in nature, the names of the Graeae suggest rather dire monsters: Deino is "the dread", Enyo, "the horror", and Pemphredo, "the alarm". They were generally depicted as old crones, having only one detachable eye and tooth between them, which they lent to each other when one of them wished to appear before the world.

Most people do not like the word "old" or being referred to as "old man/woman", which is therefore replaced by a more polite term "senior citizens". The word "senile" and the prefix "geront-" both denote "old age" in English. Here are some words with such word elements: *gerontic*, *gerontocracy*, *geriatrics*, *gerontophobia*, *senile plaque*, *senile dementia*.

格里伊也是三姐妹,她们既是戈耳戈的姐妹,也是她们的仆人。作为女巫,格里伊姐妹的名字听上去非常可怕:狄诺是"害怕",厄尼俄是"恐怖",佩佛瑞多是"战栗"。通常他们都被描绘成干瘪丑陋的老太婆,共享唯一一只可以取下的眼睛和牙齿,如果三姐妹中有人要外出的话,就把这只眼睛装上。

大多数人都不喜欢"老"这个词或者被别人称作"老人",因此,取而代之的是 senior citizens(年长公民)这个更加礼貌的词汇。单词 senile 和词缀 geront-在英语中都表示"老",以下举几个例子:gerontic(老年期)、gerontocacy(老人统治的政府)、geriatrics(老年病学)、gerontophobia(恐老症)、senile plaque(老年斑)、senile dementia(老年性痴呆)。

The Myths 神话故事

Acrisius, king of Argos, consulted far-shooting Apollo at Delphi and was foretold by the oracle that a son born of his daughter Danae would kill him. Attempting to evade this, Acrisius imprisoned his dear daughter within an underground chamber of bronze, leaving only a narrow aperture through which Danae took her meals and breathed sweet air. However, Zeus, who conceived a passion for Danae, turned himself into a shower of liquid gold, and poured himself through the slit. Thus the great god lay in love with Danae.

In due course of time, a secret son was born, and Danae named him Perseus. One day, Acrisius heard the metallic echoes of the infant and Danae's secret was discovered. Acrisius locked both mother and child in a wooden chest and tossed them into the sea so that he would be absolved of their deaths. Luckily, the frail vessel caught in the net of a fisherman called Dictys, who took Danae and Perseus to his home on the island of Seriphos and treated them with respect.

Favored by the gods, Perseus grew up lithe and sleek. The honest Dictys had a brother Polydectes, who was the king of Seriphos. Lusted after fair Danae, Polydectes decided to rid of Perseus who was seen as a barrier in his way. Polydectes invited Perseus to a banquet, during which every guest provided a horse to the king. Perseus, not rich enough to own one, asked Polydectes to name a gift, which he would manage to fetch for him. The king then demanded the head of Medusa, the only mortal Gorgon, which, he was certain, was an impossible mission.

Perseus' quest began in despair. When he was wandering on a lonely part of the island, thinking where to find the snake-haired monster, he saw two mighty gods, Hermes and Athena, in front of him. Hermes gave him a wickedly sharp sword, which showed no reflection of the moonlight, and a pair of winged sandals, which could enable him to fly as swift as any bird. Athena handed him her own aegis, a mirror-like shield. They told him to find first the three Graeae who would tell him how to defeat the Gorgons.

When Perseus reached the distant seashore where the Graeae lived, he discovered that the three perpetually-old women shared only one eye and depended on it utterly. An idea occurred to him. When the eye was in transit from one Graeae to another, Perseus grabbed it and pretended to walk away with it. Faced with the fatal threat, the desperate Graeae then agreed to help Perseus by directing him to find the Hesperides, the sea nymphs, who graciously loaned him a cap of darkness, and a special satchel.

Equipped with all the magical gifts, Perseus soon spotted the foul Gorgons from on high. He then donned his cap of invisibility and swooped down. Acting on the advice of Athena and Hermes, he used his bronze shield as a mirror to avoid the direct gaze of Medusa. Even with this handicap, Perseus managed to cut off her head cleanly, with one slice. Immediately, through the Gorgon's severed neck, leapt her children by Poseidon: the winged horse Pegasus, and the horse's human twin, Chrysaor, the father of Geryon.

Perseus quickly stuffed the head of the Gorgon into the satchel and flew off, leaving the hideous twin sisters of Medusa screeching and raving futilely. On the way back to Seriphos, Perseus caught sight of a beautiful girl struggling helplessly against chains that bound her to a jagged rock, so close to the water's edge that salt spray mingled with the tears on her face. The girl was Andromeda, an Ethiopian princess and the daughter of the king Cepheus, who sacrificed his child in order to save his land from being ruined by a sea monster.

Perseus slew the sea serpent and set Andromeda free without hesitation. Together they flew back to Seriphos, where, Danae and Dictys, having been abused by the king, greeted the returning hero with tears of hope. Perseus strode into Polydectes' palace, where the king was at a banquet surrounded by his supporters. "Did you get me the Gorgon's head?" the king taunted. Perseus reached in and pulled the ghastly object out of his satchel, while averting his gaze. Polydectes and all the others were instantly turned to stone, the mocking laughter frozen forever on their sneering lips.

After he had returned the magical sword and the winged sandals to Hermes, Perseus gave the Gorgon's head to Athena, who set it in the middle of her aegis forever. Hearing of the heroic deeds of his grandson, Crisius fled in guilt and fear. But Perseus caught up with him and the two reconciled. As there is no escaping the word of fate, Perseus took part in an athletic competition one day, and the discus he threw accidentally struck and killed a spectator—his grandfather.

阿尔戈斯国王阿克里修斯到特尔斐的阿波罗神庙求取神谕，得到的预言是他女儿达那厄所生的儿子会杀了他。为了阻止预言的发生，阿克里修斯将自己的女儿囚禁到了地下的一间铁牢里，只留出一条狭窄的缝隙用于送饭和空气对流。然而，宙斯被美丽的达那厄所吸引，变身为金水，从那条门缝中流进了地牢，并成功地让公主怀上了龙种。

不久之后，一个神秘的男孩降生了，达那厄为他取名珀尔修斯。这天，阿克里修斯听到铁牢里传来婴儿的声音，发现了这个秘密，他将母子俩锁进一个大木头箱子里，投入了大海，期待他们能自生自灭。幸运的是，这个箱子落入了渔夫狄克提斯的渔网，好心的渔夫将母子俩带回塞里福斯岛自己的家里，并以礼相待。

有了神的眷顾，珀尔修斯出落得一表人才。老实人狄克提斯有一个哥哥波吕得克忒斯，是塞里福斯岛的国王。他垂涎于达那厄的美貌，决定杀死她的儿子，以清除障碍。波吕得克忒斯邀请珀尔修斯参加王宫的宴会，席间，所有的客人都献给国王一匹骏马作为礼品。珀尔修斯没有钱，也没有马，于是他让波吕得克忒斯自己说一件礼物，然后他便会设法为他取来。国王表示他想要戈耳戈中唯一的凡人美杜莎的头，因为他相信这是一项不可能完成的任务。

珀尔修斯踏上了冒险之旅。这天，当他正独自徘徊在岛上，思忖着究竟该到哪里去寻找蛇发女妖的时候，赫耳墨斯和雅典娜出现在他面前。赫耳墨斯递给他一把锋利的宝剑和一双有翼凉鞋，这把剑在月光下也不会反光，而那双有翼凉鞋可以助他飞得比鸟还快。雅典娜则将自己的羊皮盾，一块有镜面的盾牌交给了他。他们建议珀尔修斯先去找到格里伊三姐妹，因为她们知道如何才能打败戈耳戈。

珀尔修斯很快在一个偏远的海岸找到了格里伊三姐妹，他发现这三位老妇共享一只眼睛。这只眼睛就是她们的命根子。珀尔修斯灵机一动，瞅准时机，趁着三人正在传递的时候，一把夺过那只独眼，佯装逃跑。失去眼睛对于格里伊姐妹来说是致命的威胁，迫于无奈，她们同意帮助珀尔修斯，并引导他找到了海洋仙女赫斯珀里蒂斯，后者爽快地将一顶隐身帽和一个特制背包借给了他。

有了这些神奇礼物的帮助，珀尔修斯很快便发现了戈耳戈姐妹的踪迹。于是，他戴上隐身帽，向着蛇发女妖俯冲下去。按照雅典娜和赫耳墨斯的建议，他把盾牌当作镜子，以免直视美杜莎的眼睛，就算无法直视，珀尔修斯还是干净利落地一刀砍下了美杜莎的头颅。顷刻之间，从那血淋淋的断头处，跃出了美杜莎和波塞冬的两个孩子：飞马珀加索斯，还有它的凡人兄弟，吉里昂的父亲克律萨俄耳。

珀尔修斯将美杜莎的头迅速塞进背包，在有翼鞋的帮助下飞离海岛，留下两个丑陋的戈耳戈姐姐在原地徒劳地咆哮嘶吼。在返回塞里福斯岛的路上，珀尔修斯瞥见一位美丽的姑娘被绑在粗糙的礁石上拼命地挣扎，四周腾起的海水混合着泪水不停地打在她的脸上。这姑娘是国王刻甫斯的女儿，埃塞俄比亚公主安德洛墨达，她的父亲为了防止海怪毁掉自己的国家而不得已把她绑在这里作为祭品。

珀尔修斯毫不犹豫地杀死了海怪，解救了公主。随后，两人一起飞回了塞里福斯岛，饱受折磨的达那厄和狄克提斯看到凯旋的英雄，激动地流下了泪水。珀尔修斯昂首阔步地走进了波吕得克忒斯的宫殿。此时，正在宾客簇拥下召开宴会的国王简直不敢相信自己的眼睛，他以嘲讽的口吻问道："你取到戈耳戈的脑袋了吗？"珀尔修斯将脑袋转向一边，从背包里取出了那个可怕的东西。波吕得克忒斯和在场的所有人瞬间变成了石头人，他们脸上的讥笑也永久地凝固了。

珀尔修斯将宝剑和有翼鞋归还给赫耳墨斯之后，又将美杜莎的头献给了雅典娜，女神将它永久地嵌在了自己的羊皮盾中央。阿克里修斯听说了自己孙子的英雄故事后，羞愧不已，提前逃离了王宫，而珀尔修斯则追上他，祖孙两人握手言和。不过，或许是命中注定阿克里修斯无法善终，一天，珀尔修斯受邀参加体育比赛，他掷出去的铁饼不幸砸中了看台上的一位观众——正是他的祖父。

Extra 拓展测试

1. Below is a pair of ordinary sandals. Could you draw a few lines to make it a pair of winged sandal?

下面是一双普通的草鞋，你能加上几笔把它变成一双有翼鞋吗？

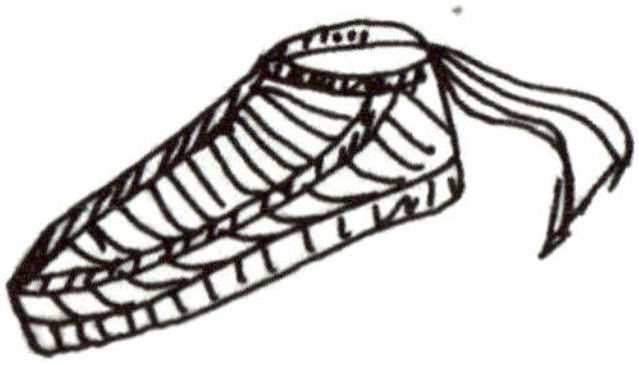

2. Andromeda is now the name of a large northern constellation between Perseus and Pegasus. It is chiefly notable for the Andromeda Galaxy, or the Great Nebula of Andromeda, a conspicuous spiral galaxy probably twice as massive as our own and located two million light years away. Do you know its Chinese name?

安德洛墨达如今是一个北方大型星座的名字,位于珀尔修斯(英仙座)和珀加索斯(飞马座)之间,它主要以“安德洛墨达星系”,或“安德洛墨达超大星云”而著称,这是一个明显的漩涡星系,很可能是我们银河系的两倍,距离我们有两百万光年。你知道它的中文名字叫什么吗?

(2.答案:仙女座)

CHAPTER 5 Bellerophon
第五章 柏勒洛丰

Word Knowledge 词汇知识

Chimaera(喀迈拉)

According to Greek mythology, the Chimaera was a monstrous fire-breathing hybrid creature of Lycia in Asia Minor. It is usually depicted as a huge monster of immortal make, lion-fronted and snake behind, a goat in the middle. It was one of the offspring of Typhon and Echidna and a sibling of such monsters as Cerberus and Lernaean Hydra. The sight of a Chimaera was an omen for disaster.

Now the term Chimaera, or chimera, has come to describe any mythical or fictional creature with parts taken from various animals, or to describe anything composed of very disparate parts, or, like what is given in the following example, a thing which is hoped for but is illusory or impossible to achieve: *China has been my passion, my calling, my own personal Shangri-la and Chimera rolled into one.*

在希腊神话中,喀迈拉是生活在小亚细亚地区,利西亚国的一只喷火怪兽,它通常的样子是狮头、蛇尾、羊身,拥有庞大的不死之躯。它是堤丰和厄喀德那的后代,与三头狗刻耳柏洛斯和勒拿九头蛇属一母同胞,喀迈拉的出现常被当作灾祸的预兆。

如今,喀迈拉(Chimaera,或拼作 chimera)可以用来描述任何由不同动物组合而成的神话或虚构的生物,也可以表示任何由不同部件嵌合而成的东西,抑或如下面的例句所给出的那样,表示某种虚幻或难以实现的愿望:"中国是我的激情和事业所系,是我心中世外桃源和幻想结的合体。”

Amazons(亚马孙人)

When Amazon is mentioned, modern people are likely to think of either the longest river in South America, or the world's largest online retailer. But the Amazons, in Greek mythology, were in fact a tribe of women warriors. Daughters of Ares and Harmonia, they were tall and strong in appearance, brutal and aggressive in character, their main concern being in war.

The Greek geographer Strabo (64 BC—20 AD) recorded the belief that the Amazons seared their right breasts to better use a bow and arrow or throw a spear. He also wrote that the Amazons were believed to live separately from men—travelling into neighbouring territories to mate—but keeping only girls to rear. With all the above in mind, please try to understand the following sentence: *Men in turn have felt threatened by the emerging Amazon women who no longer seem to need them and they may slip into a form of complacency.*

提到亚马孙,现代人可能首先想到的是南美最长的亚马孙河,或者世界上最大的网络零售商。然而,在希腊神话中,亚马孙人其实是一个部落,她们是战神阿瑞斯和哈耳摩尼亚的女儿,是一群外表高大强壮、性格好斗冷酷的女战士,她们的主要爱好就是打仗。

据古希腊地理学家斯特拉柏记载,亚马孙人为了能更好地使用弓箭或投掷长矛,不惜烧焦自己的右侧乳房。他还写道:一般认为,亚马孙人是和男人分开居住的。她们会到周边部落寻找男人进行交配,但是她们只会将女孩留下来抚养长大。请根据上述介绍尝试解读下面这个句子:“反之,亚马孙(独立强悍的)女人的出现令男人们深感威胁,他们似乎不再被需要,而渐渐沦为某种安慰剂似的存在。”

Bellerophon was the son of Glaucus, king of Corinth, and grandson of Sisyphus, but his mother told him that he was the child of Poseidon. In consequence of an accident killing of a brother, Bellerophon was compelled to leave the land of his birth, and settled in Tiryns, where he was kindly received by King Proetus, who purified him from his crime.

Stheneboea, the wife of Proetus, was so charmed with the handsome youth that she tried to seduce him, but Bellerophon refused her. The infuriated Stheneboea then came to her husband and falsely accused the innocent of attempting to rape her. Blinded by his desire for revenge, Proetus sent Bellerophon to his father-in-law, Iobates, king of Lycia, with a sealed letter containing Stheneboea's charges and the request that Iobates get rid of his young visitor, permanently.

Judging by the appearance that the guest must be of noble birth, Iobates feasted with Bellerophon for nine days before opening the letter. Then he became horror-struck upon reading the message. As he could not make up his mind to murder the guest he had grown to esteem, he decided to set him to cleanse Lycia of its plague. By rights, any one of the tasks should kill him. Iobates could only win: either Bellerophon would die, or, if he succeeded, Lycia would at least have been free from terror.

Bellerophon, however, was watched over by the gods, who, in answer to his prayer, sent him Pegasus, the white, winged horse that had sprung from Medusa's severed neck. But the divine animal was wild and untamed, and nothing Bellerophon could do would make the proud steed obedient to his commands.

Noticing the boy's trouble, Athena appeared to him in a dream and presented him with a magic bridle, with which he was eventually able to mount and control the splendid creature.

The first task the Lycian king gave Bellerophon was to kill the Chimaera, a huge fire-breathing monster with the face of a lion, the body of a goat and the tail of a snake. Mounted on Pegasus, the young hero flew high up to the sky and soon spotted the whereabouts of the Chimaera. Without hesitation, he swooped down and shot three deadly arrows in quick succession, one for each of the creatures that made up its body.

Succeedingly, he was sent to conquer the neighboring Solymi tribe, which was Iobates' traditional enemy. After putting down the rebellion of the barbarian Solymi in the east, Bellerophon was immediately ordered to quell the Amazons in the north, for the warrior women were raiding Iobates' territory. The third labor met with success.

Having single-handedly done all that Iobates wanted, Bellerophon set out in triumph back to the king's palace. But a plot was afoot to get rid of him for good. As he was approaching the Lycian capital, fifty royal warrior jumped down on him. However, not one of the ambushers returned alive, and at last Iobates was forced to recognize that Bellerophon was under the special protection of the gods.

Realizing that his daughter had been lying, the king, in recompense, gave Bellerophon half his kingdom and his younger daughter's hand in marriage. When she learnt that her shamelessness and lies had been revealed, Stheneboea killed herself rather than live with the humiliation. Bellerophon succeeded to the throne after the king died and became increasingly intoxicated with pride and vanity.

One day, Bellerophon rode on Pegasus and attempted to fly to Olympus. To punish him for his impiety and such a foolish enterprise, Zeus sent a gadfly to sting the steed, who became so restive as to buck his rider off to the ground. Bellerophon, maimed and blind, found himself on a vast expanse of wilderness where no one had ever set foot since creation. After wandering for some time, he died a miserable death.

柏勒洛丰是科林斯国王格劳科斯的儿子,西西弗斯的孙子,而他母亲则说他是波塞冬的孩子。由于无意间杀死了自己的兄弟,柏勒洛丰被迫离开自己的祖国,来到了梯林斯,在那里,他不仅得到了国王普洛托斯的盛情款待,还洗清了自己的罪过。

普洛托斯的妻子斯塞尼波尔对这位英俊少年一见倾心,试图诱惑他,但遭到了拒绝。于是,盛怒之下的王后来到丈夫面前诬告这位年轻人想要强奸她。普洛托斯信以为真,他决定让自己的岳父,利西亚国王伊俄巴忒斯来帮助自己除掉这个年轻人。他把这一想法写在了一封密信里,让柏勒洛丰带过去。

伊俄巴忒斯见来访的客人一表人才,断定其出身不凡,于是,并没有着急看信,而是连续设宴款待了柏勒洛丰九天。第十天,当他读到信里的内容,伊俄巴忒斯惊慌不已。此时对于这位客人他已心生好感,并不愿动手杀他。他决定派柏勒洛丰去完成几项任务。按理说,其中任何一项都足以要了他的命,而伊俄巴忒斯则不会有任何损失:要么就是柏勒洛丰死去,要么就是利西亚国从此获得太平。

然而,柏勒洛丰是众神眷顾之人,得知他有难处,他们为他送来了飞马珀加索斯,就是那匹从美杜莎的断头处跳出来的白色飞马。不过,这匹桀骜不驯的神兽可不容易驾驭,柏勒洛丰尝试了无数方法都没有成功。而这一切,雅典娜都看在眼里。这天夜里,女神悄悄来到他的梦中,将一根神奇的马缰交到他的手里,有了这件宝物,柏勒洛丰最终骑上了马背,得以驾驭这匹骏马。

利西亚国王交给柏勒洛丰的第一项任务是杀死怪兽喀迈拉:一头拥有狮头、羊身、蛇尾,能够喷火的巨型妖怪。有了珀加索斯的帮助,柏勒洛丰飞上蓝天,迅速锁定了怪物的行踪。说时迟,那时快,他驾驶飞马俯冲而下,三支利剑嗖嗖嗖地分别射入妖怪身体的三个致命部位。

接下来,他被派去征讨邻近的索利米部落,伊俄巴忒斯的宿敌。成功击败东部地区野蛮的索利米族叛乱分子之后,柏勒洛丰又立刻接到命令,去迎战北部地区的亚马孙人,不能让这群彪悍的女人在伊俄巴忒斯的土地上肆意妄为。柏勒洛丰再次完成了任务。

单枪匹马地完成国王交给他的所有任务后,柏勒洛丰凯旋。然而,一场阴谋正在悄然进行,就在他距离利西亚都城越来越近之时,五十名埋伏的皇家杀手突然向他扑来。不过,这些刽子手没有一个能活着回去。伊俄巴忒斯终于意识到柏勒洛丰是被众神宠爱之人。

同时,国王也意识到自己的女儿说了谎,作为补偿,他决定将小女儿嫁给柏勒洛丰,并附赠一半的国土作为嫁妆。斯塞尼波尔听说此事,羞愧难当,自刎而死。柏勒洛丰最终继承了王位,成了利西亚国王,渐渐地,他变得越来越骄奢狂妄。

这天,柏勒洛丰突发奇想,骑上珀加索斯,试图飞上奥林匹斯山。这种愚蠢而不敬的行为令宙斯心生不快,他放出一只牛虻,在飞马的身上叮了一口,受惊的马儿猛地腾起,将背上的骑手掀翻在地。经此一摔,柏勒洛丰变得又瞎又残,他落到了一片杳无人烟的地方。孤独地徘徊了一段时间后,凄惨地结束了自己的生命。

Extra 拓展测试

1. Could you find an obvious mistake in the following Chimaera?
   你能在下面这幅喀迈拉的画上发现一处明显的错误吗?

2. According to the myth, when Bellerophon arrived in Lycia, King Iobates did not inquire his name and errand. Instead, he entertained the young visitor, in the most princely and hospitable manner, for

nine days. In Greek mythology, number 9 is a magical and sacred number. We are all familiar with the nine Muses, but do you know that Leto labored nine days and nine nights to give birth to her twins: Apollo and Artemis? Myth has it that it would take nine days for an anvil to fall from heaven to earth. Do you know how long it would take for it to fall from earth to Tartarus?

传说柏勒洛丰到达利西亚之后,国王伊俄巴忒斯并没有询问他的姓名或来访目的,而是根据传统,以最隆重的方式款待了他九天时间。在希腊神话中,9是一个神奇且神圣的数字。九位缪斯女神大家一定都不陌生,可是你知道勒托花了九天九夜才费力地生下了她的龙凤胎阿波罗和阿耳尔忒斯吗?传说一只铁锤需要九天时间才能从天堂坠落到人间,那么你知道它还需要多久才能从人间坠落到地狱吗?

(1. 答案:喀迈拉应是羊身)

(2. 答案:同样是九天时间)

FURTHER READING
A Procrustean Bed
延伸阅读　强盗之床

In ancient China, there was a well-known fable about a stupid man who tried to cut his feet or toes in order to fit a pair of shoes that was small for him. We now often use the idiom to satirize those who handle things mechanically without considering the real situation. There is a similar expression in English, a Procrustean bed, which was derived from a Greek myth concerning the hero Theseus and a robber Procrustes.

The myth goes like this. On his way to Athens, Theseus encountered a giant man Procrustes, who was said to be a son of Poseidon. Procrustes kept a stone house by the side of the road where he offered hospitality to passing strangers, who were invited in for a pleasant meal and a night's rest in his very special bed. When Theseus arrived there, he received warm welcome and was likewise asked to stay for that night.

"It is not often that travelers pass this way. But you shall sleep on a wonderful bed which I have—a bed which fits every guest and cures him of every ill," said Procrustes. "Now I will go in and make the bed ready for you." When he had gone into the house, Theseus looked around him to see what sort of a place it was. Just at this moment, a young girl appeared and whispered to him: "Noble stranger, do not lie down on his bed, for those who do so never rise again."

"Who are you?" asked Theseus, "What is so special about his bed?" "Well, I am just a slave of him. Did he not tell you that the bed fits all guests?" said the girl, "And most truly it does fit them, for if a traveler is too long, Procrustes hews off his legs until he is of the right length; but if he is too short, as is the case with most guests, then he stretches his limbs and body with ropes until he is long enough. It is for this reason that men call him the Stretcher."

The very next moment Procrustes came back. "My dear young friend, the bed is ready, and I will show you the way." Theseus followed him to an inner chamber, where he saw an iron bed, very curiously wrought, and upon it a soft couch, seeming to invite him to lie down and rest. "Is this your wonderful bed?" asked Theseus. "Yes, it is," answered Procrustes, "and you need to lie down upon it, and it will fit you perfectly."

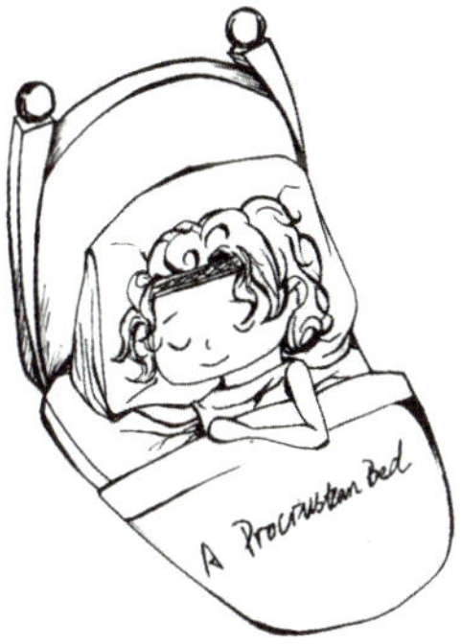

"But you must lie upon it first," said Theseus, "and let me see how it will fit itself to your stature." Before Procrustes could respond, Theseus seized his waist and threw him by force upon the bed. No sooner was he prone upon the couch than curious iron arms reached out and clasped his body in their embrace so that he could not move hand and foot. The evildoer shrieked and cried for mercy, but Theseus turned away.

"You are caught," said Theseus, "in the trap which you set for others and for me. There is no mercy for the man who shows no mercy." He went out of the room, leaving the wretched scoundrel to perish by his own cruel device. Then the girl whose fair face Theseus had seen before, came running into the house. She seized the young hero's hands and blessed and thanked him because he had rid the world of the cruel bandit.

The word "Procrustean" is now used to describe situations where different lengths or sizes or properties are fitted to an arbitrary standard. "The bed of Procrustes" or "a Procrustean bed" has become a common proverb to mean something designed to produce conformity by unnatural or violent means. Here is an example: "*Never stiffen your idea and never act in a Procrustean way for the stale regulations and queer ideas*."

在中国古代，有一则著名的寓言故事，讲的是一个愚蠢的人为了穿上一双尺码偏小的鞋子，竟然要把自己的脚指头剁掉。如今，我们常用“削足适履”这个成语来讽刺那些做事机械古板，不考虑实际情况的人。在英语中也有一个类似的表达，那就是“普罗克汝斯忒斯之床”。它源自一则希腊神话，讲的是英雄忒修斯和一个名叫普罗克汝斯忒斯的强盗的故事。

故事是这样的。在忒修斯前往雅典的路上，他遇到了一个名叫普罗克汝斯忒斯的巨人，据说他是海神波塞冬的儿子。普罗克汝斯忒斯住在路边的一栋石屋里，每当有客人经过时，他就会热情相迎，邀请对方到他的屋中享用美餐，并在他那奇特的床上度过良宵。当忒修斯经过时，他同样受到了热烈欢迎，还被挽留在那儿住上一夜。

“我这儿不常有客人来，既然来了，就体验一下我那张神奇的大床吧——这是一张适合所有客人，包治百病的床。”普罗克汝斯忒斯如是说，“现在我去收拾一下，你也可以早点休息。”说完，他走进了里屋，忒修斯环顾四周，想看看这究竟是怎样一个地方。就在这时，一个年轻的姑娘出现了，她悄悄告诉忒修斯：“尊敬的客人，千万不要睡到他的床上去，否则你就再也起不来了。”

“你是谁？”忒修斯问道，“那张床究竟特殊在哪里？”姑娘答道：“我只不过是个奴隶。难道他没有告诉过你那张床适合所有人吗？因为如果睡在上面的人太高的话，普罗克汝斯忒斯就会把他多余的腿砍掉，而如果像大多数人那样不够高的话，他就会用绳子硬把你的腿或身子拉长，这就是人们称他为‘强扯者’的原因。”

过了不久，普罗克汝斯忒斯返回屋子，说道：“年轻的朋友，床已铺好，请跟我来吧。”忒修斯跟着他来到了里屋，那里摆着一张造型奇特的铁床，上面铺着柔软的床垫，看上去很舒服的样子。忒修斯问道：“这就是那张神奇的大床吗？”“是啊，你只要一躺上去，它就会百分百地适合你。”普罗克汝斯忒斯回答。

“可是你得先自己躺上去，让我看看它究竟如何适应你的体型。”忒修斯说。没等普罗克汝斯忒斯回答，忒修斯猛地抓住他的腰部，将他扔到了那张床上，说时迟，那时快，强盗的身体刚一贴到床垫上，"咔嚓"一声，他的手臂和双腿便被床上的机关牢牢卡住，再也动弹不得了。尽管他大声尖叫、哭喊，请求忒修斯放了他，但是英雄却转身扬长而去。

临走之前，忒修斯说道："这是你为别人和我准备的陷阱，如今陷进去的却是你自己，这就叫自作孽不可活。"说完，他大踏步地走出了屋子，留下那个坏蛋在自己所设的陷阱中挣扎。此时，先前曾出现过的美丽姑娘再次来到忒修斯面前，她握住英雄的手，感谢他为民除了大害。

今天，我们用 Procrustean 这个词来描述那些强求一致的情况，而"普罗克汝斯忒斯（强盗）之床"已经成了一种常见的表达，用来指借助非自然或强迫的手段来达到统一的行为，例如："千万不要让你的思想僵化，不要为了那些陈规旧俗、怪异理念而削足适履。"

Extra 拓展测试

In the myth about Procrustes, the robber adopted a method of "one-size-fits-all", fatally adjusting his guests to fit his iron bed. Can you guess what a Procrustean solution is?

在关于普罗克汝斯忒斯的神话故事中，他用了一种致命的方式来使客人的身体适应他的铁床，也就是"用一个尺寸来适应所有人"的方法。那么你能猜出来什么是"普罗克汝斯忒斯式的解决办法"吗？

（答案：强求一致的解决办法）

PART Ⅷ　Myth and Legend

第八部分
神话与传奇

扫一扫，听本部分音频

CHAPTER 1 The Labors of Hercules
第一章 大力神的故事

Word Knowledge 词汇知识

The Choice of Heracles(海格立斯的选择)

There is a classic anecdote about Heracles recorded by Xenophon, a friend and pupil of Socrates, in the *Memorabilia*. It goes as follows. When Heracles reached his manhood, he felt it necessary to decide for himself how to make use of the extraordinary powers. One day, wandering in the heart of the forest, he was confronted by two females of great beauty. One was Vice, the other Virtue. The former, full of artificial wiles and fascinating arts, offered him a pleasant and easy life, whilst the latter, of noble bearing and modest mien, depicted a severe but glorious life. After mature deliberation, Heracles decided to follow in the paths of virtue, and henceforth to honor the gods, and bent his strength to the direction of good.

Vice and virtue are not only antonyms but also words with similar initial consonants. In rhetoric, such pairs of words can be very impressive because they are both alliteration and antithesis. Here are some examples like this: *fauna and flora*, *weal and woe*, *friend or foe*, *saints or sinners*, *medicare and medicaid*. Frederick J. Turner, a famous American historian, once said, "We shall esteem virtue, though in a foe; and adhor vice, though in a friend."

色诺芬是古希腊哲学家苏格拉底的学生兼好友,在他的《回忆苏格拉底》一书中,记录了一段关于海格立斯的经典趣闻。趣闻讲述的是成年后的海格立斯有一天在森林深处徘徊，思考着自己那身非凡的能力如何才能有用武之地，正在这时，他遇见了两位美貌女子：一位是恶德，一位是美德，前者满是花言巧语、虚假魅惑，承诺给他轻松享乐的生活，而后者端庄高贵，为他描绘出了一幅充满艰辛与荣耀的人生画卷。一番深思熟虑之后，海格立斯选择追随美德之路，为了神的荣耀向善努力。

恶德与美德不仅是一对反义词，同时也是两个拥有相同辅音开头的词汇。在修辞当中，这样兼具头韵和对照功能的组合可以给人留下非常深刻的印象。类似的例子还有：fauna and flora（动植物）、weal or woe（福祸）、friend or foe（是敌是友）、saints or sinners（圣人抑或罪人）、medicare and medicaid（医疗照顾和医疗补助）。美国著名的历史学家弗雷德里克·特纳曾经说过："敌之美德仍应尊敬；友之恶德亦遭痛恨。"

Herculean Effort(海格立斯般的努力)

The myth of Heracles being obligated to fulfill twelve tasks, known as the labors of Heracles, not only entertained and inspired numerous writers and artists throughout the world but also contributed to the English language such expressions as "Herculean task" and "Herculean effort". If associated with the myth and the labours, a "Herculean task" can easily be understood as an extremely difficult task. Likewise, any effort we nowadays deem as tremendous might be described as "Herculean", or great. Here are two examples: 1) *Reaching a commercial agreement was a Heraclean task*. 2) *Science means honest, solid knowledge, allowing not and iota of falsehood, and it involves Herculean effort and grueling toil*.

海格立斯完成十二项艰巨任务的神话故事不仅为全世界的作家津津乐道，为无数的艺术家提供了创作的素材，同时也为英语贡献了诸如"大力神的任务"和"海格立斯般的努力"这样的表达。假如你知道这个故事，你就很容易理解什么是"大力神的任务"了。而我们今天觉得需要付出大量艰辛努力的工作都可以用海格立斯般的（Herculean）来表达。

举两个例子:1)“达成商业协议是一项海格立斯般的(极其艰巨)的任务。”2)“科学是老老实实的学问,来不得半点虚假,需要付出海格立斯般(艰巨)的努力。”

Leave No Stone Unturned(翻遍所有的石头)

This catch-phrase had been included in a play by Euripedes, one of the three ancient Greek tragedians. It was related to Eurystheus, the king of Argos who was responsible for Heracles' twelve labors. After Heracles died, he tried to eliminate the hero's children, saying that he wanted "no stone left unturned" in finding and killing them. So "to leave no stone unturned" is now used to mean to search in all possible places or do all one can do to complete a task. Here is an example: *I left no stone unturned when I was searching my thesis topic. I think I checked out every book on it that the library had.*

这句流行语最早出现在古希腊三大悲剧家之一的欧里庇得斯所撰写的一部作品当中。作品讲述了负责给海格立斯分配任务的阿尔戈斯国王欧律斯修斯,在英雄死后,试图追杀他的孩子,叫嚷着“翻遍所有石头也要找到他们、杀死他们。”所以,“翻遍所有石头”如今就被用来指“不遗余力地找遍所有地方”或“尽一切可能完成任务”。举例:“为了我的论文题目我可谓不遗余力了,图书馆所有相关的书我几乎都翻遍了。”

The Myths 神话故事

Being a son of Zeus, Heracles had a powerful enemy Hera. Myth has it that no sooner had Heracles been born than Hera sent two slithering vipers into his chamber, intending their poisonous fangs to make short work of this bastard baby. But the mighty infant grasped a snake in each of his chubby hands and squeezed them to death. In fact, his name Heracles simply means "Hera's glory" because Hera sent him a lifetime of difficulty and challenges, which made Heracles suffer greatly, but he also achieved tremendous victories that led to everlasting fame and glory.

With the jealous eyes of Hera always on him, Heracles was destined to have a dangerous and difficult future. When he reached his manhood, Heracles was married and had three lovely children, but one day, in a fit of madness induced by Hera, he threw his own kids into the fire and slew his beloved wife. To do penance, he did the bidding of gods and became a ten-year servant of his step-brother Eurystheus, king of Argos. Under this weakling king, Heracles performed twelve stupendous labors, which ultimately won his way to heaven.

The first labour Eurystheus demanded was the skin of a lion that was ruining men's livelihoods in the hills around Nemea. The lion, raised specifically by Hera to be a trial for Heracles, was so powerful that its hide could not be penetrated by iron, bronze or stone. Seeing his arrow bounced off the lion, Heracles wrestled the creature with his bare hands. After killing the ferocious lion, he made a hooded cloak out of the lion's impenetrable skin, which was to become Heracles' special uniform.

Over the next decades, the king sent Heracles far and wide, on ever more difficult and dangerous missions. He defeated a terrible swamp monster called a Hydra; he trapped an enormous wild boar; he drove out a menacing flock of birds that were terrorizing a whole village. He single-handedly captured a herd of fierce cattle. The more the king tried to get rid of Heracles, the more he enhanced the young man's reputation.

In order to retrieve the golden apples of the Hesperides, Heracles sought advice from the old sea god Nereus, who alone knew the way to the Garden of the Hesperides. As the sea god was unwilling to cooperate, the mighty hero grabbed him so tightly that after various metamorphoses, Nereus was compelled to give the information required. Eventually, with both great strength and intelligence, Heracles got the apples with the help of Atlas.

Being the hardest labour, the twelfth and final mission of Heracles was to go down to the underworld and drag the three-headed Cerberus up to light. Like Nereus, Hades was furious at the hero's presumption and reluctant to let Cerberus go. However, Heracles shot him in the shoulder, and for the first time the god of the Hell experienced the agony of mortal suffering. Heracles then got the consent and caught hold of the monstrous gate-keeper with his bare hands and brought it to the upper air.

Heracles, a living man, had entered the underworld and come back again, which was such an extraordinary feat only Orpheus and Theseus would ever match. With the twelve labours coming to an end, Heracles' trials by no means finished. However, this process of a virtuous struggle against the odds brought him both everlasting fame and immortality. When he died at the age of 900, the mortal part of him descended into Hades, but his spirit was taken up to Olympus by Athena, where Zeus gladly accepted him among the company of the gods.

作为宙斯的儿子,海格立斯一出生就遭遇了劲敌赫拉的诅咒。传说为了让海格立斯消失,赫拉派了两条毒蛇溜进海格立斯睡觉的房间。然而,这个小婴儿竟用两只胖胖的小手一把掐死了两条毒蛇。事实上,“海格立斯”这个名字的意思就是“赫拉的荣耀”,因为虽然赫拉带给了他一生的艰难挑战,令他痛苦不已,但与此同时,通过战胜这一系列的艰难挑战,他也收获了永久的声望与荣耀。

由于赫拉嫉妒的双眼始终盯着海格力斯,他的未来注定充满了危险与挑战。成年后的海格立斯结婚并有了三个可爱的孩子,有一天,赫拉令他失去心智,以致他在狂暴中将自己的孩子扔进了火堆,并亲手杀死了自己的妻子。为了赎罪,他接受了神的旨意,开始了长达十年的为其继兄、阿尔戈斯国王欧律斯修斯服役的生活。在这个懦弱的国王手下,海格立斯一共完成了十二项令人惊叹的任务,实现了自己通往天堂的祈愿。

欧律斯修斯交给海格立斯的第一项任务是去尼米亚附近的山上杀死扰民的猛狮,取回狮皮。这头狮子是赫拉为了试探海格立斯而专门喂养的,不但凶猛异常,而且其皮毛刀枪不入。海格立斯眼见自己射出的箭碰到狮子的身体后被弹了回来,只好徒手与猛兽展开肉搏。得胜之后,他用那块刀枪不入的兽皮为自己做了一件连帽斗篷,这也成了海格立斯独有的战袍。

在接下来的数十年间,国王不断地把海格立斯派往各地,去完成一项又一项艰巨的任务。他打败了名为海德拉的沼泽怪兽九头蛇;捕获了一头庞大的野猪;赶走了一大群威胁村民的怪鸟;徒手擒住了一群疯牛。国王越是想除掉海格立斯,越是助其名声远扬。

为了从赫斯珀里得斯那里取回金苹果,海格立斯向老海神涅柔斯寻求帮助,因为只有他才知道通往赫斯珀里得斯果园的道路。然而,老海神起初并不配合,于是,大力神紧紧地抱住他不放,任凭老海神千变万化也无法脱身。无奈之下,他只好将秘密告诉了海格立斯。最终,凭借自己的智慧和力量,加上阿特拉斯的帮助,海格立斯成功地取回了苹果。

第十二项、也是最后一项任务是最艰难的,那就是去地狱抓回三头狗刻耳柏洛斯。和涅柔斯一样,哈迪斯起初也不情愿,并且对于海格立斯的想法大为光火。然而,海格立斯一箭射中了他的肩膀,令冥王首次品尝了凡人的痛苦,他不得不同意放行,眼看着大力神徒手抓起他的看门狗扬长而去。

海格立斯作为一个生者,却能进入冥界并成功返回,这样的壮举只有俄耳甫斯和忒修斯才能完成。十二项任务虽然告一段落了,但海格立斯所面临的挑战却并未完结。不过,这段不断战胜艰难险阻的义举之旅为他带来了不朽的生命与荣耀。据说,海格立斯活到了九百岁,死后他的肉体坠入冥界,而他的灵魂却被雅典娜带上了奥林匹斯山,在那里,宙斯欣然接受他为众神的一分子。

Extra 拓展测试

1. Which of the following do you think is Hydra?
你认为以下哪一幅图是海德拉？

A　　　　B

2. On the eleventh of his twelve labors, while in search of the golden apples of Nesperides, Heracles passed by Prometheus who was still bound to the Caucasus. Heracles killed the eagle that had tormented the Titan for so long and set Prometheus free. Prometheus then gave the hero valuable information by advising him to send Atlas to retrieve the apples instead of himself.

Prometheus Unbound is a four-act lyrical drama created by a famous Romantic poet in 1820. Do you know the name of this English poet?

在完成第十一项任务，也就是在寻找赫斯珀里得斯的金苹果途中，海格立斯碰到了仍被绑在高加索山上的普罗米修斯。他杀死了那只长久以来折磨巨人的老鹰，解救了普罗米修斯。于是，普罗米修斯建议他让阿特拉斯去找金苹果，而不要自己去，这一建议非常关键。

《解放的普罗米修斯》是一部四幕的抒情诗剧，由一位著名的浪漫诗人创作于 1820 年，你知道这位英国诗人叫什么名字吗？

（1. 答案：B）

（2. 答案：雪莱）

CHAPTER 2 The Apple of Discord

第二章 纷争果

Word Knowledge 词汇知识

Apple of Discord(纷争果)

An apple of discord is a reference to the Golden Apple of Discord left by Eris, the goddess of Strife, in the midst of the feast at the wedding of Peleus and Thetis. As the apple was inscribed "For the fairest", it sparked a vanity-fueled dispute among Hera, Athena and Aphrodite, which eventually led to the Trojan War. Thus the "apple of discord" is used to signify the core or crux of an argument, or a small matter that could lead to a big dispute. Look at the following example: *The question of income tax was the apple of discord among the senate.*

纷争果指不和女神厄里斯在珀琉斯和忒提斯的婚宴上留下的那只金苹果。由于苹果上刻着"给最美的人"几个字,它在赫拉、雅典娜和阿芙洛蒂忒三位女神之间引起了一场虚荣之争,并最终导致了特洛伊战争的爆发。因此,"纷争果"就被用来形容争论的核心或症结所在,或指一件能够引起较大争端的小事。举例:"所得税问题在参议院的议员之间引起了争论。"

The Judgment of Paris(帕里斯的决定)

Paris, the Trojan prince, was given the impossible task of deciding which goddess, Athena, Aphrodite, or Hera, was the most beautiful. All three tried bribes, of which Aphrodite's, the love of the most beautiful mortal woman in the world, was the most enticing to the young man. After that, Paris (and Troy) gained the other goddesses' animosity, and the judgment of Paris proved fatal to his city. Therefore, if a decision is referred to as the judgment of Paris, it involves a lot of controversies and would probably be extremely difficult to make. The decision made by King Edward VIII, the Duke of Windsor, to give up his throne for the love of his wife Willis Simpson is a most typical example of this.

特洛伊王子帕里斯接到了一项不可能完成的任务：决定赫拉、雅典娜和阿芙洛蒂忒三位女神中谁最美丽。三位女神均以不同的好处来贿赂他，而其中阿芙洛蒂忒给他的承诺——世界上最美丽女子的爱情，对于这位年轻人来说最具诱惑力。此后，帕里斯（以及特洛伊城）便成了另外两位女神的仇敌，帕里斯的决定对于他的城邦来说是致命的。因此，假如一项决定被比作"帕里斯的决定"，那么其中一定包含着许多矛盾，很可能是一项艰难的抉择。温莎公爵、英国国王爱德华八世为了和辛普森结合而放弃王位的决定就是一个最典型的例子。

The Face that Launched a Thousand Ships
（发动了千艘战船的容颜）

This idiom originated from a poem by Christopher Marlowe, an English playwright, poet and translator of the Elizabethan era. It is a direct reference to Helen of Troy, the most beautiful woman in the world. The abduction of her by the Trojan prince Paris caused Menelaus, her husband, to declare war on Troy. Because of prior alliances, eventually all of the Greeks were involved, thus Helen's beauty had "launched a thousand ships" into war. The idiom might be used like this: *When he looked backward to the corner, he found a face that launched a thousand ships.*

这句谚语最早出现在伊丽莎白女王时期英国的剧作家、诗人和翻译家克里斯托弗·马洛所创作的一首诗歌中，指的就是特洛伊的海伦——这位世界上最美丽的女人。帕里斯带走了她，从而促使海伦的丈夫墨涅拉俄斯向特洛伊宣战。由于之前缔结的盟约，最终所有的希腊城邦都加入了进来，造就了“海伦的美丽发动了千艘战船”的壮丽场景。如今，这句谚语可以这样使用：“当他回过头去望向街角，他看到了一张倾国倾城的脸。”

The Myths 神话故事

Thetis was a beautiful sea nymph, one of the fifty daughters of the sea god Nereus. She was courted by both Zeus and Poseidon, but neither of them married her, out of fear of a prophecy that she would bear a son who would outstrip his father, however great he was. An idea was then conceived that Thetis should join in wedlock to a human being. Peleus, the son of King Aeacus, became the ideal candidate.

The wedding between Peleus and Thetis was celebrated on Mount Pelion. All the gods and goddesses deigned to descend from Olympus to attend, each bringing some unique wedding gifts. Everyone seemed to be happy with the way things were, except Eris, the goddess of Strife, who had not been invited and, therefore, was in a foul mood at being overlooked. In no more than a few minutes, she sowed an evil that would yield countless deaths.

There, rolling on the floor in the middle of the hall where the gods and goddesses were feasting, was a golden apple, wheedled from the Hesperides and was inscribed “For the Fairest”. Hera, Athena, and Aphrodite immediately fell to quarreling, each claiming to be the rightful possessor of the beautiful bauble. The argument became so heated that Zeus had to step in and commanded them to be silent.

It was not long when Zeus came up with a solution. He sent Hermes, together with the three contestants, down to Mount Ida to find a shepherd boy there. The boy, Paris by name, was the Trojan prince who had been abandoned at birth due to an oracle that he would bring destruction to the country. Being raised by some kind herdsmen, Paris grew up to be an innocent young man with noble blood and astounding good looks, which was simply the reason why he was given the important mission.

Confronted suddenly with this impossible judgment, Paris leapt to his feet and paled in terror. So Hermes, the messenger of the gods, had to explain to him in a limpid voice so that he was assured of their good will. Realizing that he had no choice in the matter, Paris calmed down and agreed to do the job. Then Hermes stood aside and watched.

The first to approach was Hera, who appeared to the country boy as a woman of queenly bearing. "If you make the apple mine," she said, "I shall grant you worldly power beyond your imaginings." Athena strode briskly forward, a keen-eyed warrior, "Should you decide to grant me the apple, I will make you invincible. You will be the greatest general ever to lead an army." The contest was beginning to seem one of bribes, not beauty.

Finally, Aphrodite glided up to Paris. Leaning forward, the goddess breathed in his ear: "If you choose me, you will win the love of the most beautiful and desirable woman in the world." As her scent filled his nostrils, it suddenly dawned on Paris that this was where his happiness lay, not in the hazards of war or rule. "But who was this woman?" he asked. "And what does she look like?"

"She is Helen of Sparta," replied the goddess, "and she looks just like me. For your eyes, I have made myself in her image." The mind of the lad was swept clean: there was nothing he wanted more than the gift of Aphrodite. He indicated to Hermes that he was ready, and the three goddesses lined up expectantly. Hermes solemnly handed Paris the apple. Without a moment's hesitation, Paris held it out to Aphrodite, who took it gracefully, with a smile of triumph.

美丽的海洋仙女忒提斯是大洋神涅柔斯的五十个女儿之一。尽管宙斯和波塞冬都曾追求过她，但是他们都不愿娶她，因为有预言说无论她嫁给谁，其子都将超越其父。于是，他们出主意让忒提斯嫁给凡人，国王埃阿科斯的儿子珀琉斯便成了最佳人选。

珀琉斯和忒提斯的婚礼在皮立翁山上举行，奥林匹斯山的众神皆屈尊前来捧场，并且各自准备了独特的结婚礼物。所有人似乎都很满意，除了不和女神厄里斯，她因为没有接到邀请而非常不快。尽管她只停留了几分钟，但是她播下的邪恶之种却将夺去无数的生命。

就在众神享用婚宴的大厅中央，地板上躺着一只金苹果，这是厄里斯从赫斯珀里得斯的苹果园里骗来的，上面刻着"给最美丽的人"。赫拉、雅典娜和阿芙洛蒂忒立刻开始了争吵，她们都觉得这个漂亮的小玩意儿应该属于自己。由于吵得太厉害了，宙斯不得不介入，命令她们住嘴。

很快，宙斯便找到了解决办法。他让三位女神跟随赫耳墨斯去伊达山找一位牧羊的男孩，这位名叫帕里斯的男孩是特洛伊的王子。由于神谕说他会给国家带来毁灭，因此他一出生便被父母抛弃了。他在一些善良的牧羊人的抚养下渐渐长大，成了一位心地单纯、血统高贵、相貌异常英俊的少年，正因为如此，这项重要的评判任务才会落到他的头上。

这项突如其来的评判任务吓得帕里斯跳了起来，脸色因惊恐而变得苍白，于是，作为神的使者，赫耳墨斯不得不用清澈的嗓音向他解释，使他确信他们的好意。帕里斯意识到在这件事上他别无选择，于是冷静下来，同意试一试。这时，赫耳墨斯退到一旁，静静地观察。

首先说话的是赫拉，在这位乡下孩子眼里，这位女神宛如一位高贵的女王。她说："如果你把苹果给我，我会赐予你世间至高无上的权力。"雅典娜看上去则像一位目光锐利的斗士，她利落地上前一步，说道："你要是把苹果给我的话，我能让你成为无可匹敌，所向披靡的大将军。"比赛的内容似乎不再关于美貌，而变成了贿赂。

最后，阿芙洛蒂忒翩然而至，她俯身贴近帕里斯，对着他的耳朵悄悄说道："你要是选了我的话，我可以让世界上最美的女人爱上你。"伴随着一阵沁人心脾的芳香，帕里斯突然感觉到了什么才是他想要的幸福，不是危险的战争或统治权。"可是这个女人是谁?"他问道，"她长什么样?"

"她就是斯巴达的海伦，"女神回答，"她长得就和我一样，你眼中看到的我，就是她的样子。"年轻人的心意已决：他只想要阿芙洛蒂忒的礼物。他示意赫耳墨斯自己已经准备好了，三位女神在他面前一字排开，赫耳墨斯将金苹果郑重地交到了他的手上。帕里斯丝毫没有犹豫，伸手就递给了阿芙洛蒂忒，女神优雅地接过苹果，嘴角掠过一丝胜利的微笑。

Extra 拓展测试

1. Could you write some words on the following apple to turn it into an Apple of Discord?
   你能在下面的苹果上加上几个字，把它变成一只"纷争果"吗?

2. The English word "melon" was borrowed from ancient Greek to mean tree fruit in general. However, when the same word was borrowed into Latin, it was translated into "apple", a synonym of "evil". As a result, the "apple" gradually evolved into a symbol of knowledge, immortality, temptation and sin. What does Adam's apple mean? And do you know why it is so named?

   英语中的 melon(甜瓜)一词是从希腊语中借来的，用来指树上结的果子。然而，这个词到了拉丁语中，被翻译成了 apple，而拉丁语中的 apple 和 evil(邪恶)是同义词。随着时间的推移，apple(苹果)一词逐渐演化成知识、永生、诱惑和罪恶的象征。那么你知道 Adam's apple(亚当的苹果)是什么吗?你知道这个名称的来源吗?

(2.答案:男子的喉结。人类的咽腔之所以被称作亚当的苹果,是因为亚当偷吃禁果时,果子卡在了咽喉部位,并造成了凸起。)

CHAPTER 3 Agamemnon
第三章 阿伽门农

Word Knowledge 词汇知识

Cassandra(卡珊德拉)

Cassandra, the daughter of Priam who was given to Agamemnon as a war prize at the taking of Troy, was famous for not having her prophecies believed. According to one myth, she initially consented to accept the proposal of Apollo in exchange for the ability to foresee the future, but she broke her promise after receiving the gift. Then the enraged god turned this into a curse by causing her prophecies, though true, to be disbelieved. She foretold that Paris, her brother, would bring about a war that would destroy the city, but her parents scorned the prophecy as worthless. Before Agamemnon's death, she had foreseen the plot of Clytemnestra and Aegisthus, but no one believed her and she reluctantly accepted her fate and was slain by the queen.

A Cassandra now means a prophet of disaster, especially one which is disregarded. The Cassandra metaphor, or variously labelled the Cassandra complex or syndrome, is a term coined by the psychologists to refer to the physical and emotional suffering of some individuals whose valid warnings or concerns are dismissed or disbelieved. One typical example of the Cassandra metaphor is the dilemma faced by some environmentalists, whose warnings of impending environmental disaster are constantly mocked and disbelieved.

卡珊德拉是普里阿摩斯的女儿，在特洛伊城沦陷后，她作为战利品被送给了阿伽门农。卡珊德拉最有名的是她那无人相信的预言能力。传说她最初答应了阿波罗的求爱，条件是阿波罗赋予她预见未来的能力，然而，能力到手之后她却食言了。于是恼怒的太阳神将她的能力变成了诅咒，尽管她说的都是真的，但是没人会相信她。她曾预言自己的哥哥帕里斯会给特洛伊城带来战争和毁灭，然而她的父母对此嗤之以鼻。尽管在阿伽门农死前，她预见到了埃癸斯托斯和克吕泰涅斯特拉的阴谋，但是没人把她的话当真。无奈，她只能接受自己的命运，成了王后的刀下鬼。

如今，卡珊德拉成了灾祸预言家的代名词，尤指那些被人无视的预言家。"卡珊德拉隐喻"，或"卡珊德拉现象""卡珊德拉情结""卡珊德拉综合征"，是一个心理学词汇，用来指那种合理的担忧或警告得不到重视时，人们所感受到的身心痛苦。一个"卡珊德拉隐喻"典型的事例就是某些环保主义者所面临的窘境：他们关于环境灾害迫在眉睫的警告不断遭人嘲笑和无视。

Leda's Children(勒达的孩子们)

Leda was the wife of Tyndareus, king of Sparta. According to the myth, Zeus appeared to Leda in the form of a swan, seducing and impregnating her. Leda produced four offspring from two eggs: Castor and Clytemnestra from one egg, and Helen and Pollux (Polydeuces) from the other. Therefore, Castor and Clytemnestra were fathered by Tyndareus, whereas Helen and Pollux, by Zeus.

The twin brothers, Castor and Pollux, were renowned for their tender attachment to each other. As Castor was mortal and Pollux was immortal, the faithful brothers chose to live on alternate days, that is, they shared Pollux's immortality between them, spending half their time below the earth in Hades and the other half on Olympus. They are known together as Dioscuri. They are often identified with the constellation Gemini.

勒达是斯巴达国王廷达柔斯的妻子。传说宙斯化身为天鹅来到勒达身旁,并诱使她怀上了身孕。勒达产下了两颗蛋,从蛋中分别诞生出四个孩子:一颗蛋里是卡斯托耳和克吕泰涅斯特拉,另一颗蛋里是海伦和波吕克斯(波吕丢刻斯)。卡斯托耳和克吕泰涅斯特拉的父亲是廷达柔斯,而海伦和波吕克斯的父亲则是宙斯。

卡斯托耳和波吕克斯这对孪生兄弟以关系亲密而著称。由于卡斯托耳是凡人,而波吕克斯是神仙,为了彼此永不分离,他们选择分享波吕克斯的不死之身,轮流在冥界和天界生活。这对忠诚的伙伴并称为狄俄斯库里,据说天上的双子星座就是他们化身。

The Myths 神话故事

Agamemnon, the king of Mycenae, or Argos (a different name of the same region), is best known in Greek mythology as the chief commander of the Greeks in the Trojan War. When he was still young, he was forced to flee Mycenae with his brother Menelaus because their father, King Atreus, had been dethroned by their cousin Aegisthus. The two young princes found refuge in Sparta, in the court of King Tyndareus, and they later married Tyndareus' daughters, Clytemnestra and Helen respectively.

Menelaus eventually became king of Sparta after Tyndareus' death, while Agamemnon managed to retake the throne of Mycenae, exiling Aegisthus and his father. Ruling over Mycenae and a large part of Peloponnesus, Agamemnon stood out as the most powerful king over all the other princes of Greece. Later, when Helen was abducted by the Trojan prince Paris, Agamemnon felt that something had to be done about it. He decided to help his brother to take back his wife and thus declared war on Troy.

Agamemnon summoned all the Greek chiefs for assistance and was chosen the undisputed leader of the expedition. After two years of preparation, the Greek army and fleet assembled in the port of Aulis in Boeotia, waiting for a favorable breeze to swell their flagging sails. But weeks had gone by and there was no trace of wind coming. Agamemnon consulted Calchas, a seer, who revealed the cause of the trouble: Agamemnon had unwittingly killed a stag which was sacred to Artemis and thus infuriated the goddess, who sent continuous calms. The only remedy recommended was to offer Iphigenia, the daughter of Agamemnon, to the goddess as an atoning sacrifice.

Although there are different versions on this part of the myth, as to whether Iphigenia accepted her fate or she was tricked thinking she would be married to Achilles, she was sacrificed in the end, or perhaps replaced with a deer at the last moment and carried off by Artemis, which no one knows for sure. Anyway, after this, a fair wind sprang up and the Greek fleet sailed to the coast of Troy. Agamemnon had one hundred ships, independent of sixty which he had lent to Arcadians.

Descended from Tantalus, Agamemnon inherited the curse of the gods on his family. The enmity between his father and his uncle still persisted in the quiet resentment that his cousin Aegisthus felt against him. In his long absence, Aegisthus moved into the palace of Mycenae and took over from him not only his kingdom but also his adulterous wife Clytemnestra. When news of his return came, the guilty pair started scheming against his life. Misfortune and ruin awaited him on his arrival

Clytemnestra feigned the greatest joy on beholding her husband and accorded him the most lavish welcome fitting for a god. Despite the urgent warnings of the prophetess Cassandra, the princess of Troy and his concubine, Agamemnon received the pretentious affection of his wife with the most trusting confidence. In her well-assumed anxiety for the comfort of the weary traveler, she prepared a warm bath for his refreshment. At a given signal from the treacherous queen, Aegisthus, who was concealed in an adjoining chamber, rushed upon the defenseless hero and slew him.

There are at least three strikes accounting for Clytemnestra's murdering of her husband. In fact, Agamemnon was not Clytemnestra's real love. She was taken by force after Agamemnon killed her first husband, the grandson of Tantalus. The second strike was her daughter's sacrifice, which was certainly unbearable pain to a mother. When Agamemnon returned from Troy, he brought with him another woman. Such flagrant disregard became the last straw to Clytemnestra.

Myth has it that Odysseus met the shade of Agamemnon in the lower world and learned of his treacherous murder. Aegisthus and Clytemnestra ruled Mycenae for seven years, and then were killed by Orestes, Agamemnon's son who took revenge on his father's death. However, this matricide caused the wrath of the Furies, who pursued unceasingly the unfortunate Orestes wherever he went until the just and powerful goddess Athena intervened finally and liberated the young man from his persecution.

在希腊神话中,阿伽门农是迈锡尼,或曰或阿尔戈斯(同一地区的另一个名字)国王,也是特洛伊战争中希腊军队的最高统帅。在他年幼时期,由于堂兄埃癸斯托斯篡夺了其父阿特柔斯的王位,他被迫和弟弟墨涅拉俄斯逃离了迈锡尼,到邻国斯巴达寻求庇护。两位小王子在斯巴达国王廷达柔斯的宫殿中长大成人,并先后娶了国王的两个女儿:克吕泰涅斯特拉和海伦。

廷达柔斯死后,墨涅拉俄斯继位成为斯巴达国王,而阿伽门农则设法从堂兄的手里重新夺回了迈锡尼的王位,并流放了埃癸斯托斯父子。此后,阿伽门农统治着迈锡尼以及伯罗奔尼撒半岛的大部分地区,成为希腊王子中权力最大的国王。后来,当海伦被特洛伊王子帕里斯带走后,阿伽门农觉得自己不能坐视不管,他决定帮助弟弟讨回妻子,于是向特洛伊宣战。

阿伽门农召集了所有希腊将领前来助阵,并毫无争议地被推举为远征军的统帅。经过两年时间的准备,希腊军队和战舰在皮奥夏的奥里斯港集结完毕，整装待发。然而，连续几个星期，海上风平浪静，船只根本无法扬帆起航。阿伽门农找来随军占卜师阿尔克斯询问缘由，得到的答案是：阿伽门农曾在无意中杀死了献祭给阿耳尔忒弥斯的一头牡鹿，惹恼了狩猎女神，才导致了持续数日的风平浪静，而唯一的解决办法是把阿伽门农的女儿依菲琴尼亚献给女神赎罪。

关于依菲琴尼亚究竟是被动接受了命运的安排，还是天真地以为父亲要把自己嫁给阿喀琉斯而欣然前往，这一段故事有不同的版本，但不管怎样，最终她成了牺牲品。也有说法认为阿尔忒弥斯在最后关头心生恻隐，用一头鹿取代了她，并把她带走了。总之，真相无人知晓。但结果是随后天空刮起了风，并一路将希腊战舰顺利地送到了特洛伊的海边。阿伽门农拥有一百艘战舰，其中还不包括他借给阿卡狄亚人的六十艘船。

作为坦塔罗斯的后代，阿伽门农从出生起便背负着众神给予其家族的诅咒。其父与叔叔之间的仇恨使得他的堂兄埃癸斯托斯始终对他充满敌意。在他离家期间，埃癸斯托斯不仅搬进了迈锡尼的王宫，取代了他的位置，还和他的妻子克吕泰涅斯特拉暗通款曲。当他凯旋的消息传来之际，这对心虚的男女便开始密谋害他，不幸的阴云笼罩着他的归途。

看见丈夫的一刻，克吕泰涅斯特拉装出一副大喜过望的样子，像迎接天神下凡般大摆宴席欢迎他。尽管特洛伊公主，当时已经成为小妾的女预言师卡珊德拉警告阿伽门农要小心，但他却对妻子浮夸的示爱深信不疑，欣然接受她的安排，沐浴舒缓旅途的劳顿。阴险的王后一个手势，埋伏在隔壁房间的埃癸斯托斯突然闯入，毫无防备的英雄转瞬间便身首异处。

至少有三层原因导致了克吕泰涅斯特拉谋杀亲夫的举动。首先，阿伽门农并不是克吕泰涅斯特拉的真爱，前者在杀死了后者的前夫，坦塔罗斯的孙子后横刀夺爱。其次，女儿成为牺牲品对于任何一位母亲都是无法承受的痛苦。再次，当阿伽门农从特洛伊返回之际，他的身边还带着另一个女人，这种对于发妻的公然漠视成了压垮克吕泰涅斯特拉的最后一根稻草。

传说奥德修斯在冥界遇到了阿伽门农的鬼魂，从而得知了他被害的故事。埃癸斯托斯和克吕泰涅斯特拉统治了迈锡尼七年时间，后来，阿伽门农的儿子俄瑞斯忒斯替父报仇，杀死了他们。可是，这一“弑母”行为令复仇三女神大为震怒，想方设法要教训这个忤逆之子，直到正义女神雅典娜出面干涉，可怜的年轻人才得以摆脱种种厄运。

Extra 拓展测试

1. Can you divide the four children of Leda into two groups and put them into two eggs below?
你能将勒达的四个孩子分成两组，然后分别填入下面的两个蛋中吗？

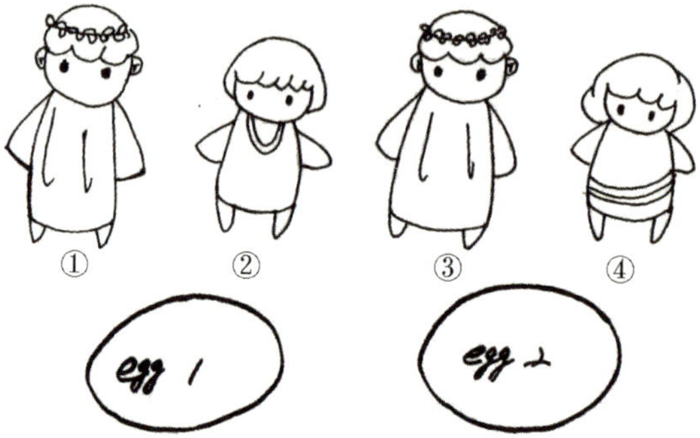

2. There is a hotel named after Agamemnon in modern Greece. Can you guess in which peninsula the hotel is located?
如今，在希腊有一家以阿伽门农命名的酒店，你能猜到这家酒店位于哪个半岛吗？

（2. 答案：伯罗奔尼撒半岛）

CHAPTER 4 Achilles
第四章 阿喀琉斯

Word Knowledge 词汇知识

Achilles' Heel(阿喀琉斯之踵)

Thetis, the sea nymph who was married to the mortal king Peleus, wanted to make her son Achilles immortal by dipping him in the sacred waters of the river Styx, one of the rivers that flowed through the Underworld. However, she did not realize that, when she was dipping the infant, his heel by which she held him was not touched by the waters, thus leaving that spot vulnerable. This is how the modern phrase "Achilles' heel" came to be, for this was also the hero's doom. Paris, the prince of Troy, shot a poisonous arrow, which was believed to have been guided by the god Apollo, and hit Achilles' heel, thus killing him.

Nowadays we use "Achilles' heel" to describe a person's weak spot, or particular vulnerability. Here is an example: *He would be an excellent candidate for the position. He has energy and knowledge, but he has got an Achilles' heel—his bad temper.* The Achilles heel cord is the strongest tendon in the human body, which enables us to walk, run, climb stairs and do all of things that we need to do every day. Stretching and proper warm up are the most general recommendations to prevent injury to your Achilles tendon. Here is an example: *Chinese hurdler Liu Xiang has arrived at a renowned private hospital in London to receive surgery on his torn right Achilles tendon.*

海洋仙女忒提斯在嫁给了人类国王珀琉斯后，希望自己的儿子阿喀琉斯能够拥有不死之身，于是把他带到冥界，将孩子的身体浸泡在冥河的神水之中。可是，她没有意识到在这个过程当中，孩子的脚踵始终在她手里，没能经过洗礼，因此，这块地方就成了他身体中最脆弱的部分。“阿喀琉斯之踵”由此而来，这是英雄致命的弱点。后来，特洛伊王子帕里斯正是在阿波罗的帮助下，将一支毒箭射中了阿喀琉斯的脚踵从而杀了他。

今天，我们用“阿喀琉斯之踵”来描述一个人的软肋或特别脆弱的地方。举个例子：“他有知识有能力，是这一职位的最佳人选，不过他有个软肋——那就是他的坏脾气。”阿喀琉斯肌腱指人身体上最强壮的跟腱，我们无论是走路、跑步、攀登，还是做其他任何事情都离不开它。要防止跟腱拉伤，最有效的方法就是运动前充分热身。举个例子：“中国跨栏运动员刘翔抵达伦敦一家著名的私立医院，对受伤的右脚跟腱进行手术。”

Achilles Reflex(阿喀琉斯反射)

Achilles reflex, also known as the ankle-jerk reflex, is a reflected action or movement, the sum total of any particular automatic response mediated by the nervous system. A reflex is built into the nervous system and does not need the intervention of conscious thought to take effect. In addition to Achilles reflex, there are also knee-jerk reflex and jaw-jerk reflex.

阿喀琉斯反射也称为跟腱反射，是一种反射运动或行为，包括神经系统对于某种外部刺激所做出的全部自然反应。这种本能反应的出现源于神经系统本身，而无须有意识的思维干涉。除了跟腱反射之外，还有膝跳反射和颌跳反射。

The Myrmidons(默米东人)

The Myrmidons were a legendary race of Greek mythology, created by Zeus from a colony of ants. They were then taken to Thessaly either by Aeacus or his son Peleus, king of Thessaly and father of Achilles. During the Trojan War, Achilles led the Myrmidons to battle as an ally of the Achaeans commanded by King Agamemnon.

When Achilles felt wronged by Agamemnon and refused to fight, his army of Myrmidons all followed him by abandoning the battle as well. Seeing the Achaeans suffering tremendous losses, Patroclus, the best friend of Achilles, borrowed Achilles' armour and led the Myrmidons return to the battlefield and soon pushed the Trojan forces back. However, Patroclus was killed by Hector, which enraged Achilles who rejoined the Trojan War to seek revenge.

The Myrmidons were known for their skill in battle and loyalty to their leaders. If someone is likened to a Myrmidon, he must be a devoted person who executes without question or scruple a master's commands.

在希腊神话中，默米东人是宙斯用一群蚂蚁造出来的传奇人种。后来，塞萨利国王埃阿科斯或者他的儿子珀修斯，也就是阿喀琉斯的父亲，将他们带到了塞萨利。特洛伊战争期间，阿喀琉斯率领默米东人加入希腊联军，成为国王阿伽门农所统领的阿卡亚人的盟友。

当阿喀琉斯对于阿伽门农的行为心生不满，决定退出战场时，他手下的默米东人都紧随他放弃了战斗。阿喀琉斯的好友普特洛克勒斯不忍心看着阿卡亚人节节败退，便借来阿喀琉斯的盔甲，率领默米东人回到战场，并很快击退了特洛伊人的进攻。然而，普特洛克勒斯却为赫克托耳所杀，好友的死激怒了阿喀琉斯，为了报仇，他重返战场。

默米东人以骁勇善战、忠心耿耿而著称。假如有人被比作默米东人的话，那他一定是一个非常忠诚的人，会坚决执行主人的命令，绝无半点疑义。

The Myths 神话故事

Achilles was the son of King Peleus and the beautiful sea nymph Thetis, who was so protective of her son that she wanted to transfer her divine powers to this mortal child. She brought the little infant to the underworld and dipped him in the River Styx in order to make his body invincible. It almost worked, except that she forgot to dip in one part—the baby's heel which she was holding at the time.

Young Achilles had been placed under the guidance of the wise centaur Chiron. One day when Thetis learned that her son was essential to the fall of Troy, but he was destined not to return from the war, she determined to shield her child by preventing him from joining the army. So she took him to Scyros, where Achilles was disguised as a girl and kept safe by Lycomedes, the king of the island.

In order to find Achilles, Agamemnon, the leader of the Greek army, sent some clever agents to Scyros, who brought various gifts for the king's daughters. All girls were fluttering around the beautiful jewels and perfume, except one, who seemed to be more interested in a sword. His true nature was revealed. Casting off his disguise, Achilles accepted the choice of a candle-brief, but glorious life.

For many years, the Trojan War raged on with no winners. The Trojan were led by the great warrior Hector, brother of Paris who had abducted Helen, while the Greek boasted Achilles, the youngest but bravest soldier who could fight for days on end without growing weary. However, being a bit of a hothead, one day Achilles got into an argument with Agamemnon, who had taken away from him a slave maid called Briseis from him by force. Feeling insulted, the furious Achilles withdrew to his tent and sulked.

As Achilles refused to fight, his men—the fearsome but loyal Myrmidon army, also refused. Soon the tide of the war turned against the Achaeans. Patroclus, Achilles' tentmate and dearest companion, was unable to stand the wanton Trojan slaughter any longer. He convinced Achilles to let him put on his armor and lead the Myrmidon army into battle. Patroclus succeeded in beating back the Trojan forces, but he was swiftly slain by Hector, prince of Troy.

The death of Patroclus became the prime motivation for Achilles to return to the battlefield. With the sole aim of avenging his friend's death, Achilles led a fierce attack against the Trojans. Finally, just outside the wall of the city, the two great champions, Achilles and Hector, met face to face. With his mighty strength, Achilles threw his spear, and the leader of the Trojan army was dead. After defeating Hector, Achilles tied his corpse by the heels behind his chariot and dragged it three times around the walls of Troy.

Deeply grieved to hear about his brother's death, Paris, though not much of a soldier himself, vowed to take revenge on Achilles. On one occasion, he followed Achilles with a poisonous arrow. On its own, Paris' arrow would never have found its mark, but he had a little help from the great archer god Apollo. Myth has it that Apollo guided the arrow to strike right into Achilles' heel, the vulnerable spot that his mother had forgot to dip in the River Styx.

Achilles, deemed as a real "man" by Hegel, was the only truly multi-faceted, complex hero, endowed with both appealing and abhorrent characteristics. In Homer's *Odyssey*, Odysseus sailed to the underworld and conversed to the shades, one of which was Achilles. When greeted as "blessed in life, blessed in death", Achilles responded, "I would rather be a slave to the worst of the masters than be king of all the dead."

阿喀琉斯是国王珀琉斯和美丽的海洋仙女忒提斯的儿子，忒提斯深爱自己的儿子，希望凭借自己的神力强化儿子的凡人之躯。于是，她来到冥界，将婴儿的躯体浸泡在冥河里。她的计划近乎完美，婴儿被河水浸泡过的身体变得刀枪不入。然而她忘记了一个地方，就是抓在她手里的孩子的脚踵。

幼年的阿喀琉斯被送到智慧的半人马喀戎那里接受培训。有一天，忒提斯听说自己的儿子命里注定会被卷入特洛伊的沦陷之战，并且将有去无回，她决定无论如何要阻止儿子加入这场战争。于是，她把儿子带到了斯库罗斯岛，并将他化装成一个女孩，交由国王吕克墨得斯照看。

为了找到阿喀琉斯，希腊联军的统帅阿伽门农派了一批聪明的特工来到斯库罗斯岛，他们给国王的女儿们献上了各种礼物。女孩子们的目光都被那些美丽的珠宝、香水所吸引，其中只有一个"姑娘"，似乎对那把剑更感兴趣。暴露了本性的阿喀琉斯脱下伪装，决定选择一条短暂而荣耀的生命之路。

特洛伊战争一打就是许多年，始终难分胜负。特洛伊方的统帅是伟大的战士赫克托耳，正是带走海伦的帕里斯的哥哥，而希腊一方则以拥有阿喀琉斯而自豪，这位最年轻最勇敢的战将能够不知疲倦地连续作战。不过，阿喀琉斯血气方刚，因为阿伽门农强行从他的帐中带走了一名叫作布里塞伊斯的女奴，阿喀琉斯和他发生了争执，并一怒之下退回营帐，不再出来。

由于阿喀琉斯拒绝参战，他手下的士兵——那些骁勇善战却异常忠诚的默米东人也拒绝拿起武器。很快，战争开始向着不利于阿卡亚人的方向发展。阿喀琉斯最亲密的伙伴和帐中好友普特洛克勒斯无法忍受希腊士兵被特洛伊人肆意屠杀，便说服阿喀琉斯，借来他的盔甲，代替他率兵出征。普特洛克勒斯成功地击退了敌军，但是他自己却很快被特洛伊王子赫克托耳斩落马下。

普特洛克勒斯的惨死促使阿喀琉斯重新返回了战场，一心为好友复仇的，阿喀琉斯率军猛攻特洛伊大营。最后，就在特洛伊城的城墙下，阿喀琉斯和赫克托耳两位大将面对面地遭遇了。阿喀琉斯挥舞起手中的长矛猛地刺向敌人，赫克托耳应声落马。阿喀琉斯将赫克托耳的双脚绑到自己的马车后方，拖着他的尸体绕着特洛伊城转了三圈。

哥哥的死讯令帕里斯伤心不已，虽然他自己并不善战，但他发誓要替兄长报仇。这天，他瞅准机会，跟踪阿喀琉斯，并将一支毒箭射入了阿喀琉斯的脚踵——他全身最脆弱的地方，那块没有被冥河水浸泡过的地方。传说，帕里斯之所以能够一箭中的是因为阿波罗暗中帮助了他，导致那支箭不偏不倚，正中阿喀琉斯之踵。

阿喀琉斯拥有既可爱又可憎的性格特征，是唯一一位真正复杂多面的英雄，黑格尔因此称他为一个真正的"人"。在荷马史诗《奥德赛》中，奥德修斯曾航行到冥界，并和众多鬼魂有过交谈，其中就包括阿喀琉斯的魂魄。奥德修斯称赞他"无论生前还是死后均为有福之人"，而阿喀琉斯却回答道："我宁愿在阳间做恶人的奴隶，也不愿在阴间做死人的君王。"

Extra 拓展测试

1. Here is a picture of Achilles. Please draw an arrow on his heel.
以下是一副阿喀琉斯的图片，请在他的脚踝部位画上一支箭。

2. The word "Hector" is not simply the name of the eldest Trojan prince, who was slain by Achilles, but could be used as a verb to mean bully or torment. Can you translate the following sentence into proper Chinese?

The teacher hectored his students incessantly.

Hector 这个词不仅仅是那个被阿喀琉斯杀死的特洛伊大王子的名字，还可以用作动词，表示“恐吓”或“折磨”。你能将下面这句话翻译成合适的中文吗？

The teacher hectored his students incessantly.

（2. 答案：那位老师不停地吓唬他的学生。）

CHAPTER 5 Odysseus' Return
第五章 十年返乡路

Word Knowledge 词汇知识

Penelope(珀涅罗珀)

Penelope was the wife of Odysseus who was known for her fidelity to her husband during his twenty-year absence. Despite having 108 suitors, she devised various strategies to delay marrying any of them. One of the excuses she gave was to weave a shroud for her father-in-law, which she would busily work on by day, but unraveled what she had woven at night. For three years she kept her admirers off with the deception.

The name Penelope has therefore become synonymous of a chaste woman and is often associated with marital fidelity. A Penelope's web or the web of Penelope is taken as a task that seems never ending, or the tactics of delaying something on purpose. Here is an example: *My work is something like the Penelope's web: never done, but ever in hand.*

珀涅罗珀是奥德修斯的妻子,以对丈夫忠贞不渝而著称。在丈夫离家的二十年间,她的身边先后出现了 108 位追求者,但是她用各种各样的对策来拖延他们的求婚。其中一个借口就是要为岳父织一件寿衣,这件寿衣她总是白天织,晚上拆,织了三年仍没有织完。

于是,珀涅罗珀这个名字就成了"贞妇"的同义词,常与"婚姻忠诚"相联系。"珀涅罗珀的织物"的意思就是一份似乎总也完成不了的工作,或指故意拖延的战术。例如:"我的工作就像珀涅罗珀的织物:永远做不完,永远在手上。"

Trojan Horse(特洛伊木马)

The Trojan Horse is a popular tale from the Trojan War about the subterfuge that the Greeks used to enter the independent city of Troy and eventually win the war. After a fruitless ten-year siege, Odysseus thought of building a great wooden horse, hiding an elite force inside, and fooling the Trojans into wheeling the horse into the city as a trophy. Then that night the Greek force crept out of the horse and opened the gates for the rest of the Greek army. The city of Troy was destroyed.

A Trojan horse has now metaphorically come to mean any trick or stratagem that causes a target to invite a foe into a securely protected bastion or place. Hence a malicious computer program which tricks users into willingly running it is referred to as a "Trojan horse" or simply a "Trojan". Meanwhile, Greek gift, which is alluded to the Trojan horse, is understood as a gift given with the intention of tricking and causing harm to the recipient. Here is an example: *The loan of his cottage turned out to be a Greek gift. The roof fell in and injured us.*

特洛伊木马是一则广为流传的故事,讲的是希腊人利用诡计攻入特洛伊城,取得了战争的最后胜利。在围攻城池十年无果的情况下,奥德修斯想出了一个办法,即建造一匹巨型木马,将一支精锐部队藏入其中,特洛伊人误以为这是希腊人留下的战利品,将木马拖入城中。那天夜里,藏在木马中的士兵悄悄爬出,打开了城门,希腊军队长驱直入,特洛伊城因而沦陷。

如今,特洛伊木马可以用来比喻任何"引狼入室"的诡计或花招,因此,诱使用户自愿运行的恶意计算机程序就被称作"特洛伊木马"或简称"木马"。同时,"希腊礼物"通常暗指特洛伊木马,用来指不怀好意或者给人带来伤害的礼物。例如:"他把小屋暂借给我们原来是不安好心,屋顶坍塌了下来,我们都受了伤。"

Man's Best Friend(人类最好的朋友)

Upon his return after twenty years, Odysseus disguised himself as an old beggar in order to secretly re-enter his palace. Argus, his beloved dog, was the only individual to recognize him. As Odysseus approached his home, he saw an old dog lying in filth there. It was his old hunting hound, Argus, which had in the good old days followed him faithfully in the chase. Argus recognized his master at once, but he had just enough strength to drop his ears and wag his tail. Unable to greet his beloved dog, as this would betray who he really was, Odysseus passed by (but not without shedding a tear) and Argus, letting out a cry, died for joy.

Domestic dogs are man's best companions. They would remain loyal to their masters, despite being neglected occasionally, until the end of their lives. Such a millennia-long history of close relations between dogs and humans is reflected in the common English phrase referring dog as "man's best friend".

二十年后,当奥德修斯重返家园时,他将自己伪装成一位年迈的乞丐,以便悄悄潜入王宫。唯一识破他伪装的是他心爱的猎犬阿戈斯。临近家门时,奥德修斯瞥见不远处躺着一只脏兮兮的老狗,那便是阿戈斯,那只曾经在往昔美好的日子里追随他四处奔跑的忠实朋友。阿戈斯一眼便认出了主人,然而,它的力气只够他耷拉下耳朵,摇一摇尾巴。奥德修斯不愿暴露自己的身份,因此并没有向他的忠犬打招呼,而是含泪从他身边径直走过。阿戈斯大叫一声,开心地死去了。

家犬是人类最好的伴侣。尽管有时人类会忽视他们,但是他们对主人的忠诚却是至死不变的。人与狗这种亲密的关系已经有了上千年的历史,而将狗比作"人类最好的朋友"恰恰反映了这样的历史。

The Myths 神话故事

Odysseus, king of Ithaca, was the hero of Homer's epic poem *Odyssey* and one of the most frequently portrayed figures in western literature. He was a man of outstanding wisdom and shrewdness. When he was first invited to join the Greek expedition against Troy, he was so reluctant to leave his loving wife, Penelope, that he feigned insanity, sowing his field with salt. But when his friends, suspecting trickery, laid his little son before the plough, he turned it aside. With his disguise stripped off, he was eventually persuaded to go to war.

Being a man of eloquence, Odysseus played a leading part in achieving the reconciliation between Agamemnon and Achilles. He fought bravely and struck fear into the hearts of the Trojans. When Troy still refused to yield after years of bitter fighting, Odysseus devised the ruse of the wooden horse, by means of which the city was sacked and houses and temples alike razed to the ground. Thus the heroes incurred the wrath of the gods. So on their way back to Greece, many of them died as victims to the vengeance of the gods.

Odysseus' wanderings and the recovery of his kingdom are the central theme of *Odyssey*. On the tenth day after leaving Troy, Odysseus and his men came to an island, where the inhabitants' sole food was lotus fruit and blossoms. The enchanted plant had such a magic spell on its eaters that it tended to blot out their recollection of the past and produce a dreamy lethargy over them. Detecting the entrancing effect of the food, Odysseus forbade his followers to touch the plant and ordered them to drag their languid companions back to the ships and had them chained to the rowing-benches. Without hesitation, they set sail, leaving the dreamy lotus-eaters behind.

Continuing their journey, Odysseus and his followers arrived at the country of the Cyclops, a race of giants having only one eye in the center of their foreheads. In need of some provisions, Odysseus, together with twelve chosen companions, entered a vast cave, the home of Polyphemus, son of Poseidon, who proved to be a savage man-eater. After six unfortunate companions were devoured by the Cyclop, Odysseus took chance to blind him by thrusting an olive-staff into the eye-ball of Polyphemus. Then they succeeded in escaping from the cave by clinging to the wool of the finest rams.

Odysseus also encountered a beautiful enchantress called Circe. She lived in a charming and fertile valley. Seemingly gracious and hospitable, she invited the visiting sailors to her magnificent marble palace and presented them with fine wine. However, once touched, the drugged wine transformed the drinkers immediately into swine. At this critical moment, Hermes came to aid. He provided Odysseus with a peculiar herb which would break the spell. For the first time the magic wine became completely nullified and Circe was astonished. At Odysseus request, she restored his companions to their human form and loaded his ship with provisions for the voyage before reluctantly biding him farewell.

Having wandered for ten years from place to place and gone from one mishap to another, Odysseus was eventually approaching his home. With the help of Athena, he transformed his own appearance to that of an old beggar. Inside the palace, he was held in ridicule by all the young suitors of his wife, Penelope, but not for long. For he shot an arrow through the holes of nine axe-heads with his own bow which all the young princes present had failed even to pull. The hero then revealed his true identity and shot all the suitors to death.

奥德修斯是伊萨卡国王，也是荷马史诗《奥德赛》中的英雄，是西方文学中最常出现的人物之一。他智慧超群、敏锐果敢，传说最初他并不愿离开自己心爱的妻子珀涅罗珀，去特洛伊征战，因此在家里装疯卖傻，把盐种到地里。他的朋友怀疑他在演戏，就把他的儿子放到犁耙前面，他立刻调转了方向。伪装被识破，最终他不得不同意随军出征。

奥德修斯能言善辩，在调和阿伽门农和阿喀琉斯的关系中起到了非常重要的作用。他骁勇善战，令特洛伊人胆寒。由于久攻不下，敌人又拒绝投降，奥德修斯想出了木马之计，并因此攻入了特洛伊城。希腊士兵在城中烧杀抢掠、滥杀无辜，惹怒了众神，因此在返回希腊的途中，他们中的许多人都遭到天谴而命丧黄泉。

奥德修斯返乡途中的流浪经历构成了史诗《奥德赛》的主要内容。在离开特洛伊的第十天，奥德修斯和他的手下来到了一个小岛，那里的居民以忘忧树的花朵和果实为食物，而这种魔性的植物能让吃它的人瞬间忘记往事，陷入一种恍恍惚惚的昏睡状态。奥德修斯察觉到了这种食物的致幻作用，严令禁止手下触碰这种植物，并将那些业已瘫软的水手拖回船上、用铁链把他们绑到凳子上。他不敢迟疑，下令立刻起航，逃离那个梦幻的小岛。

接着，奥德修斯和手下航行到了独眼巨人的领地，这些巨人的额头中央只有一只眼睛。为了寻找补给，奥德修斯率领十二名勇士进入了一个巨大的山洞，这是波吕斐摩斯的家，他是波塞冬的儿子，也是一个吃人的恶魔。先后有六名勇士都不幸成了他的腹中餐，奥德修斯最终抓住机会将一根橄榄枝插入他的独眼，戳瞎了他，并和其余的手下躲在羊肚子下面成功溜出了洞穴。

奥德修斯还遇到了一位名叫喀耳刻的美丽女巫。她住在一个迷人而富饶的山谷里。表面上看，她既好客又慷慨，不仅邀请来访的水手参观她那富丽堂皇的大理石宫殿，还为他们端上美酒佳肴。然而，一旦喝了她的毒酒，水手们就会立刻变成猪。关键时刻，赫耳墨斯前来帮忙。他给了奥德修斯一种特殊的草药，可以解除魔咒。喀耳刻的魔酒第一次失效了，震惊之余，她按照奥德修斯的要求，将其手下又变回人形，并为他们备足了补给，很不情愿地放他们走了。

十年间，奥德修斯游历了一个又一个地方，经历了一次又一次磨难，最后终于快要到家了。在雅典娜的帮助下，他将自己变成了一位年迈的乞丐。宫殿之中聚集着珀涅罗珀众多的追求者，他们纷纷嘲笑这个又老又丑的家伙，可是，这种嘲笑并没有持续多久，因为奥德修斯用一支箭射穿了九把斧头的斧心，而那些年轻的王公贵族们却连那把弓都拉不开。露出真容的英雄结束了在场所有追求者的性命。

Extra 拓展测试

1. Which of the following do you think is a Penelope's web?
以下哪一幅图画的是珀涅罗珀的织物？

A

B

2. In Latin, Odysseus was known as Ulixes, or Ulysses in English. *Ulysses* is also a modernist novel about a Dublin businessman named Leopold Bloom, whose life in one day turns out to bear many elaborate parallels to Odysseus' ten years of wandering. This novel was written by a famous Irish novelist. Do you know his name?

在拉丁语中，奥德修斯被称作尤利西斯（拉丁文拼法：Ulixes，英文拼法：Ulysses），而《尤利西斯》也是一部现代主义小说，讲的是一位名叫利奥波德·布卢姆的都柏林商人的生活。故事发生在一天当中，却与奥德修斯十年的漂泊生涯不谋而合。这部小说由一位爱尔兰作家所创作，你知道他叫什么名字吗？

（1. 答案：A）

（2. 答案：詹姆斯·乔伊斯）

FURTHER READING
Sword of Damocles
延伸阅读　达摩克利斯之剑

The famed "sword of Damocles" dates back to an ancient moral parable popularized by the Roman philosopher Cicero around 45 B.C. The tale centers on Dionysius II, a tyrannical king who once ruled over the Sicilian city of Syracuse during the fourth and fifth centuries B.C.

Though rich and powerful, Dionysius was supremely unhappy. His iron-fisted rule had made him many enemies, and he was tormented by fears of assassination—so much that he slept in a bedchamber surrounded by a moat and only trusted his daughters to shave his beard with a razor.

The king's dissatisfaction came to an end one day after a friend of his, and a court flatterer, Damocles by name, showered him with compliments and remarked how blissful his life must be. "Since this life delights you," the annoyed Dionysius replied, "do you wish to taste it yourself and make a trial of my good fortune?"

"Oh, no, not that, my king!" said Damocles in a nervous manner, "but I think, that, if I could only have your riches and your pleasures for one day, I should not want any greater happiness." "Very well," said the king. "You shall have them."

So the next day, when Damocles entered the palace, he was seated on a golden throne, with a host of servants waiting on him. He was treated to succulent cuts of meat and lavished with scented perfumes and ointments. Damocles couldn't believe his luck. Resting himself among soft cushions, he felt that he was the happiest man in the world.

But just as he was starting to enjoy the life of a king, he chanced to raise his eyes toward the ceiling. What was it that was dangling above him, with its point almost touching his head? It was a razor-sharp sword! Suspended only by a single strand of horsehair! What if the hair should break? There was danger every moment that it would do so.

The smile faded from the lips of Damocles. His face became ashy pale. His hands were trembling. From that moment on, the courtier's fear for his life made it impossible for him to savor the opulence of the feast or enjoy the servants. After casting several nervous glances at the blade dangling above him, he asked to be excused, saying that he no longer wished to be so fortunate.

"What is the matter?" asked the king. "That sword! That sword!" cried Damocles. He was so badly frightened that he even dared not to move. "Yes," said Dionysius, "I know there is a sword above your head, and that it may fall at any moment. But why should that trouble you? I have a sword above my head all the time. I am every moment in dread lest something may cause me to lose my life."

"Let me go," said Damocles. "I now see that I was mistaken. The rich and powerful are not so happy as they seem. Let me go back to my old home in the poor little cottage among the mountains." When the permission was granted, Damocles fled immediately. So long as he lived, he never again wanted to be rich, or to change places, even for a moment, with the king.

The tale of Dionysius and Damocles represented the idea that those in power always labor under the specter of anxiety and death, and that "there can be no happiness for one who is under constant apprehensions." The parable later became a common motif in medieval literature, and the phrase "sword of Damocles" is now commonly used as a catchall term to describe a looming danger.

Likewise, the saying "hanging by a thread" has become shorthand for a fraught or precarious situation. One of its more famous uses came in 1961 during the Cold War, when President John F. Kennedy gave a speech before the United Nations in which he said that "Every man, woman and child lives under a nuclear sword of Damocles, hanging by the slenderest of threads, capable of being cut at any moment by accident or miscalculation or by madness."

著名的"达摩克利斯之剑"源于公元前45年左右,古罗马哲学家西塞罗所撰写的一则寓言故事。故事的主人公是一位有名的暴君小狄奥尼西奥斯,也就是在公元前4至5世纪期间,曾统治西西里城邦锡拉库萨的国王。

虽然小狄奥尼西奥斯有权有势,但他一点也不快乐。由于铁血统治为他树敌无数,他一直担心自己会遭人暗算,以至于不得不在寝宫之外挖了一条护城河来保护自己,他甚至只允许自己的女儿帮他修面。

这天,国王的痛苦终于告一段落了,因为王宫里来了位客人。这位谄媚的朋友名叫达摩克利斯,在一番阿谀奉承之后,他表示国王的生活一定是非常幸福的。小狄奥尼西奥斯听了不免有点恼火,于是说道:"既然你这么喜欢这种生活,那你愿意试试和我交换一下位置,亲身体验一下吗?"

"哦,不,不,陛下!我没那个意思!"达摩克利斯略显紧张地说,"不过,我想,假如能拥有您的财富和快乐一天的话,我就别无所求了。""很好,"国王说道,"你会有的。"

于是,第二天,当达摩克利斯走进王宫之后,他被安排坐上了国王的金色宝座,一大群奴仆围绕着他,为他端上美味佳肴,奉上香氛珠宝。达摩克利斯简直不敢相信自己有这样的福分,坐在松软的椅垫上,他感觉自己就是世界上最幸福的人了。

就在他开始享受国王的待遇时,他无意中瞥了一眼天花板——那个悬在他头顶上的东西是什么?它的尖端几乎要碰到他的脑袋了!那是一把锋利的宝剑!而用来悬挂宝剑的仅仅是一根马鬃!如果那马鬃断了可怎么办?这种危险随时都存在。

达摩克利斯嘴角的笑容消失了,他的脸色变得惨白,他的双手开始颤抖。从那一刻起,这位弄臣由于担心小命不保,已无心享用美味佳肴和奴仆侍奉了。在紧张地瞥了几眼头上的刀刃后。他再也坐不住了,请求国王能原谅他，让他做回寻常百姓。

“怎么了？”国王问道。“那把剑！那把剑！”达摩克利斯大叫道。他吓得不轻，动都不敢动。“没错，”狄奥尼西奥斯说道，“我知道你头上有一把剑，而且随时有可能掉下来，但那又怎样呢？我的头上无时无刻都悬着一把剑，每一分钟我都处在恐惧中，担心有人会要了我的命啊。”

“让我走吧，”达摩克利斯说道，“现在我知道自己错了，有钱有势的人并非像他们看起来那样幸福。还是放我回家，让我回到山里那个小破屋去吧。”得到国王的应允，达摩克利斯拔腿就跑。在他活着的时候，他再也不想成为有钱人了，再也不愿和国王交换哪怕一刻的位置了。

小狄奥尼西奥斯和达摩克利斯的故事告诉我们，那些拥有权力的人往往会处在死亡和疑惧的阴影之中，而“始终处在忧虑之中的人根本没有幸福可言”。后来，这则寓言成为中世纪文学的常见主题，“达摩克利斯之剑”这个词组也成了一个含义甚广的表达，常用来描述“隐约可见的危险”。

与此相似，“命悬一线”作为一种简略说法，用来指令人担忧、岌岌可危的情况。关于这一词组最著名的一个用法出现在1961年冷战期间，时任美国总统的肯尼迪在联合国发表演讲时说：“每一个男人、女人和孩子都生活在一把名为达摩克利斯的核剑之下，这把剑用最细的线悬挂着，一个意外，一次误判，一场疯狂的行为都有可能使其断裂。”

Extra 拓展测试

In *The Canterbury Tales*, the author refered to the sword of Damocles, which the knight described to hang over Conquest. Do you know who wrote *The Canterbury Tales*?

在《坎特伯雷故事集》中，作者曾借骑士之口，以达摩克利斯之剑来描述征服者需面对的危险。你知道《坎特伯雷故事》是谁写的吗？

（答案：杰弗雷·乔叟）

Index
人名索引

	English 英文名	Chinese 中文名	Sex 性别	Note 备注
	Individual Names 单名			
1st Generation 一代主神	Gaea	盖亚	F	Mother Earth
	Uranus	乌拉诺斯	M	Father Sky
	Erebus	埃里伯斯	M	Darkness
	Nyx	尼克斯	F	Night
	Aeolus	伊俄勒斯	M	God of the winds
	Aether	埃忒尔	M	Brightness
	Atlas	阿特拉斯	M	Titan
	Ceos	西耳斯	M	Titan
	Crios	克瑞耳斯	M	Titan
	Cronus	克罗诺斯	M	Titan (heaven)
	Eos	厄俄斯	F	Goddess of the dawn
	Epimetheus	厄庇墨修斯	M	Brother of prometheus
	Helios	赫利俄斯	M	God of the sun
	Hemera	赫墨拉	F	Day
	Hyperion	许珀里翁	M	Titan (sun)
	Hypnos	修普诺斯	M	Sleep
	Iapetus	伊阿珀托斯	M	Titan
	Mnemosyne	摩涅莫辛涅	F	Goddess of memory
	Oceanus	俄刻阿诺斯	M	Titan (ocean)
	Phoebe	福柏	F	Titan (moon)
	Prometheus	普罗米修斯	M	Titan
	Rhea	瑞亚	F	Titan
	Tethys	蒂锡斯	F	Titan
	Thanatos	塔纳托斯	M	Death
	Theis	忒弥斯	F	Titan
	Themis	西弥斯	F	Goddess of justice

（续表）

	English 英文名	Chinese 中文名	Sex 性别	Note 备注
2nd Generation 二代主神	Anteros	安忒洛斯	M	Brother of Eros
	Aphrodite	阿芙洛蒂忒	F	Goddess of love
	Apollo	阿波罗	M	God of the sun
	Ares	阿瑞斯	M	God of war
	Artemis	阿尔忒弥斯	F	Goddess of the moon
	Asclepius	阿斯克勒庇俄斯	M	God of medicine
	Athena	雅典娜	F	Goddess of wisdom
	Boreas	波瑞阿斯	M	God of the north wind
	Deimos	戴墨斯	M	Son of Aphrodite and Ares
	Demeter	得墨忒耳	F	Goddess of agriculture
	Dionysus	狄俄尼索斯	M	God of wine
	Eris	厄里斯	F	Goddess of strife
	Eros	厄洛斯	M	God of love
	Eurus	欧洛斯	M	God of the east wind
	Hades	哈迪斯	M	God of the underworld
	Hebe	赫柏	F	Goddess of youth
	Hephaestus	赫菲斯托斯	M	God of blacksmith
	Hera	赫拉	F	Wife of Zeus
	Hermes	赫耳墨斯	M	Messenger of the gods
	Hestia	赫斯提	F	Goddess of the hearth
	Khione	开俄尼	F	Goddess of snow
	Lucina	鲁西娜	F	Goddess of childbirth
	Metis	墨提斯	F	1st wife of Zeus
	Nemesis	内密西斯	F	Goddess of revenge
	Nereus	涅柔斯	M	God of the sea
	Notus	诺托斯	M	God of the south wind
	Pan	潘神	M	God of fertility
	Persephone	珀耳塞福涅	F	Wife of Hades
	Poseidon	波塞冬	M	God of the sea
	Phobos	弗伯斯	M	Son of Aphrodite and Ares
	Selene	塞勒涅	F	Goddess of the moon
	Tmolus	特摩洛斯	M	God of woods
	Zephyrus	仄斐若斯	M	God of the west wind
	Zeus	宙斯	M	God of the Gods

（续表）

	English 英文名	Chinese 中文名	Sex 性别	Note 备注
Minor Divinities 小神	The Nine Muses 缪斯女神			
	Calliope	卡利俄珀	F	Muse (epic poetry)
	Clio	克利俄	F	Muse (history)
	Melpomene	墨尔波墨涅	F	Muse (tragedy)
	Thalia	塔利亚	F	Muse (comedy)
	Erato	埃拉托	F	Muse (love poetry)
	Euterpe	欧忒耳珀	F	Muse (lyric poetry)
	Terpsichore	特耳西科瑞	F	Muse (dance and song)
	Urania	乌拉尼亚	F	Muse (astronomy)
	Polyhymnia	波吕许谟尼亚	F	Muse (sacred hymns)
	The Horae 时序女神			
	Thallo	塔罗	F	Horae (spring)
	Auxo	奥克索	F	Horae (summer)
	Carpo	卡波尔	F	Horae (autumn)
	The Moirai/Fates 命运女神			
	Atropos	阿特洛波斯	F	Moirai (thread cutter)
	Clothos	克洛索	F	Moirai (spinner)
	Lachesis	拉基西斯	F	Moirai (drawer of lot)
	Nymphs 仙女			
	Daphne	达芙妮	F	A nymph
	Echo	厄科	F	A mountain nymph
	Eupheme	欧斐墨	F	A nymph
	Eurynome	欧律诺墨	F	One of the Oceanides
	Harmonia	哈耳摩尼亚	F	Daughter of Aphrodite
	Leto	勒托	F	Lover of Zeus
	Maia	迈亚	F	Nymph, lover of Zeus
	Melissae	梅丽西	F	nymph
	Orithyia	欧丽泰亚	F	Wife of Boreas
	Philyra	斐莱拉	F	nymph & mother of Chiron
	Psyche	普赛克	F	Wife of Eros
	Salmacis	萨耳玛西斯	F	A water nymph
	Syrinx	绪任克斯	F	A nymph loved by Pan
	Thetis	忒提斯	F	Sea nymph

（续表）

	English 英文名	Chinese 中文名	Sex 性别	Note 备注
Minor Divinities 小神	Other Divinities 其他			
	Acis	埃西斯	M	Son of a river god
	Amninos	阿尼诺斯	M	A river god
	Charon	卡戎	M	Boatman in Hades
	Chiron	喀戎	M	A wise centaur
	Chrysaor	克律萨俄耳	M	Brother of Pegasus
	Circe	喀耳刻	F	a beautiful enchantress
	Hermaphroditus	赫墨芙洛狄忒斯	M	Son of Hermes & Aphrodite
	Medusa	美杜莎	F	One of the Gorgons
	Minos	弥诺斯	M	Judge in Hades
	Orion	俄里翁	M	Friend of Artemis
	Rhadamanthus	拉达曼堤斯	M	Judge in Hades
	Polyphemus	波吕斐摩斯	M	A giant Cyclops
	Pythia	皮提亚	F	A priestess at Delphi
	Silenus	塞列努斯	M	Tutor of the wine god
Mortal Beings 凡间生物	Strange Creatures 怪物			
	Argus	阿耳戈斯		A one-hundred-eyed monster
	Cerberus	刻耳柏洛斯		Three-headed dog
	Chimaera	喀迈拉		A hybrid creature
	Hydra	海德拉		A nine-headed serpent
	Minotaur	弥诺陶洛斯	M	Half-man-half-bull monster
	Parthenope	帕耳忒诺珀	F	Siren (the eldest)
	Pegasus	珀加索斯		The flying horse
	Python	皮同		A dreadful serpent
	Sphinx	斯芬克司	F	a monstrous creature
	Mortals of Unknown Origin 人类（所属不明）			
	Adonis	阿多尼斯	M	Mortal lover of Aphrodite
	Aristaeus	阿瑞斯泰俄斯	M	Half-brother of Orpheus
	Battus	巴图斯	M	An old shepherd
	Coronis	刻洛尼斯	F	Wife of Apollo
	Cycnus	席古拿斯	M	Friend of Phaethon
	Demophoon	得摩富翁	M	Son of Celeus
	Deucalion	丢卡利翁	M	Son of Prometheus

（续表）

	English 英文名	Chinese 中文名	Sex 性别	Note 备注
Mortal Beings 凡间生物	Strange Creatures 怪物			
	Dictys	狄克提斯	M	A fisherman
	Epaphus	厄帕福斯	M	Friend of Phaethon
	Eurydice	欧律狄刻	F	Wife of Orpheus
	Galatea	伽拉忒亚	F	Wife of Pygmalion
	Io	艾奥	F	Mortal over of Zeus
	Narcissus	那喀索斯	M	A handsome youth
	Orpheus	俄耳甫斯	M	Most gifted musician
	Pandora	潘多拉	F	1st mortal woman
	Phaethon	法厄同	M	Mortal son of Helios
	Pygmalion	皮格马利翁	M	a talented sculptor
	Pyrrha	皮拉	F	Wife of Deucalion
	Semele	塞默勒	F	Mortal lover of Zeus
	Mortals from Athen 雅典			
	Aegeus	埃勾斯	M	King of Athens
	Helen	海伦	F	Wife of Menelaus
	Menelaus	墨涅拉俄斯	M	Brother of Agamemnon
	Theseus	忒修斯	M	A hero of Athens
	Mortals from Argos 阿尔戈斯			
	Acrisius	阿克里修斯	M	King of Argos
	Adrastus	阿德拉斯托斯	M	King of Argos
	Aegisthus	埃癸斯托斯	M	Cousin of of Agamemnon
	Aegyptus	埃古普托斯	M	Brother of Danaus
	Aeson	埃宋	M	Father of Jason
	Agamemnon	阿伽门农	M	King of Mycenae/Argos
	Alcmene	阿尔克墨涅	F	Mother of Heracles
	Amphiaraus	安菲阿拉俄斯	M	A seer adn one of the Seven
	Atreus	阿特柔斯	M	Father of Agamemnon
	Capaneus	卡帕纽斯	M	One of the Seven
	Clytemnestra	克吕泰涅斯特拉	F	Wife of Agamemnon
	Danae	达那厄	F	Daughter of Acrisius
	Danaus	达那俄斯	M	King of Argos

（续表）

	English 英文名	Chinese 中文名	Sex 性别	Note 备注
Mortal Beings 凡间生物	Mortals from Argos 阿尔戈斯			
	Eurystheus	欧律斯修斯	M	King of Argos
	Galanthis	伽兰西斯	F	Servant of Alcmene
	Heracles	海格立斯	M	Demigod
	Hippomedon	希波墨冬	M	One of the Seven
	Hypermnestra	许珀耳涅斯特拉	F	The eldest of the Danaids
	Iphigenia	依菲琴尼亚	F	Daughter of Agamemnon
	Jason	伊阿宋	M	Leader of the Argonauts
	Lynceus	林瑟斯	M	Husband of Hypermnestra
	Orestes	俄瑞斯忒斯	M	Agamemnon's son
	Pelias	珀利阿斯	M	Uncle of Jason
	Perseus	珀尔修斯	M	A hero of Argos
	Tydeus	提丢斯	M	One of the Seven
	Mortals from Corinth 科林斯			
	Bellerophon	柏勒洛丰	M	Prince of Corinth
	Creon	克瑞翁	M	King of Corinth
	Glauce	格劳刻	F	Daughter of Creon
	Merope	美罗珀	F	Wife of Polybus
	Polybus	珀吕波斯	M	King of Corinth
	Sisyphus	西西弗斯	M	Son of Aeolus
	Mortals from Thebes 底比斯			
	Antigone	安提戈涅	F	Daughter of Oedipus
	Creon	克瑞翁	M	Jocasta's brother
	Eteocles	厄忒俄克勒斯	M	Son of Oedipus
	Eurydice	欧律狄刻	F	Wife of Creon
	Haemon	希门	M	Son of Creon
	Ismene	伊斯墨涅	F	Sister of Antigone
	Jocasta	伊俄卡斯	F	Wife of Laius
	Laius	拉伊俄斯	M	King of Thebes
	Oedipus	俄狄浦斯	M	Son of Laius
	Polynices	波吕尼克斯	M	Son of Oedipus
	Mortals from Thessaly 塞萨利			
	Achilles	阿喀琉斯	M	Son of King Peleus

（续表）

	English 英文名	Chinese 中文名	Sex 性别	Note 备注
Mortal Beings 凡间生物	Briseis	布里塞伊斯	F	A slave maid
	Patroclus	普特洛克勒斯	M	Achilles' tentmate
	Peleus	珀琉斯	M	Son of King Aeacus
	Ixion	伊克西翁	M	King of Thessaly
	Mortals from Sparta 斯巴达			
	Castor	卡斯托耳	M	Son of Leda & Tyndareus
	Hyacinthus	雅辛托斯	M	A Spartan prince
	Leda	勒达	F	Wife of Tyndareus
	Pollux	波吕克斯	M	Son of Leda and Zeus
	Tyndareus	廷达柔斯	M	King of Sparta
	Mortals from Arcadia 阿卡狄亚			
	Arcas	阿尔卡斯	M	Son of Callisto
	Atalanta	阿塔兰忒	F	An Arcadian princess
	Callisto	卡利斯托	F	Daughter of Lycaon
	Hippomenes	希波墨涅斯	M	Husband of Atalanta
	Lycaon	吕卡翁	M	King of Arcadia
	Parthenopaeus	帕耳忒诺派俄斯	M	Son of Atalanta
	Mortals from Troy 特洛伊			
	Cassandra	卡珊德拉	F	Daughter of Priam
	Hector,	赫克托耳	M	Brother of Paris
	Laomedon	拉俄墨冬	M	King of Troy
	Paris	帕里斯	M	Trojan prince
	Priam	普里阿摩斯	M	King of Troy
	Mortals from Crete 克里特			
	Ariadne	阿里阿德涅	F	Daughter of Minos
	Daedalus	代达罗斯	M	A famous architect
	Minos	弥诺斯	M	King of Crete
	Mortals from Babylon 巴比伦			
	Pyramus	皮拉摩斯	M	A young man in Babylon
	Thisbe	提斯柏	F	Lover of Pyramus
	Mortals from Other Places 其他地区			
	Aeetes	埃厄忒斯	M	King of Colchis
	Althaea	阿尔泰娅	F	Mother of Meleager
	Andromeda	安德洛墨达	F	An Ethiopian princess

（续表）

	English 英文名	Chinese 中文名	Sex 性别	Note 备注
Mortal Beings 凡间生物	Cepheus	刻甫斯	M	King of Ethiopia
	Epaphus	厄帕福斯	M	Son of Io
	Hero	海洛	F	A maiden in Sestos
	Iobates	伊俄巴忒斯	M	King of Lycia
	Leander	利安得	M	A youth in Abydos
	Lycomedes	吕克墨得斯	M	King of Scyros
	Medea	美狄亚	F	Daughter of Aeetes
	Meleager	墨勒阿格尔	M	Son of Oeneus
	Midas	迈达斯	M	King of Phygia
	Odysseus	奥德修斯	M	King of Ithaca
	Oeneus	俄纽斯	M	King of Aetolia
	Penelope	珀涅罗珀	F	Wife of Odysseus
	Phrixus	佛里克索斯	M	Prince of Boeotia
	Pierus	庇厄洛斯	M	King of Macedon
	Polydectes	波吕得克忒斯	M	king of Seriphos
	Proetus	普洛托斯	M	King of Tiryns
	Stheneboea	斯塞尼波尔	F	Wife of Proetus
	Tantalus	坦塔罗斯	M	A Lydian king
Collective Names 合名				
Giants 巨人	Centimani	百臂巨人	M	Giants
	Cyclopes	独眼巨人	M	Giant monsters
	Titans	提坦巨人	F/M	Giants
Nymphs 仙女	the Amnisiades	阿尼西阿得斯	F	Daughters of Amninos
	the Dryades	德律阿得斯	F	Tree nymphs
	the Hamadryades	哈墨德律阿得斯	F	Wood nymphs
	the Heliades	赫利阿得斯	F	Daughters of Helios
	the Hesperides	赫斯珀里得斯	F	Sea nymphs
	the Hyades	许阿得斯	F	Cloud nymphs
	the Limoniades	利墨尼阿得斯	F	Meadow nymphs
	the Meliades	弥利阿得斯	F	Nymphs of fruit-trees
	the Naiades	那伊阿得斯	F	Water nymphs
	the Napaeae	那庇伊	F	Valley nymphs
	the Nereides	涅瑞伊得斯	F	Sea nymphs
	the Oceanides	俄刻阿尼得斯	F	Ocean nymphs
	the Oreades	俄瑞阿得斯	F	Mountain nymphs

（续表）

	English 英文名	Chinese 中文名	Sex 性别	Note 备注
Deities 兄弟/姐妹神	Anemoi	阿涅摩伊	M	Wind gods
	the Boreades	波瑞阿蒂斯	M	Sons of Boreas
	the Furies	复仇三女神	F	Three deities in Hades
	the Graces	美惠三女神	F	Three deities
	the Horae	霍莉(时序女神)	F	Three deities of hours
	the Moirai	摩伊拉(命运女神)	F	Three deities of fates
Others 其他	the Gorgons	戈耳戈	F	Three snake-haired sisters
	The Graeae	格里伊	F	Three old sisters
	the Harpies	哈比	F	Three eagle-like divinities
	the Sirens	塞壬	F	Three sea nymphs
Mortals 凡人	the Amazons	亚马孙人	F	the warrior women
	the Danaids	达那伊得斯	F	Daughters of Danaus
	the Propoetides	普罗珀艾提得斯	F	First prostitutes

Index 2
地名索引

English 英文	Chinese 中文	Note 说明
Abraham	亚伯拉罕河	A river in Lebanon
Abydos	阿拜多斯	An Egyptian city
Acheron	阿刻戎	A river (sorrow)
Aegean Sea	爱琴海	East of Greece
Aeolian Island	伊奥利亚岛	Kingdom of wind
Arcadia	阿卡狄亚	Greek state
Argos /Mycenae	阿尔戈斯/迈锡尼	Greek state
Athens	雅典	Greek state
Aulis	奥里斯	A port
Peloponnesus	伯罗奔尼撒半岛	A peninsula
Black Sea	黑海	An interior sea
Boeotia	皮奥夏	Greek city state
Bosporus	博斯布鲁斯海峡	A strait
Tartarus	塔尔塔罗斯	Deep abyss in Hades
Caucasus	高加索	A mountain
Cocytus	科赛特斯	A river (lamentation)
Colchis	科尔基斯	Greek state
Corinth	科林斯	Greek city state
Crete	克里特	An island state
Cyprus	塞浦路斯	Greek city state
Delos	得洛斯	A floating island

（续表）

English 英文	Chinese 中文	Note 说明
Delphi	特尔斐	Temple of Apollo
Elysium	伊利索姆	A blissful place
Eridanus	波江	A river
Helicon	赫利孔	A mountain
Hellespont	赫勒斯滂	A strait
Hippocrene	灵泉	A sacred spring
Ithaca	伊萨卡	Greek city state
Iolcus	伊奥克斯	Greek city state
Ladon	拉冬	A river
Lethe	勒忒(忘川)	A river (oblivion)
Lycia	利西亚	Greek city state
Macedon	马其顿	Greek city state
Marathon	马拉松	Greek state
Mediterranean	地中海	West of Greece
Memphis	孟斐斯	A city in Egypt
Nysa	倪萨山	A mountain
Othrys	俄特里斯	A mountain
Phlegethon	佛勒革同	A burning river
Phoenicia	腓尼基	Greek city state
Olympus	奥林匹斯	A mountain
Pactolus	帕克托洛斯	A river
Phygia	弗里西亚	A state in Asia Minor
Scyros	斯库罗斯岛	An island
Sparta	斯巴达	Greek city state

（续表）

English 英文	Chinese 中文	Note 说明
Seriphos	塞里福斯	An island
Sestos	塞斯托斯	Greek city state
Stymphalian	斯廷法罗斯	Shrine of Artemis
Styx	斯堤克斯	A river（darkness）
Tiryns	梯林斯	Greek city state
Thebes	底比斯	Greek city state
Thessaly	塞萨利	Greek city state
Troy	特洛伊	Greek city state

References
参考文献

[1] American Museum of Natural History. 2016. Mythic Creatures. New York: Sterling Publishing Co. Inc.
[2] Berens E M. 2009. The Myths and Legends of Ancient Greece and Rome. 上海:世界图书出版公司.
[3] Bulfinch T, Stuart B. 2008. The Age of Fable. Beijing: Foreign Language Teaching and Research Press.
[4] 常耀信. 2017. 希腊神话、圣经故事及亚瑟王传奇. 天津:南开大学出版社.
[5] Graves R. 1992. The Greek Myths—the Complete and Definitive Edition. Penguin Random House UK.
[6] 柯克. 2017. 希腊神话的性质. 刘宗迪译. 上海:华东师范大学出版社.
[7] 梁德润. 2015. 希腊罗马神话和圣经专名小词典. 北京:商务印书馆.
[8] Greek Mythology. Taipei: SPEEDCORE Enterprise Co., Ltd.
[9] 顾爷. 2016. 小顾聊神话. 北京:北京联合出版公司.
[10] Rose H J A. 1990. Handbook of Greek Mythology. New York: Routledge.
[11] Waterfield R, Waterfield K. 2013. The Greek Myths—Stories of the Greek Gods and Heroes Vividly Retold. London: Querus.